The Archaeology of Garden and Field

The Archaeology of Garden and Field

edited by Naomi F. Miller and
Kathryn L. Gleason

PENN

University of Pennsylvania Press

Philadelphia

10 9 8 7 6 5 4 3 2 1

Published by
University of Pennsylvania Press
Philadelphia, Pennsylvania 19104-4011

Library of Congress Cataloging-in-Publication Data

The archaeology of garden and field / edited by Naomi F. Miller and
    Kathryn L. Gleason.
        p.   cm.
    Includes bibliographical references and index
    ISBN 0-8122-3244-5 (cloth)   ISBN 0-8122-1641-5 (pbk)
    1. Garden archaeology. 2. Landscape archaeology. I. Miller,
    Naomi Frances. II. Gleason, Kathryn L.
SB 466.7.A73 1994   94-1603
635'.09—dc20   CIP

For

Abraham and Mildred Miller

Dorothy Chamberlain Joslyn,
Clark Hough Gleason, Jr.,
and
Paul Chamberlain

Contents

Figures

Tables

Preface

Fields and gardens are increasingly the subject of archaeological investigation by practitioners in several disciplines and theoretical schools. Archaeologists of all types (prehistoric, biblical, classical, and historical), historic preservationists, landscape architects, in fact any of us interested in the landscape history of our own "back yard" would like to know specific techniques for investigating sites of past cultivation. Yet no researcher is conversant with all the specialties relevant to garden archaeology, and few have the time or library resources to follow the methodological advances in more than one or two areas of the world.

The need for a reader and sourcebook on the archaeology of gardens and fields that would bring together information about practical approaches to the study of cultivated land for use by researchers working in different archaeological traditions and world areas had become apparent to the editors by 1987. Miller, whose research ordinarily focuses on archaeobotanical studies of Near Eastern sites, began working in the mid-1980s on plant macroremains from two eighteenth-century garden sites: the Calvert Site in Annapolis, Maryland, and Morven, in Princeton, New Jersey (both excavated by Anne Yentsch). Other archaeologists soon began calling for advice on how to excavate their own garden sites, little realizing that Miller was not that much more experienced than they in the particular problems of garden archaeology. Gleason's introduction to the field of landscape archaeology was a bit more direct. An archaeologist trained as a landscape architect, she was looking at ways classical archaeologists could locate, study, and interpret remains of ancient Roman gardens and designed landscapes traditionally overlooked by scholars. Inspired by the interdisciplinary efforts of Wilhelmina Jashemski at Pompeii and Herculaneum and Barry Cunliffe at Fishbourne, she was excavating gardens of Herod the Great's palaces at Jericho, Masada, and Herodium, with various degrees of success, as well as undertaking landscape studies of a villa at Castle Copse in Wiltshire, England, and design analyses of a large first-century B.C. public park in Rome, the Porticus of Pompey.

It was with this background that the editors decided to organize a symposium on "The Archaeology of Garden and Field" at the annual meeting of the Society for American Archaeology in Atlanta in March, 1989. Several of the authors included in this volume presented papers in that venue (Ford et al., Erickson, Gleason, Yentsch, and Pulsipher). The symposium generated considerable enthusiasm for a volume that would focus on the identification and analysis of gardens and fields as places where people grew plants for pleasure and provender.

Following an introduction to landscape archaeology and the archaeology of cultivation, several overview articles deal with techniques and problems in world perspective, examples from diverse geographical areas and time periods, and questions that researchers typically ask about the value of various techniques or problems: Miller and Gleason discuss the importance of fertilizer, Fish presents the problems and potential of pollen analysis, Bevan surveys remote sensing techniques, and Treacy and Denevan discuss terracing. John Treacy prepared much of his paper on terracing before his sudden death. We are grateful to his former dissertation supervisor, William Denevan, for completing the manuscript for inclusion in this volume, an important tribute to a young scholar whose work held much promise.

Then case studies are presented which illustrate the variety of approaches and techniques that archaeologists use to delve into cultivated landscapes of the past (Ford, Bowen, Gaffney, and Mees on "Celtic fields" in England, Erickson on Andean raised field agriculture, Yentsch and Kratzer on eighteenth-century pleasure gardens on the east coast of the United States, and Pulsipher on Caribbean slave gardens). The authors of these articles evaluate in practical terms their own experiences with different techniques. Because one cannot divorce anthropological and historical questions from research design, these chapters also demonstrate how one puts the technical study of past gardens and fields in a social context.

A number of collections have been published in the past ten years on the archaeology of gardens and fields. Carole Crumley and William Marquardt (1987) present a cross-disciplinary group of essays on the Burgundian landscape. Others concentrate on historic periods in the United States (Kelso and Most 1990, Yamin and Metheny 1994) and landscape archaeology in Great Britain (Brown 1991) and continental Europe (Guilaine 1991; MacDougall and Jashemski 1981).

Other books deal with prehistoric fields (Denevan et al. 1985, Groene-man-van Waateringe and Robinson 1988). Lacking, however, is a volume that 1) introduces basic concepts necessary to understand the technical literature, 2) deals with many practical issues of research design and execution, and 3) pulls together information from a variety of sources, many of which are available only in major academic libraries. Until a textbook is offered on this subject, we hope that *The Archaeology of Garden and Field* will address this need.

The editors are grateful to the Museum Applied Science Center for Archaeology (MASCA) at the University Museum of Archaeology and Anthropology and to the Department of Landscape Architecture and Regional Planning at The University of Pennsylvania for their support of this project, particularly to Stuart J. Fleming, Anne Whiston Spirn, Dan Rose, and Patricia Smith for their advice in the development of this volume, and Elena Brescia, Ruth O'Brien, and Tyrone Hoffman for technical and editorial assistance. The thoughtful criticism offered by Wilhelmina Jashemski and Deborah M. Pearsall has improved the text and enhanced the book's value for students. We would like to thank the Samuel H. Kress Foundation of New York City for providing a subvention for publication, and Josephine A. Hueber for her kind support toward the preparation of the illustrations.

References

Brown, A.E. (editor). 1991. *Garden Archaeology*. CBA Research Report 78. Council for British Archaeology, London.

Crumley, C.L. and W.H. Marquardt (editors). 1987. *Regional Dynamics: The Burgundian Landscape in Historical Perspective*. Academic Press, San Diego.

Denevan, W.M., K. Mathewson, and G. Knapp (editors). 1985. *Pre-Hispanic Agricultural Fields in the Andean Region*. British Archaeological Reports, International Series 359. Oxford.

Groeneman-van Waateringe, W. and M. Robinson (editors). 1988. *Man-Made Soils*. British Archaeological Reports, International Series 410. Oxford.

Guilaine, J. (editor). 1991. *Pour une archéologie agraire*. Armand Colin, Paris.

Kelso, W.M. and R. Most (editors). 1990. *Earth Patterns: Essays in Landscape Archaeology*. University Press of Virginia, Charlottesville.

MacDougall, E.B. and W.F. Jashemski (editors). 1981. *Ancient Roman Gardens*. Dumbarton Oaks, Washington, DC.

Yamin, R. and K.B. Metheny (editors). 1994. *Case Studies in Landscape Archaeology: Methods and Meanings*. CRC Press, Boca Raton, FL. (forthcoming)

Chapter 1
To Bound and to Cultivate: An Introduction to the Archaeology of Gardens and Fields

Kathryn L. Gleason

The study of relict gardens and fields is part of the growing discipline of landscape archaeology, which examines patterns of human use and perception of land over time. Landscape would seem to be a diffuse topic for archaeological study. Yet in the English language it is "landscape" not "land" that expresses the cultural dimension within which landscape architects design, and the cultural domain that anthropologists, geographers, and historians study. "Land" has form and physically transforms over time. Its social meaning, too, exhibits continuity and change, through legal ownership for instance. "Landscape" shows many of the same qualities and, additionally, signifies the whole realm of perception (Appleton 1980:1). The definition of this area of archaeology marks a shift in focus from land as a contextual setting for artifacts and buildings to landscape as a subject of investigation in its own right.

Eagerly taken up after its introduction into English in the late sixteenth century, "landscape" initially referred to painted scenes of the Dutch "landschap" (Stilgoe 1982:24–25; Tuan 1974:133). It now captures the full spectrum of perception: from wilderness areas perceived but essentially unaltered by humans (e.g., "lunar landscapes") to landscapes offered as purely metaphorical places without reference to actual physical places. One is tempted to say, therefore, that not all areas of cultural landscape study are appropriate for archaeological investigation; however, "archaeology," too, refers not simply to the study of physical remains but to the layering of knowledge and thought (Duncan 1990:14; Foucault 1972:6–7). Non-physical dimensions of the definitions of archaeology and landscape structure our theoretical interpretation of past gardens and fields as an activity inevitably situated in the present, directed by our current concerns and influenced by the interpretations of others before us (Lowenthal 1985:412). Our archaeological excavation and interpretations, in turn, become part of the history of the landscape.

The Garden and the Field: Bounding and Cultivation

Gardens and fields are human constructions defined by two fundamental characteristics: they are bounded and they are cultivated. The cultural limits of language preclude more specific definition than this. As this collection of essays explores, gardens and fields can be further explicated only within the context of the culture and time in which they were tended.[1] Comparing Pulsipher's and Erickson's use of these English terms (this volume), for example, one sees that gardens for one culture are fields for another, depending on their scale and location in relationship to such concepts as public and private, individual and communal, sacred and secular, utility and amenity.[2] Other bounded, cultivated places—woods, orchards, groves, cemeteries, and parks—are part of the continuum, though they are not included in this discussion. This introduction sets out some basic aspects of the archaeology of gardens and fields that are appropriate to the investigation of prehistoric and historic cultures throughout the world.

Gardens, fields, and other constructed landscapes are unique products of the building arts and crafts in that they combine made materials with living plants and animals. Gardens and fields are never finished projects. Their hourly, daily, seasonal, and annual changes inspire delight, curiosity, anticipation, awe, and the fear of crop failure. Most societies understand these changes in terms of cycles that govern both cultivation and culture. To build a field or garden is to enter into a constant interaction with natural processes. By definition, gardens and fields will remain identifiable as such only through con-

1. The examples in this introduction are drawn primarily from the author's own work with gardens of the ancient Roman world.

2. One point is worth emphasizing. Most recent literature on garden history and archaeology strongly differentiates utility from ornament in the garden or field. While it is important to address this distinction where it is known to have existed, in many cultures fertility, utility, and abundance are synonymous with beauty, and the structure of a field or vegetable garden holds potential for readings other than the purely functional. Consider, for example, the dining couches and small shrines Jashemski (1979) has found in the vineyards and market gardens of ancient Pompeii.

tinued cultivation within the cycles of change. Thus gardens, fields, and other designed landscapes defy characterization as static "objects" or, in archaeological terms, "artifacts," although their ordering principles may be interpreted similarly.

Recent Theoretical Approaches

Land is the medium that preserves the evidence of most archaeological remains, but for gardens and fields it is both the relic and the context: to dig the dirt is to penetrate the very canvas of the landscape. Recently scholars have begun to refer to landscape as "text" (Duncan 1990:14; Foucault 1972:6), and while this metaphor is of limited relevance for the many landscapes of nonliterate peoples, it conveys the point that land is the primary evidence for landscape, a fact that is just now being addressed in archaeology. The essays in this collection reflect the nascent stage of archaeology's contribution to the interpretation of landscapes. The first portion of this volume, therefore, focuses on specific techniques for detecting evidence of relict gardens and fields in the land itself. The second provides case studies that emphasize the techniques used as well as the interpretation gathered from the evidence.

The difficulty of fully reconstructing a garden or field to the extent one might a broken flint, a Greek vase, a colonial house, or even a text may be an important factor in the previous dearth of archaeological research on built landscapes. Yet, as this book explores, bounding and cultivation are acts that give land a particular structure and form. That form may then be investigated in part with the empirical methods developed to address architecture and artifacts within the context of larger cultural patterns of ordering society and environment. Given the paucity of artifacts in most cultivated contexts, acquiring sufficient evidence necessitates use of the most rigorous methods of stratigraphic excavation and the full range of techniques employed by environmental archaeologists.

The ever-expanding variety of analytical techniques available to archaeologists help one reconstruct the spatial and perceptual environment ancient people would have experienced in the built landscape. Deetz has pointed out that in the three dimensions of archaeology (form, time and space) the spatial dimensions of landscape have received little attention (Deetz 1990:1). Among the reasons for this he cites the difficulty of excavating the large land area of many gardens and most fields, as well as the traditional view of many archaeologists, who regard the land between artifacts, buildings, and prominent landmarks as interstitial open space, or "context." Archaeologists find what they are looking for, and, it is difficult to look for "context." But definable places such as gardens, sports grounds, cemeteries, parks, fields, hunting parks all exhibit identifiable patterns of organization, whose relict structures, like artifacts, can be interpreted to shed light on such cultural issues as political power, leisure, economy, colonization, or subsistence.

Finally, because the evidence for cultivated land is inherently partial and subject to extensive interpretation, landscape archaeologists must use the tools of critical theory that encourage awareness of cultural bias.[3] These tools are particularly important when a garden or field is restored on paper or by physically re-creating the place. The difficulty of getting past one's own cultural blindness is exemplified by a standard architectural exercise that asks students to draw one of the villas described in rich detail by Pliny the Younger (*Letters* 2.17; 5.6 [A.D. 100–109]); collections of their interpretations from the past two hundred years give a better sense of the architectural principles of the time in which they were drawn than they do of the ancient Roman architecture and gardens that Pliny perceived (e.g., Tanzer 1924). Current archaeological theory permits a view of relict landscapes that is dynamic and complexly textured, one that can challenge simplistic interpretations of cultivated land.

The Archaeology of Bounding

The act of creating boundaries establishes a framework for gardens or fields. Bounded land shares three properties with most artifacts. First, it is designed: the ordering framework is conceived and planned prior to being built. Plans may be drawn or painted on paper, scratched in the dirt, recorded in clay or marble, or simply discussed verbally. The plan is then surveyed, staked out, or otherwise plotted onto the land itself. As the word "design" suggests, the form the bounding takes is a sign of the individual or culture. In the Mediterranean, for example, geometry has long governed the surveying of land as well as many other aspects of culture such as philosophy, art,

3. In a review of philosophic approaches to archaeology, Preucel (1991 : 28) suggests that the three currently diverging branches of theory, with the goals of explanation (positivism), understanding (hermeneutics), and self-understanding (critical theory), are in fact mutually reinforcing. Preucel's position seems most appropriate in the excavation and interpretation of gardens and fields.

architecture, and engineering (Dilke 1971). According to Herodotus (2.109), the origins of geometry, literally land measurement, lay in Egypt, where the annual flooding of the Nile obliterated field boundaries, necessitating a system of surveying by "scribes of the fields" to re-mark the land when the waters retreated.

Second, these designs are built in some respect, and frequently with a high level of craft. The requirements of property ownership, the need to keep out predators, the physical limits of human, animal, and mechanical endurance combine to specify the nature of the boundary, in both the conceptual and executed phases. The physical act of bounding leaves an archaeological record of the conceptual act of design, adapted to the realities of the terrain and the requirements of cultivation.

Third, the executed design becomes the focus of human activity as cultivation begins. More than a site, it becomes a specific entity, a place that is named: the garden, the field, Cabey Piece, Knighton Bushes, or the Porticus Pompeiana, to use examples from this book. As long as it is cultivated, and sometimes well after, the bounded place retains the name regardless how the planting, paths, ornamentation, and other internal features change over time.

Archaeologists often assume that evidence for the boundaries and internal structure of ancient gardens and fields, as well as the activities that took place within, is as ephemeral as the plants, lost to the processes of time and nature.[4] Most archaeological landscapes, however, do not lose the marks of time so completely. At this point in the development of garden and field archaeology, the primary task is to locate the remains; interpretive studies that make finer distinctions between boundary types on the basis of archaeological evidence alone are still in the future for sites without historical documents. The discussion that follows, therefore, stresses the methods of detecting and understanding built boundaries and subdivisions of gardens and fields.

Boundary Features Preserved in the Archaeological Record

The perimeter of a garden or field may lie on level ground, or it may be expressed by a change in grade. The latter can be used to delimit fields even on flat terrain, as evidenced by raised fields in the Lake

---

4. Garden archaeologists of the United States who have recently expressed concern about the overemphasis on studying the form of the garden rather than the people and plants may be an exception (Beaudry 1994).

Titicaca basin (Erickson, this volume). Terracing, discussed by Treacy and Denevan (this volume), is a more common way of bounding both gardens and fields, whether to define formal garden parterres (Yentsch and Kratzer, this volume), to create fields with steep hand-hewn terraces (Pulsipher, this volume), or to impede erosion on the slight terraces formed by lynchets (Ford et al., this volume). Other forms of earthworks use change of level to bound gardens and fields: banks and ditches, such as the "ha-ha" sunken fences of the English landscape garden, separate fields from roads, paddocks, houses, and settlements.

Fencing around fields and gardens can be difficult to detect, but careful excavation has produced ample evidence for postholes in a variety of gardens. Living fences—hedgerows or windbreaks—have proven very difficult to recognize by excavation alone. Archaeobotanists have used pollen, waterlogged clipped branches, or a preponderance of hedgerow species among charred remains to posit the presence of hedgerows (Clapham and Gleason 1994; Murphy and Scaife 1991).

Many gardens are found in courts bounded by buildings, the design of which creates an interplay with the planted forms. The peristyle gardens of Pompeii are the most extensively preserved archaeological remains of this type, also seen elsewhere in the Roman world (Cunliffe 1971; Gleason 1987/88; Jashemski 1979; MacDougall and Jashemski 1981). The courtyard garden is a ubiquitous type, and archaeological findings are increasingly widespread (Ruggles and Kryder-Reid 1994).

The act of bounding includes the subdivision of internal features of a garden or field system. Planting beds, paths, irrigation channels or drains, internal fences and hedges all delimit spaces for cultivation and can leave distinctive remains (see below). Paths and water features are typically built, but sometimes even earthworks can be detected by careful observation of changes and patterns in the soil. Intensively managed plots, more likely to be characterized as gardens than as fields, exhibit more elaborate structure in built features as well as in patterns of soil cultivation and planting.

Ascertaining the basic materials and functions of the boundaries and internal framework of a garden or field leads to an interpretation of the three-dimensional character of the site. Though archaeological deposits usually lie on an essentially horizontal plane, roughing out the vertical dimension of a landscape begins to give a sense of the spatial volumes and visual relationships that the human eye can discern from within or without the garden. Knowing what can be seen from, of, or within a garden or field suggests physical and human relationships that can be interpreted (Ruggles and Kryder-Reid 1994). Excavation may reveal details of construction that establish the probable height of walls and fences, trees or shrubs, although the exact treatment or design may be impossible to discover without historical documents. Figure 1.1 shows the public park built by Pompey the Great in Rome. Surrounded by architecture, the garden is known only from a cryptic plan engraved in marble, several brief passages in ancient poetry, and its silhouette in the urban form of modern Rome. Yet by combining this evidence it is possible to establish basic visual relationships that lead to an interpretation of Pompey's lofty political ambitions and their expression in terms of garden art and architecture (Figure 1.2) (Gleason 1990, 1994).

Locating Relict Boundaries

Aerial photography is the primary means of detecting the presence of landscape boundaries. The images are often extraordinary testaments to the persistence of landscape design over time (Taylor 1983; Wilson 1991:20–35). Given the scale of many gardens and field systems, no other method of observing the land surface allows the archaeologist to see the overall order and condition of relict gardens and fields. Various forms of remote sensing have enabled archaeologists to detect the boundaries of gardens and fields otherwise invisible from the ground (Bevan, this volume; Bradford 1957; Bussi 1983; Romano and Schoenbrun 1993).

Though their materials or even uses may change, boundaries make enduring marks on the landscape, which aerial photographs can record. In the country, roads replace hedges, paths mark old fence lines; later ecclesiastical boundaries follow old park impalements and vice versa; housing developments contort to fit within legal bounds of an old field. In the city, the floor plans of houses may retain the lines of ancient public gardens (Gleason 1990); while in city and country alike, modern streets may follow ancient roads (Hoskins 1955).

The two-dimensional patterns evident in maps and aerial photographs serve effectively as diagrams or symbols of the ordering system used in land survey and agriculture. Striking differences between the central Italian and English countryside, visible to this day, express a long history of contrasting practices of land survey and management. Broadly speaking, the centuriated[5] Roman landscape and the

5. Centuriation was the ancient Roman practice of surveying land into a grid of *centuries*, i.e., inheritable land units, for apportionment to veterans (Dilke 1971).

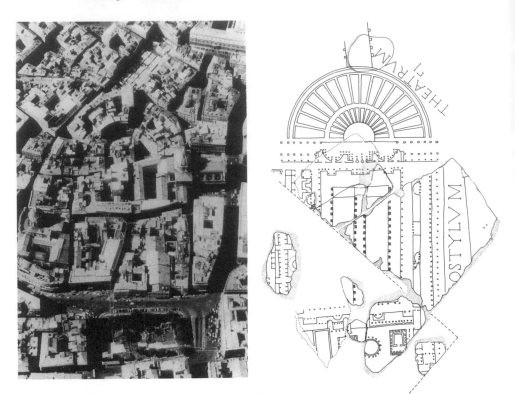

1.1. The Porticus and Theater of Pompey in Rome. The remains of this popular ancient Roman park and theater are evident in the aerial view of the medieval neighborhood (left) and an ancient plan of the complex incised in marble c. A.D. 210 (right). (photograph courtesy of Fototeca dell'Unione 5796; drawing by K. L. Gleason after Carettoni et al. [1960] and Rodriguez-Almeida [1981])

formal patterning of Roman gardens (in both ancient and Renaissance periods) exhibit a concern with geometry, whereas the English agricultural landscape and the gardens of the seventeenth century retained an ancient practice of topographically-oriented bounding (Figure 1.3).

Evaluation of the underlying topography, geology, soils, and archaeological remains provides a fuller picture. Here, aerial photographs are examined to interpret boundaries in a three-dimensional context. For example, Figure 1.4 shows a study undertaken to detect centuriation in cardinally oriented field systems, roads, and villages near the Roman villa at Castle Copse in Wiltshire, England (Hostetter

1.2. The perspective view through the park along the central axis of the Porticus of Pompey demonstrates the strong relationship between the Temple of Venus Victrix atop the theater and the senate house just behind the viewer. (L. Cockerham)

1994). A Geographic Information System (GIS) computer mapping program was used to layer the information from geological maps, topographic surveys, aerial photographs, historic maps, and field observations.[6] After combining various layers, the fields and roads were seen to conform to the underlying landforms rather than to Roman practices of land surveying.

Field survey is useful as a means of checking information gleaned from aerial photographs, ascertaining the state of preservation of boundary features, and gathering surface evidence for cultivation

6. I am grateful to Eric Hostetter and Indiana University for permission to use this information.

1.3. Contrasting aerial views of the fields around Padua, Italy (Bussi 1983) and Great Bedwyn, Wiltshire (facing page) (courtesy of University of Cambridge) suggest ways of ordering land that are correspondingly reflected in the gardens of both regions.

(see below). Aerial photographs can reveal features that have been ploughed out or otherwise rendered invisible on the ground, but field checking is necessary to establish the location of segments that can be studied by excavation. Ford et al. (1990; this volume) offer a case study from a field system not far from Castle Copse.

Finally, excavation can be employed to achieve three objectives: to establish a date for the boundary, to determine the materials and construction techniques of the boundary, and to retrieve artifacts and environmental evidence that typically accumulate around the margins of a garden or field. The latter are helpful for identifying the inside and outside of a field or garden, the soils and materials used in its construction, and the patterns created by cultivation and by the pro-

cess of abandonment. All evidence contributes to an understanding of the spatial properties of a garden or field.

The Archaeology of Cultivation

Not content with simply knowing the skeletal framework of a field or garden, archaeologists generally ask what was cultivated there. Yet,

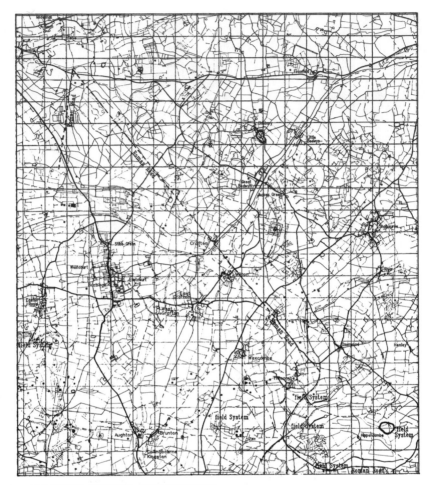

CASTLE COPSE, WILTSHIRE

CENTURIATION
Oriented to Cunetio town plan

Legend

	Parish Bounds
	Roads, Lanes, Tracks, and Paths
	Field Boundaries
	Cities/Villages
	Farmsteads

N

0 1 2 3 km

1.4. A study of possible centuriation (Roman surveying) at Castle Copse, Wiltshire using Microstation, a type of geographic information system. (J. Poor)

except under extraordinary "Pompeii" conditions, soil preserves few remains of a plot's vegetation. In the absence of historical evidence, the archaeologist must look at every aspect of the soil and its contents, as well as indirect evidence from other locations to piece together a body of information that may lead to a hypothesis about what was cultivated. A multi-faceted exploration of the process of cultivation can reveal such diverse spatial, social, and economic dimensions of the garden or field that determining the specific plantings may become a secondary issue. Throughout this book, the authors explore some of the ways that the land holds remains of the practices of manuring, tilling, ploughing, pruning, weeding, harvesting, and ornamenting, as well as those myriad activities that took place in cultivated settings.

The archaeology of cultivation is grounded in ecology (Dimbleby 1978:11; Willey and Sabloff 1980:191). A field or garden is an artificial but often complex ecosystem made up of air, water, soils, soil organisms, plants, molluscs, insects, fish, amphibians, reptiles, birds, mammals, and humans. Cultivation is a system of continuing human intervention whose factors, impact and problems are generally understood. Thus the archaeological remains of any one piece of the system potentially offer evidence for another piece or for the whole (Dimbleby 1978; Pearsall 1989). Environmental archaeology, the branch of archaeology that deals with this study of the past environment of human culture, is crucial to the study of landscape archaeology (Evans 1978:xiii; Shackley 1981): with it, climate, geology, soils, hydrology, vegetation, fauna, and diseases are set within the dynamics of space and time (Evans 1978:2). Environmental archaeology is also characterized by the study of the highly dynamic interrelationship of organisms and their environment at scales ranging from the microscopic to the global. Knowledge of the past environment is thus gleaned from evidence as minute as phytoliths and pollen grains and as grand as LANDSAT satellite imagery. For example, Erickson's study of Andean raised fields (this volume) uses data collected at many different scales, from aerial photography down to pollen analysis and thermoluminescence dating.

A fully environmental approach is as important in the study of cultivation practices as it is in determining the boundaries. A field may exist in isolation or it may be part of a wider system, and in either case the external factors at play on the practice of and evidence for cultivation must be evaluated. Pollen studies, for example, can be fine-tuned to a specific cultivated land surface most effectively by knowing what plants outside the garden or field might have contributed to the record. The environmental samples taken from a garden or field are related to conditions inside and outside the garden area, as well as above and below in the stratigraphic sequence of the soil. This study of the environment helps to identify contaminants as well as to establish patterns for analysis and interpretation.

The Excavation of Cultivated Land

Once a garden or field site is identified, areas of good preservation should be evaluated. The aim is to find the surface of the garden buried intact under upper layers of soil. To do this is not as obvious as it sounds: many archaeologists have dug down to the subsoil before recognizing a garden from the drainage channels or planting pits. Wall edges or other areas where there is a fairly thick deposit from collapse, fill, landslide, or destruction protect buried cultivated soils, although extra time is needed to document the overburden.

After a promising site is identified for excavation, some form of test sampling or "previewing" is necessary. The soil is not simply the context of artifacts but is itself the feature for study. There is little sense in beginning excavation blindly. Yentsch and Kratzer (this volume) evaluate a number of techniques whose utility varies according to the size of the site and extent of the preserved area.

Every archaeologist has a preferred approach to the layout of trenches, but a few points are worth noting. Open area excavation allows the cultivated surface to be completely exposed, enabling the documentation of the original grading, irrigation ditches, and planting furrows (Figure 1.5) (Cunliffe 1971). Differential weathering within a well-cleared expanse can also indicate the presence of planting pits, plant supports, trellises, and fence posts. On the other hand, baulks or vertical sections are essential as stratigraphical guides—and to help keep evaluation in three dimensions—especially to locate the surface of the garden topsoil in the preliminary phases of excavation (Chapter 2, Figure 2.2). Furthermore, if the preservation conditions are poor or the garden had several phases, baulks can be particularly valuable for sorting out irregularities and stratigraphic discontinuities.

Soil stratigraphy, the physical record of the natural and archaeological layers, is the most important and most complex evidence available for analyzing the structure of ancient gardens and fields; in many places it may be the only evidence. Archaeologists detect planting pits, stake holes, fence postholes, bedding patterns, irrigation contouring, and depth and quality of garden soil by distin-

1.5. This open area excavation in the courtyard of the Roman villa at Fishbourne revealed a central path, elaborate bedding trenches, and pits for espaliered (?) trees and supporting posts (Cunliffe 1971). (courtesy of Fishbourne Roman Palace/Sussex Archaeological Society)

guishing nearly imperceptible to highly contrasting patterns in soil types. Given the destructive nature of archaeological excavation, if these features are not recognized on the spot, they are lost. Thus, digging may proceed more slowly than is usual on archaeological sites to enable the archaeologist to view the dirt in varying conditions of light, soil moisture and weathering. Careful documentation of soil changes in the form of trench plans and baulk sections is critical.

Implements of Cultivation

Gardens and fields are notoriously artifact-poor. Some artifacts, such as potsherds, coins, and other objects, come to the soil in fertilizer (Miller and Gleason, this volume). Tools are occasionally found, but, to my knowledge, horticultural implements are not often discussed or catalogued, although experimental archaeological study with such evidence would shed important light on gardening practices (Jashemski 1979; Moorhouse 1991; White 1970). Agricultural implements have received much more attention (Ferdière 1991:81–102; Rees 1979; White 1970). Experimental archaeologists using reproductions of ancient tools at Butser Farm have contributed to the discussion of crop cultivation, stratigraphy, and technological development in ancient agriculture (Reynolds 1987). There is important work to be done on this topic in many areas of archaeology.

One of the more exciting developments in ancient Mediterranean garden archaeology in recent years is the discovery, identification, and publication of planting pots (known to the Romans as *ollae perforatae*) (Figure 1.6; Messineo 1983/84). Perforated pots used for displaying plants have been found at the Minoan sites of Knossos and Mallia on Crete, Olynthos in northern Greece, and the Etruscan site of Poggio Civitate. Elsewhere, flower pots from the Roman period have been identified in Pompeii (Jashemski 1979) and Jericho (Gleason 1987/88; 1993); their use extended from England to as far east as Sri Lanka (J. Howell, pers. comm.; Vann 1987). Undoubtedly more flower pots and pot fragments remain unidentified in excavation and museum storerooms, perhaps misidentified or considered too utilitarian to publish.

As ceramic pots are used in both the propagation and transportation of plants (Varro 52.1–2), archaeometric analysis of the clays may, in turn, help identify the source of the plant. Plant size can be estimated from the dimensions of the pot, and planting layout can be measured and judged in its relationship to any architectural features,

View & Section

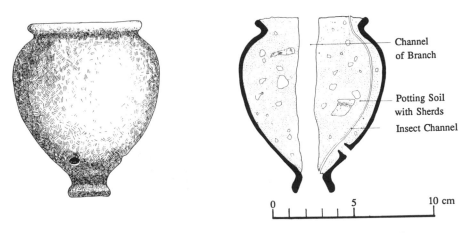

Channel
of Branch

Potting Soil
with Sherds

Insect Channel

0   5   10 cm

1.6. A ceramic planting pot found in a garden of Herod the Great's palace at Jericho. (K.L. Gleason, courtesy of Anglo-Israel Archaeological Society)

supporting postholes, or ornaments. Root channels rarely preserved in soils may be protected in the pots, thus allowing at least a partial identification of the plant (Figure 1.7).

Botanical Remains

As noted above, plant remains are generally scant. Few gardens in full bloom perish suddenly in a manner that would preserve their remains, whether by carbonization (burning), freezing, or waterlogging. Important exceptions are at Pompeii (Jashemski 1979; Meyer 1988) and Cerén, El Salvador (Sheets 1979; Sheets and McKee 1989), where deep and catastrophic deposition of volcanic ash permanently buried gardens and prevented further human habitation. Phytoliths are very promising for garden studies at present (Piperno 1988), and along with pollen and carbonized remains (Hastorf and Popper 1988) may occasionally be preserved on some buried field surfaces. The caveats in interpreting their use are discussed in the following chapter, while Fish (also this volume) discusses the value and limitations of pollen analysis.

Taking casts of the cavities of plant roots has been so successful at

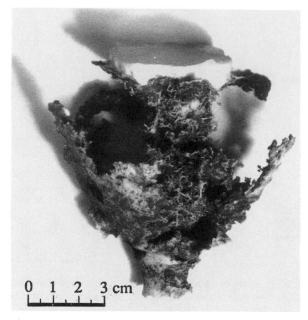

1.7. Latex impressions of a rooted branch propagated in a ceramic pot at the Herodian winter palace at Jericho. (K.L. Gleason)

Pompeii and Cerén, and so important in the interpretation of those gardens, that the possibility of uncovering preserved root channels at other sites is intriguing. While the planting holes of large trees and shrubs sometimes can be located, especially if they are deliberately dug, rarely do soil conditions permit the identification of smaller cavities or root channels.

Other evidence comes from plant remains found in related, non-field features like kitchen hearths, rubbish pits, or ditches and land-fills. These sources provide data for the various types of plants used in the vicinity, and ecological studies may enable the botanist to determine the habitat of each plant, its use, the stage of processing it was in when deposited, and whether it grew locally or was imported. Excellent texts on paleoethnobotany and phytolith analysis have recently been published (Pearsall 1989; Piperno 1988), and both discuss how these important forms of evidence may be collected, analyzed, and interpreted to understand agricultural practices, whether or not actual garden and field surfaces can be identified.

Faunal Analysis

On or near most cultivated lands, even in the most ornamental gardens, a variety of livestock may be raised for culinary and aesthetic purposes. Wild species, too, may colonize cultivated land when it replicates their natural environment or provides suitable food sources (Murphy and Scaife 1991:93–95). Molluscs, beetles, amphibians, reptiles, and small mammals from archaeological sites are studied to provide detailed information on habitat (Evans 1972). As the requirements of these creatures are often narrow, their remains can provide important information about the structure and species composition of the vegetation in a landscape (see Ford et al., this volume).

Artifacts and environmental remains offer a small window into the structure, activities, and appearance of the garden or field. Brought together, they can provide vital evidence for the workings of the whole system of cultivation. Specialist analyses are expensive and often difficult to coordinate. Miracles cannot be expected of the material; on the other hand, excavation without analysis cannot bring the dynamic dimension of explanation to gardens and fields.

Gardens and agricultural landscapes are not only reflections of their makers but agents of social transformation as well (Duncan 1990:11). Historically, the requirements of cultivation as well as the power of design itself have catalyzed change within society. In recent years, scholars studying prehistoric and nonliterate cultures have sought the means to observe similar processes by looking at the archaeological evidence alone (Erickson, this volume; Treacy and Denevan, this volume). In turn, their methods offer archaeologists of historical periods an independent means of evaluating textual evidence.

The Interpretation and Restoration of Relict Gardens and Fields

The history of the interpretation of a place may be as stratified as the site itself, for "every study of a landscape further transforms its meaning, depositing yet another layer of cultural representation" (Daniels and Cosgrove 1988:1).

This is not the place to synthesize the interpretations of relict gardens and fields, as there is not yet enough archaeologically produced evidence to integrate information across cultures, let alone across the disciplinary boundaries separating the archaeologies of the different scholarly traditions—anthropology, classics, history, and geography.

Interpretation must be culture and site-specific before a work such as this can identify commonalities across time and space.

Landscape archaeologists are beginning to interpret the remains of gardens and fields: their various forms and their relationships to each other, to individual buildings, to settlements, and to the greater landscape. The archaeological evidence is strongest for boundaries, which express the relationships among people in their physical environment. The traditional value of landscape as the domain, or context, within which other types of archaeological data can be interpreted is enhanced when gardens and fields are themselves the subjects of study. The work in this volume demonstrates how the study of bounding and cultivation offers new insights into many fields of scholarly investigation of past and contemporary cultures.

Once a garden or field has been located, excavated, and studied, opportunities may arise for interpretive reconstruction, whether on paper or the site itself. Physical reconstruction is, in fact, impossible. The resumption of cultivation on a relict garden or field site destroys any original fabric left after the archaeological excavation. Thus, a physical presentation is always a re-creation, and the decision to cultivate for present day purposes must be weighed against the loss of future archaeological discoveries prompted by methodological advances.

This dilemma has recently been addressed with regard to the preservation of historic battlefields (Deetz 1990:3). Battles have frequently been fought on agricultural fields or pastures, which are often left untilled thereafter as memorials. Archaeologists are beginning to use principles of landscape archaeology to establish details of the battles that took place on those fields. But how should such places be portrayed to the public? Resumed ploughing and planting would destroy evidence of the historical events, as well as of the field that was present at the time, yet the typical treatment of battlefields, with lawns and mown meadows, shady trees and interpretive signage, gives little sense of the place at the time of the event memorialized.

Preservation practice applied to gardens, fields, and other landscape features faces similar conflicts (Meier and Chittenden 1990), and the conservation of excavated garden and field surfaces is virtually unexplored. As discussed above, re-creating a former or current living feature raises methodological problems that were not considered when conservators established the principles for restoration of art objects and architecture. Most gardens develop over time, exhibiting a variety of plants of different ages and correspondingly diverse effects. The result is that, almost invariably, preservationists re-create gardens in a manner that speaks more of the time in which the re-creation took place than of the time in which the garden was first bounded and cultivated.

This said, re-creation of gardens and fields for the purposes of experimental archaeology has substantially contributed to our knowledge of past cultivation. At Butser Farm in England (Reynolds 1987) and the desert agricultural experiment station at Avdat in Israel (Evenari et al. 1971), researchers used ancient techniques on the past cultivation sites in order to establish the nature and effectiveness of the older practices. Erickson's work (this volume) has enabled the present-day inhabitants to reintroduce the more productive agricultural methods of their ancestors.

Educating the public about past uses and aesthetics of landscape is an important reason for re-creating garden and field sites. In many industrialized cultures, where people perceive that they have lost their connection to the land, historic re-creations are offered to enrich their sense of the possibilities of interaction and aesthetic appreciation (Beaudry 1994; Yentsch 1994).

Recent advances in computer technology permit considerable experimentation with reconstruction and simulation without physically intervening in the ground. Computers can accommodate vast quantities of archaeological data, both quantitative and visual, and juggle the temporal and spatial variables that characterize the growth and appearance of gardens and fields in different lighting conditions, in different seasons, under different owners. Computer-based virtual reality environments can provide a visually and aurally rich three-dimensional experience of a past landscape that draws on our modern ability to immerse our perceptions in electronic imagery. Multi-media programs connect the varied data used in a reconstruction and allow the viewer to navigate through the full range of textual and visual variables based upon that data. Of course, electronic portrayals cannot capture the aromas, the subtle changes of temperature, and the complex associations that past individuals and societies had in their gardens and fields, and thus may have the undesirable effect of contributing to the modern sense of dissociation from the land.

Clearly we cannot accurately portray the totality of what a person experienced in the past, but must we do so to achieve some understanding or empathy for past cultures? As Lowenthal (1985) has pointed out, the past is a foreign country, and few foreigners ever fully come to know the places they visit. As the essays in this book show, scholars and designers of landscapes seek a vision of land that is scientifically informed but not culturally impoverished. Archaeology can offer the perspective that, conceptually and physically, landscapes are composed of stratified layers that represent cultural order, made both continuous and discontinuous over time by the nature of cultivation. To study a relict landscape is to work with a subject that has changed constantly from the moment of its conception. We gain rich insights into the relationship of people to the land within their evolving paradigms of nature and order, but our view is composed of fragmentary glimpses. To make the intellectual and imaginative journey of seeing a landscape in the eyes of a past culture is to return renewed and enriched, with a different vision of the present.

It is a pleasure to thank my colleagues Naomi F. Miller, Ehud Netzer, Barbara Burrell, Ann Kuttner, and the members of the Penn Computers in Archaeology Group for their contributions to this discussion.

References

Appleton, J. 1980. *Landscape in the Arts and Sciences*. University of Hull, Hull.

Beaudry, M.C. 1994. Why Gardens? In *Case Studies in Landscape Archaeology: Methods and Meanings*, ed. R. Yamin and K.B. Metheny. CRC Press, Boca Raton, FL. (forthcoming)

Bradford, J.S.P. 1957. *Ancient Landscapes*. G. Bell and Sons, London.

Bussi, R. 1983. *Misurare la terra: centuriazione e coloni nel mondo romano*. Edizione Panini, Modena.

Carettoni, G.F., A.M. Colini, L. Cozza, and G. Gatti. 1960. *La Pianta Marmorea di Roma Antica*. M. Danesi, Rome.

Clapham, A. and K.L. Gleason. 1994. The Archaeobotanical Evidence. In *The Roman Villa at Castle Copse*, by E. Hostetter. Indiana University Press, Bloomington. (forthcoming)

Cunliffe, B. 1971. *Excavations at Fishbourne*. Vol. I. Society of Antiquaries, London.

Daniels, S. and D. Cosgrove. 1988. Introduction: Iconography and Landscape. In *The Iconography of Landscape*, ed. D. Cosgrove and S. Daniels, pp. 1–4. Cambridge University Press, Cambridge.

Deetz, J. 1990. Landscapes as Cultural Statements. In *Earth Patterns: Essays in Landscape Archaeology*, ed. W. Kelso and R. Most, pp. 1–6. University of Virginia Press, Charlottesville.

Dilke, O.A.W. 1971. *The Roman Land Surveyors: An Introduction to the Agrimensores*. Barnes and Noble, New York.

Dimbleby, G.W. 1978. *Plants and Archaeology*. 2nd edition. John Baker, London.

Duncan, J. 1990. *The City as Text: The Politics of Landscape Interpretation in the Kandyan Kingdom*. Cambridge University Press, Cambridge.

Evans, J.G. 1972. *Land Snails in Archaeology*. Seminar Press, London.

———. 1978. *An Introduction to Environmental Archaeology*. P. Elek, London.

Evenari, M., L. Shanan, N. Tadmor. 1971. *The Negev: The Challenge of a Desert*. Harvard University Press, Cambridge, MA.

Ferdière, A. 1991. Gaulois et Gallo-romains: techniques et outillages agricoles. In *Pour une archéologie agraire*, ed. J. Guilaine, pp. 81–102. Armand Colin, Paris.

Ford, S., M. Bowden, V. Gaffney, and G. Mees. 1990. Dating Ancient Field Systems on the Berkshire Downs in England. *Expedition* 32(2):44–51.

Foucault, M. 1972. *The Archaeology of Knowledge*. Translated by A.M. Sheridan Smith. Harper and Row, New York.

Gleason, K.L. 1987/88. Garden Excavations at the Herodian Winter Palace in Jericho. *Bulletin of the Anglo-Israel Archaeological Society* 7:21–39.

———. 1990. The Garden Portico of Pompey the Great. *Expedition* 32 (2): 4–13.

———. 1993. The Royal Gardens of Herod the Great at Jericho. *Landscape Journal*.

———. 1994. The Porticus Pompeiana: A New Perspective on the First Public Park of Ancient Rome. *Journal of Garden History* 4(1).

Hastorf, C. and V. Popper. 1988. *Current Paleoethnobotany*. University of Chicago Press, Chicago.

Herodotus. 1921/24. *Herodotus*, tr. A.D. Godley. Loeb Classics, Harvard University Press, Cambridge, MA.

Hoskins, W.G. 1955. *The Making of the English Landscape*. Hodder and Stoughton, London.

Hostetter, E. 1994. *The Roman Villa at Castle Copse*. Indiana University Press, Bloomington. (forthcoming)

Jashemski, W.F. 1979. *The Gardens of Pompeii: Herculaneum and the Villas Destroyed by Vesuvius*. Caratzas Brothers, New Rochelle, NY.

Lowenthal, D. 1985. *The Past Is a Foreign Country*. Cambridge University Press, Cambridge.

MacDougall, E.B. and W.F. Jashemski (editors). 1981. *Ancient Roman Gardens*. Dumbarton Oaks, Washington, DC.

Meier, L. and B. Chittenden (compilers). 1990. *Preserving Historic Landscapes: An Annotated Bibliography*. National Park Service, U.S. Department of the Interior, Washington D.C.

Messineo, G. 1983/84. Ollae Perforatae. *Xenia* 9:65–82.

Meyer, F. 1988. Food Plants Identified from Carbonized Remains at Pompeii and Other Vesuvian Sites. In *Studia Pompeiana et Classica in Honor of Wilhelmina Jashemski*, ed. R.I. Curtis, pp. 183–230. Caratzas Brothers, New Rochelle, NY.

Moorhouse, S. 1991. Ceramics in the Medieval Garden. In *Garden Archaeology*, ed. A.E. Brown, pp. 100–117. CBA Research Report 78. Council for British Archaeology, London.

Murphy, P. and R.G. Scaife. 1991. The Environmental Archaeology of Gardens. In *Garden Archaeology*, ed. A.E. Brown, pp. 83–99. CBA Research Report 78. Council for British Archaeology, London.

Pearsall, D.M. 1989. *Paleoethnobotany: A Handbook of Procedures*. Academic Press, San Diego.

Piperno, D.R. 1988. *Phytolith Analysis: An Archaeological and Geological Perspective*. Academic Press, San Diego.

Pliny the Younger. 1915. *Letters*, tr. Betty Radice. Loeb Classics, Harvard University Press, Cambridge, MA.

Preucel, R. (editor). 1991. *Processual and Postprocessual Archaeologies: Multiple Ways of Knowing the Past*. Southern Illinois University, Carbondale.

Rees, S. 1979. *Agricultural Implements in Prehistoric and Roman Britain.* 2 vols. British Archaeological Reports, British Series 69. Oxford.

Reynolds, P.J. 1987. *The Butser Ancient Farm Year Book.* The Butser Ancient Farm Project Trust, Hampshire.

Rodriguez-Almeida, E. 1981. *Forma Urbis Marmorea.* Quasar, Rome.

Romano, D.G. and B.C. Schoenbrun. 1993. A Computerized Architectural and Topographical Survey of Ancient Corinth. *Journal of Field Archaeology* 20:177–190.

Ruggles, D. and E. Kryder-Reid (editors). 1994. *Sight and Site: Vision in the Garden. Journal of Garden History* 14(1), special issue.

Shackley, M. 1981. *Environmental Archaeology.* George Allen and Unwin, London.

Sheets, P.D. 1979. Maya Recovery from Volcanic Disasters: Ilopango and Cerén. *Archaeology* 32(3):32–42.

Sheets, P.D. and B.R. McKee. 1989. 1989 Archaeological Investigations at the Cerén Site, El Salvador: A Preliminary Report. Department of Anthropology, University of Colorado, Boulder. (bound photocopy)

Stilgoe, J.R. 1982. *Common Landscape of America, 1580 to 1845.* Yale University Press, New Haven, CT.

Tanzer, H.H. 1924. *The Villas of Pliny the Younger.* Columbia University Press, New York.

Taylor, Christopher. 1975. *Fields in the English Landscape.* J.M. Dent, London.
———. 1983. *The Archaeology of Gardens.* Shire Publications, Ltd., Aylesbury.

Tuan, Yi-Fu. 1974. *Topophilia: A Study of Environmental Perception, Attitudes and Values.* Prentice-Hall, Englewood Cliffs, NJ.

Vann, L. 1987. The Palace and Gardens of Kayayapa at Sigiriya, Sri Lanka. *Archaeology* 40(4):34–41.

Varro. 1935. *De Re Rustica.* In *Cato & Varro, De Re Rustica,* tr. H.B. Ash, E.S. Forster, and E. Heffner, pp. 159–529. Loeb Classical Library, Havard University Press, Cambridge, MA.

White, K.D. 1970. *Roman Farming.* Cornell University Press, Ithaca, NY.

Willey, G.R. and J.A. Sabloff. 1980. *A History of American Archaeology,* 2nd ed. W.H. Freeman, San Francisco.

Wilson, D.R. 1991. Old Gardens from the Air. In *Garden Archaeology,* ed. A.E. Brown, pp. 20–35. CBA Research Report 78. Council for British Archaeology, London.

Yentsch, A.E. 1994. Close Attention to Place: Landscape Studies by Historical Archaeologists. In *Case Studies in Landscape Archaeology: Methods and Meanings,* ed. R. Yamin and K.B. Metheny. CRC Press, Bocan Raton, FL. (forthcoming)

Chapter 2
Fertilizer in the Identification and Analysis of Cultivated Soil

Naomi F. Miller and Kathryn L. Gleason

Many archaeological traditions treat soil simply as the medium in which artifacts or environmental remains are embedded, the context rather than the object of study. For the archaeologist of gardens and fields, the soil itself reveals traces of ploughing, fertilizing, terracing, and other human actions that turn land into landscape. Studies of stratigraphy, soil chemistry, artifacts, and environmental inclusions provide critical evidence that can strengthen and augment interpretations based on surface survey and aerial photography.

Cultivated land is commonly improved land, because agricultural activities can degrade soils. Farming cultures have long understood that dung and organic debris may enhance or restore soil productivity. By detecting the ancient use of fertilizer, an archaeologist can recognize a buried land surface or archaeological deposit as cultivated. Inorganic inclusions in fertilizer such as potsherds, coins, and other artifacts are not uncommon and help date the cultivation site. Charcoal and highly organic soils can be radiocarbon-dated directly (see Stein 1992). For historical periods, texts documenting the nature and application of fertilizer potentially shed light on many archaeological situations. In the absence of texts, it is possible to reconstruct these practices through stratigraphic, chemical, and botanical analysis. In turn, studies of fertilizer can reveal aspects of past gardening practices and local environment.

Finding loci of probable past cultivation is the first step in garden and field archaeology, but one must then demonstrate the soil was once cultivated. The structure of cultivated soils is distinctive: frequent disturbance by digging and ploughing tends to even out the distribution of soil particles and prevents the natural development of soil horizons. (On the use of remote sensing to detect these changes, see Bevan, this volume.) A common characteristic of these cultivated soils is that fertilizer has been worked into them.[1] Fertilizer usually consists of material that has been redeposited from elsewhere, and so possesses features that reflect its circumstances of origin. Therefore, plant materials, notably phytoliths, pollen, and seeds found in situ are at least as likely to have originated in fertilizer as from the plants grown on the plot. Careful examination of these materials can reduce some of the uncertainties inherent in the interpretation of cultivated soils.

Although it can be difficult to identify and interpret the practices that produced characteristic features of cultivated soils, the task is made easier if one takes control samples from outside the former cultivated area. In the context of garden and field archaeology, such soil samples should be treated as any other sample for a given analysis. A control sample may be taken from a modern, known situation that is analogous to the presumed ancient conditions. Other types of control samples may be taken from an ancient surface where it is thought cultivation did not occur, or from the modern surface at the top of the excavation, in order to enable the analyst to assess the significance of the materials found in the deposit of interest or to test for differences in the chemical characteristics of the soils (see Sandor and Eash 1991:32 for an example of how one might define suitable control samples for soils analysis). Analogue and other control samples are discussed below and in later chapters in the context of specific studies.

Soil as a Medium for Plant Growth

Soil is a substance that has mineral and organic components and a characteristic structure (see Buol et al. 1980; Limbrey 1975; Steila 1976; Young 1976). Soil development is a result of regular chemical and mechanical processes operating on a parent material over time; it is influenced by climate and vegetation. Different "zonal" soils, which have developed enough to reflect climate and other soil-forming processes, characterize the major climatic regions of the world; "azonal" soils consist of sediments, perhaps transported from elsewhere by wind, water, or gravity, that have not had time to develop characteristic horizons. Describing the results of the regular course of soil development, soil scientists identify various soil horizons, including "O" (humic) horizon on top, which consists of organic matter; "A" horizon (accumulation of organic matter in a mineral

1. For a discussion of techniques used in traditional European agriculture see Murphy and Scaife (1991).

horizon); "E" horizon, from which some particles of clay, iron, or aluminum are lost; "B" horizon, a mineral horizon that accumulates the particles translocated from above. The zone containing unaltered or slightly altered parent material is called the "C" horizon. Cultivation disturbs the O and A horizons. Where ploughing occurs, an agricultural horizon may be recognized as a subcategory of the A horizon (see Holliday and Goldberg 1992) (Figure 2.1).

Fertilizing affects the soil factors critical for plant growth, which include nutrients as well as soil texture and structure. Soil texture refers to the relative proportions of different size mineral particles (clay, silt, and sand), and soil structure is the "arrangement of primary soil particles into secondary . . . units" (Steila 1976:203). Fertilizing therefore not only adds nutrients but may also improve a plant's ability to use air, water, and nutrients to full advantage.

Fertilizer

Many of the farming cultures of the world, both past and present, have intentionally improved the soils on which they planted (see Erickson, this volume). Edgar Anderson has even argued that food production began on (unintentionally) fertilized soils on the "dump heaps" surrounding settlements (Anderson 1967). Archaeologists can test such hypotheses by studying the nutrients that fertilizers add to the soil, especially phosphorus, nitrogen, and potassium. Phosphorus, for example, persists in inorganic form by chemically bonding with the calcium, iron, and aluminum in the soil. The soils around dwelling areas, middens, and burials have been shown to be high in phosphate concentration (e.g., Eidt 1984; Woods 1984), as have some ancient fertilized fields (e.g., Sandor 1992:240).

Of course, in ancient times, chemicals were not added directly to the soil. Common "packages" were animal dung, trash, and settlement debris. Other organic-rich materials like leaf litter and sod have also been used. Animal dung adds nitrogen and phosphorus, but it also contains plant residues of several sizes: straw and seeds, phytoliths, pollen, and spherulites (see below). Household trash typically includes residues of food preparation and fireplace sweepings, which contain charred macroremains (wood and, if dung was burned, seeds, straw, and other plant materials). Plants that grew nearby or some distance away have also been recognized as a source of fertilizer in ancient fields (e.g., Dimbleby and Evans 1974). Though *uncharred* macroscopic plant parts tend not to be preserved in such deposits, pollen and phytoliths might be. Fertilizer originating in settlement debris may also include items not particularly useful to the plants but

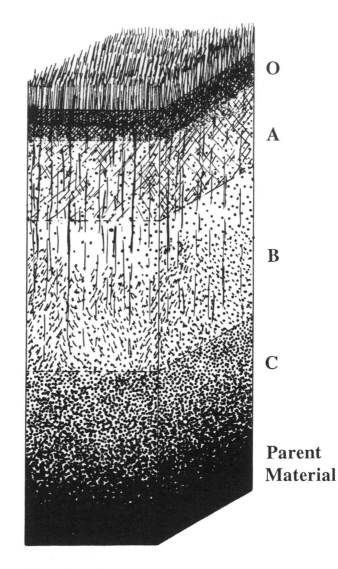

O

A

B

C

**Parent
Material**

2.1. Soil profile. See text for explanation of
the horizons. (E. Brescia)

very useful to the archaeologists, like potsherds, coins, and other datable objects (see Ford et al., this volume).

The distinctive composition and structure of fertilizer thus allows the archaeologist to distinguish cultivated land from surrounding soils (Figure 2.2), but the contents of fertilizer are not solely products of the garden or field itself. Since manures and other fertilizers may incorporate environmental remains originating outside the plot, such evidence is not a direct reflection of the ecological processes taking place within it. Particularly unambiguous examples of fertilized soils are seen in the Roman gardens at Fishbourne and at Jericho (Cunliffe 1971:125; Gleason 1987/88). The importance of this practice for the identification of garden beds on archaeological sites cannot be overstated.

Phosphate

Soil phosphates are derived from decomposed organic matter that is converted into a nearly insoluble inorganic form (see Eidt 1984; Hamond 1983; Woods 1975). Soil contains both organic and inorganic phosphate, though most is inorganic. By binding with calcium, iron, and aluminum, organic phosphate not utilized by plants is converted to an insoluble, inorganic form that accumulates in soil. An advantage of inorganic phosphate analysis is that once phosphorus becomes unavailable to plants, it tends to remain in place in soil as long as the sediments stay there. Phosphate "available" to plants is of interest to farmers, but the total inorganic phosphate concentration is at least as important for archaeologists trying to identify ancient fertilized fields.

Bone is particularly rich in phosphorus, as are other animal parts and products. Plants concentrate it in lesser proportions. Burials are therefore notoriously rich in phosphate, and settlement debris also generally shows high concentrations. Fields, refuse pits, fertilized planting pits, paddocks, trackways, and burials have all been identified using phosphate analysis (Cook and Heizer 1965; Mees 1982), but the interpretation of phosphates in fields is particularly complex.

Cultivated soils generally show lower concentrations than settlements, and depending on farming practices, less or more than surrounding uncultivated areas. For example, phosphorus is soon depleted from unfertilized fields, which therefore exhibit lower concentrations than comparable uncultivated ground (Sandor et al. 1990; cf. Eidt 1984:29). Fertilized fields, on the other hand, tend to show higher concentrations than uncultivated land, but lower concentrations than settlements (Eidt 1984:31). If the natural phosphate

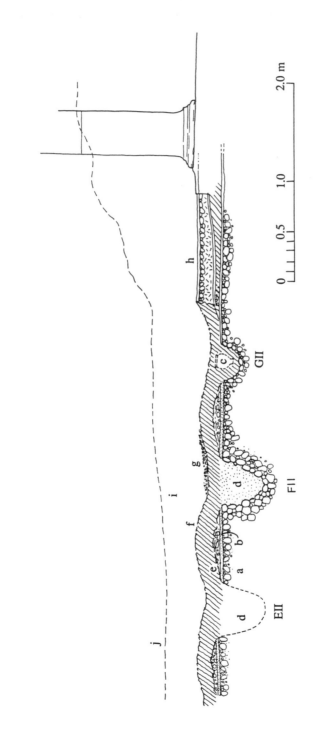

2.2. Ancient garden soil profile at the Herodian palace at Jericho. (a) alluvial subsoil; (b) plaster construction surface; (c) ceramic planting pot; (d) planting pit with humic soil; (e) fertilized garden soil; (f) garden surface contoured for irrigation; (g) fluvial deposition of pebbles; (h) perimeter walk; (i) destruction debris; (j) modern surface before excavation. (K. L. Gleason, courtesy of the Anglo-Israel Archaeological Society)

level in the parent soil is low, then fairly small additions from human or animal use can be readily detected. Complications arise if land is used after the period under investigation, as any additions of phosphorus will give an incorrect high reading. Hamond (1983) points out that if there is little vertical movement of phosphorus in the soil, more accurate measurements can sometimes be made on buried soils than on the surface. It is, however, possible for phosphorus to move downward below the A horizon (Sandor and Eash 1991).

Several methods have been developed for measuring phosphorus, though the experts disagree on their utility. A simple field spot test for detecting relative quantities of inorganic phosphate in soils is useful in non-destructive surveys of landscape features. It involves adding a chemical to a small soil sample (ca. 50 mg), putting it on some filter paper, and measuring the intensity of the blue color that forms. The spot test is quick, easy, and cheap (Hamond 1983). It is not as precise as the fractionation method for garden and field interpretation, but it has proven useful as a rough measure of intensity of settlement. At Castle Copse, England, phosphate analysis was used initially in an attempt to locate the gardens. Unfortunately the readings on the building walls gave far stronger readings than the soil areas themselves (Hostetter forthcoming); this proved to be the case at Jericho as well.

The fractionation method distinguishes three types of inorganic phosphate (I, II, III), and gives the total concentration (Eidt 1984). It requires at least 5 to 10 g of earth per sample (Woods 1975:12). For the intermediate phosphate levels associated with fields, one can look at the proportions of the three types, and match with modern samples to interpret the results. Eidt (1984:59) gives an example from the site of Billar, Colombia, where residential sediments showed very high total phosphate compared to garden soil; the garden soil showed very high type I phosphate and total phosphorus comparable to that found in analogue samples taken from modern fields of traditional crops (Table 2.1).

Archaeologists frequently use phosphate analysis to define settlement boundaries or to identify features, especially burials where the bone has decayed. When gardens surround a settlement, phosphate analysis can be used to define the area, or, in conjunction with other data, to confirm the presence of fertilized ground. The most appropriate way to sample is to take soil samples along transects. The interpretation of a phosphate analysis may require a general soils analysis. Also, it is important to take control samples to determine the concentration of the naturally occurring phosphorus in the area.

TABLE 2.1. Phosphate Analysis from Billar, Colombia, with Modern
          Comparison[a]

Sample	Phosphate fractions[b] (%)			Total phosphate (ppm)
	I	II	III	
Billar 1 (garden)	81	11	8	110
Billar 2 (residential)	66	10	24	615
Jiguales (yuca-maize)	83	12	5	116
Jiguales (yuca-plátano)	80	14	6	115

[a]Source: Eidt (1984:59)
[b]Fraction I: P moderately available to plants
Fraction II: P occluded within Al and Fe oxides and hydrous oxides
Fraction III: P occluded in calcium phosphates and apatite (Sandor et al. 1986; pers. comm. 1993)

At North Thoresby, Lincolnshire, high phosphate readings were obtained from an irregular grid pattern of ditches dated by Roman pottery and other refuse (Webster and Petch 1967). These were interpreted as planting ditches, perhaps for grape vines. At Kurban Höyük, in southeastern Turkey, soil phosphate analysis yielded only weak correlation with sherd scatters thought to have resulted from manuring with sherd-rich settlement debris (Wilkinson 1990b:73–78). A more conclusive study of an Iron Age farm site in Norway documented a zone of elevated phosphorus concentrations over an area larger than could be accounted for as a "haphazard accumulation of organic waste." As high phosphate concentrations could not be associated with sheep pens, either, the best hypothesis was that the areas of high phosphate concentration had been cultivated, fertilized fields around the farmstead (Provan 1973).

Dung

Animal dung is a common fertilizer. The dung of domesticated herbivores is sometimes found in situ on archaeological sites. If it has not disintegrated, it is readily recognized in comparison with modern specimens. It is well worth overcoming squeamishness and enduring the ridicule of colleagues in order to collect and study the dung of living animals. One can observe, for example, that sheep and goat pellets are fairly distinctive, short cylinders, flat on one end and coming to a small point on the other. They are somewhat larger than, say, gazelle scats and about the same size as those of deer. Cowpies are unlikely to be found whole, but their fibrous mass of incompletely digested straw and other vegetal material can be recognized. Courty et al. (1989 : 114) describe it thus: "The faecal residues of herbivores have a high porosity and contain many undigested plant fragments and amorphous dark brown organic matter that act as a type of binding matter." Even if worked into the soil, dung fragments might be recognizable, especially with a micromorphological study of soil thin sections (cf. Courty et al. 1989).

The grasses eaten by herbivores contain phytoliths, which remain in the dung (see below). Herbivore dung also contains spherulites, which are calcite bodies formed in the gut of some herbivores. They can be recovered from soil samples, and are good evidence for the presence of dung (Brochier 1991), though this type of analysis is not yet widely known or practiced.

Troels-Smith (1984) recognized an ancient field contemporary with and adjacent to the Neolithic lake village at Weier, in Switzerland, that dates to about 3100 B.C. (Robinson and Rasmussen 1989). In addition to charred plant material and sherds, he saw some housefly pupae. Since "houseflies do not place their eggs in cowpats . . . it is evident that the manure has been carried out from the stables along the plank-road unto the terraced field," which supported the interpretation that the animals had been stall-fed (Troels-Smith 1984 : 23).

Dung would be most likely on sites of cultures that had domesticated, penned animals, though in some situations one can imagine it to have been collected from free-ranging animals, like bison (cf. Miller and Smart 1984). If the material comes from a site where dung was used for fuel, residues of burnt dung might nonetheless wind up in the fields as part of household trash (see below). The ash would still be rich in phosphorus because combustion concentrates the phosphorus in the ash of dried cow manure (Anon. 1908; Sandor, pers. comm. 1993).

The mere identification of dung on an archaeological site is insufficient to document a field, for animal pens and dung piles are rich in the same materials. In a cultivation situation, however, one would not expect the dung to be found in a thick uniform layer. But even if fragments are found broken and mixed in with the sediments, additional argument is necessary to identify a deposit as cultivated.

Plant Macroremains

Macroremains are plant materials that are large enough to see without a microscope, though low magnification (up to about 50x) may be necessary to identify them. Seed and wood remains are the most commonly encountered types. Fertilizer may include plant materials introduced directly into the soil (leaf litter, green manure) or incorporated in dung or trash from a settlement, in charred or uncharred form. One is unlikely to find evidence of plants that actually grew in the plot of land under excavation because those plants were harvested and removed.[2] Even if a crop plant drops seeds, uncharred seeds will decay; if they did not, there would soon be more seeds in the soil than dirt. For organic materials to be preserved, biological, chemical, and mechanical degradation must be stopped. Over the long term, and barring unusual circumstances of preservation, macroscopic uncharred remains are unlikely to persist, as they are food for soil organisms. On relatively recent sites, woody seeds of fruits like grape, peach, walnut may be an exception. At Morven, for example, a peach pit was found about a foot below the modern lawn in a nineteenth-century deposit (Miller 1989).

Charred remains are not subject to organic decay, but physical effects of moisture and abrasion can break them up. Even though cultivated soil is not the ideal medium for preservation, bits of wood charcoal and charred seeds and plant parts in ancient soils probably originated in efforts to fertilize the soil, a practice mentioned in classical literature (e.g., Pliny *Natural History* 17.50 and Columella 2.14.5).

Macroscopic plant remains can be retrieved by flotation, which concentrates the plant remains by separating them from the sediment matrix. Even so, ancient cultivated soils tend to have very low quantities of preserved macroremains. Flotation and screening for macroremains mechanically separate the plant materials from the dirt, stones, and artifacts. No special laboratory facilities are required, and indeed, it is most efficient if soil samples are floated during the course of excavation near the field site. For detailed instructions and discussion of different flotation systems, see Pearsall (1989).

The analysis of an assemblage of macroremains includes identification and quantification. Identification is usually based on shape. The degree of specificity possible to reach varies from plant to plant and from plant part to plant part. Some items are only identifiable at the very gross level of plant family, while others may be identified even to variety. Unfortunately, many specific and varietal distinctions are based on flower morphology, and flowers are only rarely preserved. One must therefore frequently be satisfied with identification to the genus level.

2. An exception might be where field stubble was routinely burned, allowing some charred seeds to avoid decay or predation. A more likely situation would be the modern practice of stubble-burning, which could introduce recent charred seeds into the archaeological record.

Plant Microremains—Pollen and Phytoliths

Pollen is the male germ cell of seed bearing plants. Produced by plants in varying quantities, it may be dispersed by wind, insects, animals, water, etc. Since some plants, like wind-pollinated pine, produce vast quantities of widely dispersed pollen, and others, like insect-pollinated orchids are very parsimonious in pollen production, palynologists take the biology of pollen production into account in reconstructing past vegetation. Spores, the germ cells of non-seed bearing plants, are recovered along with pollen (see Fish, this volume; Pearsall 1989).

Most pollen analyses are done on lake and bog sediments, and focus on reconstructing local and regional vegetation patterns. Under conditions that are neither very wet nor very dry, soil organisms, mechanical abrasion, and exposure to oxygen in disturbed soils (like gardens!) reduce pollen preservability. High in protein, pollen is eaten by earthworms. Pollen's distinctive exoskeleton can survive, but will be distorted by abrasion. However, under anaerobic, undisturbed conditions, the exoskeleton is virtually indestructible. As is true of macroremains, some pollen types are more distinctive than others. For example, members of the daisy family are generally not distinguishable from one another—all have spiny pollen, and the only distinction is between high spine and low spine pollen. But many members of the pine family, with two air sacs, can be distinguished from other conifers (see Fish, this volume, Dimbleby 1985, Pearsall 1989). Pollen has been used to identify olive orchards at Pompeii (Jashemski 1979) and maize fields in the southwestern United States (Fish, this volume).

Archaeological pollen profiles from settlements or fields are usually unsuitable for direct comparison with lake cores that are based on the overall "pollen rain." Not only are most archaeological sediments unsuited to pollen preservation, but the air currents and other means of pollen transport and deposition associated with lakes and settlements are not comparable to the processes that form archaeological deposits. In archaeological garden and field deposits, one would have to distinguish air-borne pollen and spores from those grains that were deposited in fertilizer, like dung and trash, or that were produced by crop plants, weeds, and vegetation growing on or near the field. For example, an analysis of sediments underlying South Street Long Barrow yielded bracken fern spores. The fact that the soil fauna in the archaeological sediments did not match that found in the modern analogue of fern-covered soils showed that ferns had not been growing on the spot before the barrow was constructed. Rather, the spores probably came from ferns added to the soil as fertilizer (Dimbleby and Evans 1974).

Like pollen, phytoliths are virtually indestructible, but unlike pollen, they tend to remain in the sediments they were initially deposited in when the source plant died (see Piperno 1988). Phytoliths are formed when plants absorb silica from the water they take in through their roots. The silica is deposited in plant tissue, and a silica body forms which takes on the shape of the particular cell. Silica is differentially deposited in plant cells, frequently in distinctive shapes. Stem tissue, especially of grasses, is particularly rich in phytoliths. Phytoliths should therefore be particularly suited for locating in situ vegetation of phytolith producing plants (e.g., rice [Barnes 1990] and maize [Siemens et al. 1988]) or at least the location of open ground (Pearsall and Trimble 1984). Most of the grass phytoliths at Thomas Jefferson's home at Monticello were most readily explained as European introductions (Rovner 1988). Rovner (1988:162) points out that "if the samples containing grass phytoliths correlate strongly with the fodder plots," documented in Jefferson's archives, in situ plantings of these grasses would be strongly confirmed. On the other hand, phytoliths may be present in soils if plant parts or animal dung containing phytoliths had been deposited as fertilizer.

Pearsall and Trimble (1984) give a thorough discussion of sampling for phytoliths in former fields, and many of their procedures would apply to sampling for pollen as well. Note, for example, the importance of taking control samples (from deposits thought *not* to be agricultural) and surface samples from different cultivation and naturally vegetated sites, to develop analogs to aid in ecological reconstruction. Although Pearsall and Trimble do not deal with fertilizer, they point out that phytolith analysis can help identify an area as a field.

In contrast to flotation analysis, pollen and phytolith extraction require special laboratory facilities (see Pearsall 1989 and Piperno 1988 for details). For pollen analysis, one tries to mechanically remove and chemically dissolve everything that is not pollen—the organic materials, silicates, and carbonates that comprise the sediment matrix. Similarly, phytolith analysis uses mechanical and chemical means to concentrate the items of interest. Since hydrofluoric acid dissolves sand (i.e., silicates) and phytoliths are made of silica, pollen analysis will destroy phytoliths. Therefore separate sediment samples are required for the two analyses.

Where cultivated soils have been fertilized with domestic refuse or dung, care is needed in interpretation: the fertilizer is more likely to contain phytoliths than the cultivated plants, as the grasses present in dung and refuse produce phytoliths abundantly.

Settlement Debris and Organic Litter: Examples from Archaeological Survey and Excavation

Sherd Scatters in the Near East

T. J. Wilkinson's archaeological surveys of surface sherd scatters around ancient settlements in Iran, Syria, Turkey, and Iraq provide evidence of ancient manuring (Wilkinson 1989, 1990a, 1990b). Settlement debris contains potsherds along with nutrient-rich soil. In the Near East, where people tended to live in houses that were more closely spaced than in many other parts of the world (Mesoamerica, for example), it is reasonable to suppose that the source of the characteristically small and weathered sherds found on the surface come from manuring practices rather than from the occupation debris of scattered settlements. Wilkinson's methodology is relatively straightforward. A set of transects was established along which a series of 10 m x 10 m squares were laid out. Sherds collected from the squares were used to date the settlement debris and measure its density (number of sherds per 100 m^2). Following this procedure, Wilkinson mapped zones of high sherd density along a 10 km stretch of the southern side of the Euphrates river valley near Kurban Höyük in southeastern Turkey. The highest densities were recorded around sites of the Late Roman-Early Byzantine period, a time of maximum population in the area. Scatters of Bronze Age sherds suggested that manuring with settlement debris occurred during the previous population peak as well. A study of phosphate concentrations around the sites provided only partial support for this interpretation of the sherd scatters.

In a subsequent study, carried out in northern Iraq, Wilkinson was able to extend the evidence for manuring in the fields around settlements to the third millennium B.C. (Early Bronze Age). He points out that a key assumption behind this work is that people fertilized fields with their own debris rather than that of abandoned settlements, so datable pottery would correspond both to the period of settlement and to the period of manuring (Wilkinson 1989:41). In the Iraq study, the scatters correlated with the age of the settlements, so, at least in this case, the assumption holds.

Further evidence for the practice of using settlement-derived debris as long ago as the second millennium B.C. in the Near East comes from minimal textual as well as excavated evidence from fields. For example, A. Leo Oppenheim (1974) considers one of the subsidiary meanings of the word for dirt in Akkadian (*eperu*) to refer to the settlement debris dug up and carried out to the fields (by boat, according to the Chicago Assyrian Dictionary). Somewhat further afield, G.N. Lisitcyna (1976) reports sherds used to date ancient buried fields in Turkmenistan—most date to the medieval period, but Late Bronze Age and Early Iron Age sherds have also been found.

Fertilizer in the Ancient Mediterranean World

Passed down to us from antiquity, the Romans' extensive writings on farming practices, from farming manuals to short references in literary texts, suggest how we might view some of the items found in Roman gardens and fields. Ancient writers on agriculture and cultivation provide a wealth of technical information for the archaeologist: propagation techniques, nursery practices, manuring and fertilizing methods, harvesting times and equipment (see White 1970 for many references). Of course, caution must be exercised in drawing from these works, as their primary function was literary rather than utilitarian. As Seneca observed, Virgil, whose writings contain a variety of unlikely plant associations, "wished not to teach farmers but to delight readers." Nonetheless, these sources offer specific detail against which to compare archaeological remains.

Gardens and fields in the Roman world were commonly fertilized with domestic debris and manure (White 1970:125–145). Fertilizer was a valued commodity; manure piles and garbage were assets, even subject to litigation (Buck 1983:29–30). Columella (10.80–85) urges gardeners not to "hesitate to bring as food for newly ploughed fallow-ground whatever stuff the privy vomits from its filthy sewers," while other authors point to refuse pits, barn cleanings, and the remains of banquets as excellent sources of fertilizers.[3]

The sources, supported by recent archaeological evidence, describe the preparation of fertilizer. Cleanings from barns, charred kitchen refuse, broken pottery and other discarded objects, and human and

---

3. Cato (5.5.8) recommends a large dung hill, from which foreign matter is cleaned before hauling it out in the autumn. Archaeological evidence suggests that such care was rarely taken. See also Cato 7.1.3, 36.1.1, 37.1.3. Varro is quite specific on the construction of such pits (*De Re Rustica* 1.13.4), and on the types and placement of manure (1.38.1–3). Virgil (*Georgics* 2.346) recommends covering young plantings with manure and a deep level of top soil, or a thick layer of porous stone or rough shells. Pliny the Elder devotes considerable discussion to the use of dung in *Natural History* 17.50–57.

animal manure were all thrown into a compost pit. The prepared compost was then used on fields and in gardens. This widespread practice produces a characteristic layer in the garden or field, one filled with carbonized remains, bone fragments, small potsherds, and even bits of metal. The material found by archaeologists is normally in poor condition, highly abraded from constant reworking as the garden or field was tilled. Furthermore, the random direction of the remains, which have never "settled" onto a surface, is a visible characteristic in baulk sections, and can be "felt" while troweling horizontal surfaces (Cunliffe, pers. comm. 1985). In the remains of the palace gardens of Herod the Great at Jericho (late first century B.C.), archaeologists have identified components that suggest refuse from a food preparation area: potsherds, charcoal from native trees and shrub species used as fuel, carbonized seeds and fruit pits from meal preparation, and butchered animal bones (Gleason 1987/88). The work of Ford et al. (this volume) on the Roman fields of the Berkshire Downs demonstrates the importance of sherd-filled fertilizer in the detection of agricultural sites through field surveys, and in the dating of those fields through a study of the pottery's stratigraphic location in test trenches. They note, too, the presence of worked flint rather than potsherds, as evidence for prehistoric manuring practices.

In short, the presence of manuring and refuse in the soil can be said to be characteristic of Roman period cultivated land and should be looked for during excavation and field surveys. Its composition must be recognized and communicated to the environmental specialists for the interpretation of environmental remains so that phytoliths, macrofossils, and other remains are distinguished from any evidence for garden plants.

Black Earth

For years, British archaeologists considered a type of compacted black soil found in urban sites to be flood deposits or cultivated soils. Micromorphological analysis has revealed that this "black" or "dark earth" is an accretion of rubbish, perhaps the enriched, disturbed soil of market gardens (Macphail 1981).

Plaggen Soils

Land reclamation, sometimes on a grand scale, has been carried out in many areas. In this volume Clark Erickson discusses how Andean peoples created fertile raised fields on the margins of Lake Titicaca.

In northern Europe, "plaggen" soils resulted when farmers built raised fields on sandy soils by applying "a mixture of animal manure and cut heather sods or other such absorbent, usually humic, material over the fields" (Heidinga 1988:21). Not only was fertility enhanced, but the structure created by the sods helped the soil retain moisture (ibid.). The agricultural system integrated plant and animal husbandry, because the soils needed continual replenishment. The anthropogenic origin of these soils is shown by inclusions of charcoal, coal, sherds, brick, and burned soil (van de Westeringh 1988:14).

Concluding Remarks

Working with the complexities of fertilizer on cultivated land can test the talents of the most interdisciplinary of researchers. Ideally, an archaeologist would have the skills of a soil scientist, chemist, archaeobotanist, paleobotanist, entomologist, and zooarchaeologist, along with superb traditional abilities in field survey, stratigraphic excavation, and artifact analysis. In practice, the excavation director can facilitate interpretation by involving specialists in the early phases of the project. Simply recognizing that potsherds, charcoal, and other items came from manure can lead to the important questions about ancient cultivation practices, land use, and labor at the site. These questions can then guide the appropriate sampling strategy for the different types of materials. In addition, soil samples of modern analogues as well as baseline samples of non-field soils can make the difference between meaningful results and guesswork. Such sampling is best undertaken during the excavation phase of the project.

Under long term cultivation, soil nutrients must be replenished, and ancient farmers developed a variety of ways to do this. Unfortunately for the archaeologist, the addition of all sorts of different materials makes an already difficult problem (Is this an ancient field? What was planted on it?) even more complex. And yet, these traces of ancient agriculture may give us the only evidence for the date a field was cultivated, or indeed, that the ground was cultivated at all. Ancient fertilizing practices may provide the clues that permit us to interpret land as the landscape of a past culture.

We would like to give heartfelt thanks to Dr. Jonathan Sandor for reading and commenting on an earlier version of this chapter. We take responsibility for any errors that remain.

References

Anderson, E. 1967. *Plants, Man, and Life*. University of California Press, Berkeley.

Anonymous. 1908. Use of Dried Cow-Dung as Fuel in India. *Indian Forester* 34(8):493–494.

Barnes, G. 1990. Paddy Soils Now and Then. *World Archaeology* 22(1):1–17.

Brochier, J.-E. 1991. Géoarchéologie du monde agropastoral. In *Pour une archéologie agraire*, ed. J. Guilaine, pp.303–322. Armand Colin, Paris.

Buck, R.J. 1983. *Agriculture and Agricultural Practice in Roman Law*. Franz Steiner Verlag, Wiesbaden.

Buol, S.W., F.D. Hole, and R.J. McCracken. 1980. *Soil Genesis and Classification*. 2nd edition. Iowa State University Press, Ames.

Cato. 1935. *De Re Rustica*. In *Cato & Varro, De Re Rustica*, tr. H.B. Ash, E.S. Forster, and E. Heffner, pp. 1–157. Loeb Classical Library, Harvard University Press, Cambridge, MA.

Columella. 1955. *De Re Rustica*. tr. H.B. Ash and W.D. Cooper, pp. 2–157. Loeb Classical Library, Harvard University Press, Cambridge, MA.

Cook, S.F. and R.F. Heizer. 1965. *Studies on the Chemical Analysis of Archaeological Sites*. University of California Publications in Archaeology 2. University of California, Los Angeles.

Courty, M.A., P. Goldberg, and R. Macphail. 1989. *Soils and Micromorphology in Archaeology*. Cambridge University Press, Cambridge.

Cunliffe, B. 1971. *Excavations at Fishbourne*. Vol. I. Society of Antiquaries, London.

Dimbleby, G.W. 1985. *The Palynology of Archaeological Sites*. Academic Press, New York.

Dimbleby, G.W. and J.G. Evans. 1974. Pollen and Land-Snail Analysis of Calcareous Soils. *Journal of Archaeological Science* 1:117–133.

Eidt, R.C. 1984. *Advances in Abandoned Settlement Analysis: Application to Prehistoric Anthrosols in Colombia, South America*. Center for Latin America, University of Wisconsin, Milwaukee.

Gleason, K.L. 1987/88. Garden Excavations at the Herodian Winter Palace in Jericho, 1985–7. *Bulletin of the Anglo-Israel Archaeological Society* 7:21–39.

Hamond, F.W. 1983. Phosphate Analysis of Archaeological Sediments. In *Landscape Archaeology in London*, ed. T. Reeves-Smyth and F.W. Hamond, pp. 47–80. British Archaeological Reports 116. Oxford.

Heidinga, H.A. 1988. Climate and Plaggen Soils. In *Man-Made Soils*, ed. W. Groeneman-van Waateringe and M. Robinson, pp. 21–33. British Archaeological Reports, International Series 410. Oxford.

Holliday, V.T. and P. Goldberg. 1992. Glossary of Selected Soil Science Terms. In *Soils in Archaeology: Landscape Evolution and Human Occupation*, ed. V.T. Holliday, pp. 247–254. Smithsonian Institution Press, Washington, DC.

Hostetter, E. Forthcoming. *The Roman Villa at Castle Copse*. Indiana University Press, Bloomington.

Jashemski, W.F. 1979. *The Gardens of Pompeii: Herculaneum and the Villas Destroyed by Vesuvius*. Caratzas Brothers, New Rochelle, NY.

Limbrey, S. 1975. *Soil Science and Archaeology*. Academic Press, New York.

Lisitcyna, G.N. 1976. Arid Soils—The Source of Archaeological Information. *Journal of Archaeological Science* 3:55–60.

Macphail, R. 1981. Soil and Botanical Studies of the "Dark Earth." In *The Environment of Man: The Iron Age to the Anglo-Saxon Period*, ed. M. Jones and G. Dimbleby, pp. 309–331. British Archaeological Reports, International Series 87. Oxford.

Mees, G. 1982. Phosphate Analysis at Claydon Pike. Unpubl. ms.

Miller, N.F. 1989. What Mean These Seeds: A Comparative Approach to Archaeological Seed Analysis. *Historical Archaeology* 23:50–59.

Miller, N.F. and T.L. Smart. 1984. Intentional Burning of Dung as Fuel: A Mechanism for the Incorporation of Charred Seeds into the Archeological Record. *Journal of Ethnobiology* 4:15–28.

Murphy, P. and R.G. Scaife. 1991. The Environmental Archaeology of Gardens. In *Garden Archaeology*, ed. A.E. Brown, pp. 83–99. CBA Research Report 78. Council for British Archaeology, London.

Oppenheim, A.L. 1974. *Ancient Mesopotamia, Portrait of a Dead Civilization.* University of Chicago Press, Chicago.

Pearsall, D.M. 1989. *Paleoethnobotany, A Handbook of Procedures.* Academic Press, San Diego.

Pearsall, D.M. and M.K. Trimble. 1984. Identifying Past Agricultural Activity Through Soil Phytolith Analysis: A Case Study from the Hawaiian Islands. *Journal of Archaeological Science* 11:119–133.

Piperno, D.R. 1988. *Phytolith Analysis: An Archaeological and Geological Perspective.* Academic Press, San Diego.

Pliny the Elder. 1945. *Natural History*, tr. H. Rackham, W.H.S. Jones, and D.E. Eichholz. Loeb Classical Library, Harvard University Press, Cambridge, MA.

Provan, D.M.J. 1973. The Soils of an Iron Age Farm Site—Bjellandsøynæ, SW Norway. *Norwegian Archaeological Review* 6:30–41.

Robinson, D.E. and P. Rasmussen. 1989. Botanical Investigations at the Neolithic Lake Village at Weier, North East Switzerland: Leaf Hay and Cereals as Animal Fodder. In *The Beginnings of Agriculture*, ed. A. Milles, D. Williams, and N. Gardner, pp. 149–163. British Archaeological Reports, International Series 496. Oxford.

Rovner, I. 1988. Macro- and Micro-ecological Reconstruction Using Plant Opal Phytolith Analysis. *Geoarchaeology* 3:155–163.

Sandor, J.A. 1992. Long-Term Effects of Prehistoric Agriculture on Soils: Examples from New Mexico and Peru. In *Soils in Archaeology: Landscape Evolution and Human Occupation*, ed. V.T. Holliday, pp. 217–245. Smithsonian Institution Press, Washington, DC.

Sandor, J.A. and N. Eash. 1991. Significance of Ancient Agricultural Soils for Long-Term Agronomic Studies and Sustainable Agriculture Research. *Agronomy Journal* 83:29–37.

Sandor, J.A., P.L. Gersper, and J.W. Hawley. 1986. Soils at Prehistoric Agricultural Terracing Sites in New Mexico: III. Phosphorus, Selected Micronutrients, and pH. *Soil Science Society of America Journal* 50:177–180.

———. 1990. Prehistoric Agricultural Terraces and Soils in the Mimbres Area, New Mexico. *World Archaeology* 22(1):70–86.

Siemens, A.H., R.J. Hebda, M. Navarrete Hernández, D.R. Piperno, J.K. Stein, and M.G. Zolá Báez. 1988. Evidence for a Cultivar and a Chronology from Patterned Wetlands in Central Veracruz, Mexico. *Science* 242:105–107.

Steila, D. 1976. *The Geography of Soils.* Prentice-Hall, Englewood Cliffs, NJ.

Stein, J.K. 1992. Organic Matter in Archaeological Contexts. In *Soils in Archaeology: Landscape Evolution and Human Occupation*, ed. V.T. Holliday, pp. 193–216. Smithsonian Institution Press, Washington, DC.

Troels-Smith, J. 1984. Stall-Feeding and Field Manuring in Switzerland about 6000 Years Ago. *Tools and Tillage* 5(1):13–25.

van de Westeringh, W. 1988. Man-Made Soils in the Netherlands, Especially in Sandy Areas ("Plaggen Soils"). In *Man-Made Soils*, ed. W. Groeneman-van Waateringe and M. Robinson, pp. 5–19. British Archaeological Reports, International Series 410. Oxford.

Virgil. 1916. *Georgics*, tr. H.R. Fairclough. Loeb Classical Library, Harvard University Press, Cambridge, MA.

Webster, P. and D.F. Petch. 1967. A Possible Vineyard of the Romano-British Period at North Thoresby, Lincolnshire. *Lincolnshire History and Archaeology* 2:55–61.

White, K.D. 1970. *Roman Farming*. Cornell University Press, Ithaca, NY.

Wilkinson, T.J. 1989. Extensive Sherd Scatters and Land-Use Intensity: Some Recent Results. *Journal of Field Archaeology* 16:31–46.

———. 1990a. Soil Development and Early Land Use in the Jazira Region, Upper Mesopotamia. *World Archaeology* 22(1):87–103.

———. 1990b. *Town and Country in Southeastern Anatolia, Vol. I: Settlement and Land Use at Kurban Höyük and Other Sites in the Lower Karababa Basin*. Oriental Institute Publication 109. Oriental Institute, University of Chicago, Chicago.

Woods, W.I. 1975. The Analysis of Abandoned Settlements by a New Phosphate Field Test Method. *The Chesopiean* 13(1–2):2–45.

———. 1984. Soil Chemical Investigations in Illinois Archaeology: Two Example Studies. ACS Advances in Chemistry 205, *Archaeological Chemistry* 3:67–77.

Young, A. 1976. *Tropical Soils and Soil Survey*. Cambridge University Press, Cambridge.

Chapter 3
Archaeological Palynology of Gardens and Fields

Suzanne K. Fish

The soils of archaeological gardens and fields hold a record of former crops, weeds, and surrounding vegetation in the form of pollen deposited at the time of cultivation. The highly resistant outer walls of these pollen grains persist over centuries and millennia, identifying the source plants through taxonomically distinctive morphology. A vegetational history of agriculture is encoded in this pollen record through a complicated series of processes involved in dispersal, transport, deposition, and post-depositional modifications. The clarity of the record is subject to factors affecting the preservation and integrity of pollen assemblages. Nevertheless, when successfully retrieved and interpreted, the pollen content of cultivated land provides unique insights into how, when, and where plant husbandry was practiced.

Examination of garden and field sediments is neither the sole, nor most common, nor earliest means by which pollen analysts have investigated the farming of the past. Indeed, in Europe where the discipline of palynology originated, it is rarely attempted. Instead, research efforts have focused on pollen of agricultural origin that was secondarily deposited in lakes, ponds, and bogs. Archaeological sites of agricultural function and aquatic regimes contain pollen assemblages representing vegetation at opposite ends of a continuum of geographic scales, from a specific planting locus on the one hand to an agriculturally altered region on the other. This polarity is reflected in the overlapping but largely complementary information that can be obtained from these archaeologically direct and indirect situations. As repositories of pollen generated by post-harvest processing and disposition of crops, non-field proveniences associated with farming activities and products round out the pollen record of agriculture. The potential for agricultural reconstructions through direct analyses of archaeological sediments has been only partially explored, but deserves the careful attention of all who wish to understand the agriculture of the past.

Indirect Approaches

Studies of Lakes and Bogs

For both historical and methodological reasons, results from indirect approaches predominate in the palynological literature concerning ancient agriculture. Palynology developed in northwestern Europe as a methodology for investigating Quaternary climatic and vegetational change through stratigraphic sequences of pollen assemblages preserved in lakes and bogs (Faegri and Iversen 1975). Lakes and bogs offer optimal conditions for pollen recovery because they exclude or inhibit destructive processes such as oxidation, microbial digestion, and mechanical abrasion. Furthermore, pollen sequences from these relatively consistent and continuous depositional regimes can be interpreted in a more straightforward manner than stratigraphic sequences from terrestrial deposits. Many palynologists, often with geological or botanical rather than archaeological backgrounds, also prefer lakes and bogs for studying past agriculture because such deposits enable them simultaneously to characterize regional vegetation and to compare results with similar analyses in surrounding areas.

For more than fifty years, European palynologists have recognized the effects of farming on regional vegetation in the pollen sequences of lakes and bogs (Faegri and Iversen 1975; Bryant and Holloway 1983). Land clearance and cultivation reduce the pollen of arboreal taxa, change the representation of tree species in keeping with forest cutting and natural or managed succession, increase the proportion of herbaceous taxa associated with different kinds of cultural land disturbance, and introduce cultigen pollen. Particularly in Europe, palynological markers have been prominent in establishing the timing of initial cultivation in a region, intervals of increasing or declining farming activity, and the manner of land use as indicated by the kinds of crops and the diagnostic weeds of active fields, fallowed land, and other agrarian habitats.

Because palynological studies are so widespread in northwestern Europe, individual stratigraphic assemblages and short sequences usually can be dated by matching them against longer sequences in the same region. Radiocarbon determinations on organic materials in cores from lakes and bogs also allow absolute dating of agricultural patterns. Although master sequences are fewer in other parts of the world, similar indirect approaches are successfully employed in diverse areas including southeast Asia (Higham and Maloney 1989), Japan (Tsukada et al. 1986), Mexico (Watts and Bradbury 1982), lowland Central America (Hanson 1990; Tsukada 1966; Vaughan et al. 1985), Canada (McAndrews 1976), and the eastern (Delcourt et al. 1986; Brugam 1978; van Zant et al. 1979) and western (Davis et al. 1985) United States.

The geographic resolution of results from lake and bog cores depends upon the catchment for pollen entering the deposits. Early models of pollen dispersal and deposition emphasized a homogenized airborne component that typified regional vegetation, conceptualized primarily as a forest type in keeping with the predominant vegetational structure where the discipline originated. More recently, increasingly sophisticated models discriminate between local and long-distance components in pollen deposition, including substantial fractions transported by surface runoff and inflowing streams. The balance among these components in deposited assemblages, documented mainly for temperate forested environments, is affected by vegetational, topographic, and taphonomic (i.e., post-depositional) variables. Pollen dispersal and deposition in conjunction with other major categories of world vegetation is more poorly understood.

The size of the pollen catchment and the relative contributions of near and distant plant communities govern the locational applicability or precision of pollen evidence for agriculture. Lakes with large watersheds and multiple tributaries encapsulate generalized vegetational trends across a region, subsuming pollen from separate land use categories at varying distances and in varying directions. Nearshore and mid-lake corings can produce different mixes of local and regional pollen, with correspondingly different probabilities of registering infrequent pollen types from localized agricultural sources (Edwards and McIntosh 1988). Very small catchments, like damp hollows or pocket bogs without incoming drainages to introduce waterborne pollen, may receive local pollen from so limited a radius that findings can be reliably linked to particular archaeological features in the immediate vicinity (e.g., Andersen 1988; Robinson 1988). Unfortunately, the likelihood of finding such specialized aquatic regimes next to agricultural features is low or nonexistent in many parts of the world.

Studies of Non-Field Proveniences

Pollen in habitation sites also offers indirect information about crops and the manner of farming. The recovery of cultigen pollen is evidence of cultivation, although distant production and subsequent transport or acquisition through exchange must be considered in attributing domesticates to the environs of a habitation site or to nearby agricultural features. An abundance of agricultural weed pollen in habitation proveniences is another line of evidence for farming in the site surroundings (Bohrer 1970; Fish 1984; Fish and Donaldson 1991). In some cases, the topography and hydrological attributes of the setting will strongly suggest a particular agricultural technology, even though fields and gardens have not been archaeologically identified. Habitation sites of limited duration, securely associated with adjacent fields or gardens, should furnish palynological evidence most closely approximating the sort that could be obtained from the agricultural features.

When a common mode of entry into a non-field archaeological provenience can be assumed for the pollen of both agricultural weeds and cultigens, as in a midden containing crop residues, attributes of field settings may be inferred. Middens in the vicinity of agricultural features are likely repositories for debris generated by initial processing of local crops (Kautz and Keatinge 1977; Pals and van Dierendonck 1988). For example, abundant pollen of maize and herbaceous species of non-salty soils was present in middens adjacent to sunken gardens in coastal Peru (Kautz and Keatinge 1977). These results demonstrate past use of the gardens for food production in spite of the fact that farmers today plant only salt-tolerant reeds in their currently saline soils.

Methodological Concerns In Direct Approaches

Questions that archaeologists hope to address through pollen analysis are often specific to a feature or location. Does a buried surface correspond to a former field? What was grown in a set of terraces? Were certain locales irrigated? Even so, lakes and bogs are often chosen for palynological investigations of agriculture over the sediments of clearly identified gardens and fields, most consistently in Europe but elsewhere as well. Disciplinary tradition and a preference for contexts with regular and predictable depositional processes and maximal preservation figure in these decisions. Furthermore, the stratigraphic integrity and representativeness of assemblages derived from terrestrial sediments, termed "mineral soils" in the the European literature, have been challenged. Although this chapter focuses on the recovery and interpretation of pollen from ancient gardens and fields, investigators contemplating such analyses should be aware of these methodological reservations.

It has been shown observationally and experimentally that some pollen types are more fragile than others and subject to differential destruction by agents such as oxidation and soil microorganisms (e.g., Bryant and Holloway 1983; Cushing 1967; Havinga 1967, 1971; Sangster and Dale 1964). Geoffrey Dimbleby (1985:1–20) has summarized concerns about these and other post-depositional processes of progressive destruction, stratigraphic mixing, and downward movement of pollen by water in terrestrial deposits, and has proposed a comprehensive model of the stratigraphic consequences. According to this model, pollen is regularly dislocated from the position of initial deposition by percolating water, although estimates of the magnitude of this transfer are inferential. Dimbleby's scheme for terrestrial soil profiles predicts that the concentration (amount of pollen per volume or weight) should decrease with depth due to the greater age of the deeper pollen and its more prolonged exposure to destructive forces. The proportion of resistant pollen types should increase with depth as the loss of fragile types progresses. Sequential assemblages should also embody the effects of downward movement of these differentially preserved pollen types.

If downward translocation is a significant factor, the assemblage in a given stratum will consist of originally deposited pollen minus subsets of disproportionately fragile types that have been destroyed and subsets that have already been transported by percolating water to greater depth. The remnants of the original stratum assemblage also will be enriched by increments of disproportionately resistant types transported into the level from younger layers above. Soil movement by earthworms and other organisms can additionally disrupt the stratigraphic order of pollen. In the extreme case, pollen in any terrestrial stratum should therefore contain an array of types biased by additions and losses that only tenuously reflects the vegetation at the time of sediment deposition.

Potential problems of assemblage integrity are reduced in permanently wet depositional regimes because destructive agents are inhibited and water does not routinely percolate down the stratigraphic sequence. In some bogs and even in many lakes of arid regions, where water tables do rise and fall seasonally or over longer intervals, high organic content may act to bind pollen in place and reduce its movement. Advantages of aquatic environments for palynological research are partially duplicated in special circumstances where prehistoric dry land surfaces have been relatively rapidly and amply capped by natural sedimentary processes or by man-made constructions such as earthen mounds. Burial of this sort decreases upper soil biota and oxygen levels. Buried surfaces beneath barrows or other massive earthen

constructions are sampled directly by palynologists who would otherwise avoid such deposits (Dimbleby 1985:45–70, 95–124). This approach is widely followed in Europe where barrows are common
and occasionally cover furrows or other recognizable signs of prior
cultivation.

A variety of evidence strongly suggests that processes threatening
the stratigraphic integrity of pollen assemblages are neither as per-
vasive nor as serious as Dimbleby's model suggests. The evidence occurs in climates of both low and high rainfall, an important variable
in percolation, biological activity, and other factors affecting pollen.
Even in temperate areas, pollen content does not necessarily conform
to a pattern of consistently decreasing concentration with depth, nor
have alternative explanations for such patterns been systematically
eliminated in the instances fulfilling the conditions of the Dimbleby
model. Reasonably sharp boundaries often occur between distinctive
assemblages in sequential strata, implying that stratigraphic mixing is
minor, if present. Most significantly for European agricultural studies, results in the few archaeological analyses of field sediments show
a strong correlation between agricultural pollen types and these proveniences (O'Connell 1986; Reynolds and Catt 1987; Sergerstrom
1991; Vorren 1986). In these temperate zones, as well as in tropical
(Wiseman 1990) and arid (Berlin et al. 1977; Fish 1989) regions, assemblages in agricultural features at even shallow depths contain
crop and weed pollen and contrast with the assemblages of uncultivated land.

Implementation of Direct Approaches

If Dimbleby's model accurately portrayed the fate of pollen in most
terrestrial deposits, palynological study of the great majority of all
archaeological contexts, including gardens and fields, would not be
worthwhile. This position and the arguments supporting it are not
universally accepted. For example, see reviews of Dimbleby (1985) by
Bryant (1986) and Schoenwetter (1987). Indeed, there are few adher-
ents of this conclusion among a large body of North American practitioners engaged in archaeological and non-archaeological research.

The following discussion of direct analyses relies primarily on
North American experience. It is far from exhaustive with regard to
the variety of world-wide agricultural remains and their settings. Investigative possibilities as well as demonstrated outcomes are included
in the hopes of stimulating innovation and expanding the range of
future applications among archaeologists and palynologists alike.

Lakes and bogs are generally restricted to higher mountains and absent in other sectors of the arid western United States. Palynologists developed methods for extracting pollen from relatively coarse terrestrial sediments in the course of pioneering studies of alluvial sequences along drainages, cave fill, and other available deposits (Anderson 1955; Mehringer 1967). Because pollen content in these sediments is usually much lower than in waterlogged deposits, larger volumes must be processed in order to extract adequate amounts. Steps designed to reduce the sediment matrix must be strengthened. Assemblages thus obtained from terrestrial stratigraphic sequences exhibit generally the same range of pollen types and frequencies as assemblages from the surfaces of modern vegetation zones (e.g., Martin 1963).

Terrestrial contexts, including archaeological sites, have been investigated over the last several decades in the western United States. By the mid-1960s, the location of a prehistoric field was inferred on the basis of recovered maize pollen (Martin and Schoenwetter 1965) and forest succession following abandonment was correlated with the rise of pine pollen in the upper part of a terrace sequence (Martin and Byers 1965). Direct agricultural studies continued and are now being pursued in a wide variety of geographic areas. Analyses in the United States, comprising the majority of such research, are largely reported in the narrowly circulating publications of governmentally mandated archaeology. Citations in this chapter, emphasizing examples in more accessible literature, only minimally represent the breadth of this work.

Indications for pollen degradation and dislocation of the sort described by Dimbleby should be carefully evaluated in any archaeological analysis. One cautionary pattern would be the absence of pollen types in older layers that are present in modern samples. Top to bottom stratigraphic decrease in both pollen concentrations and types known to be fragile would be another. Palynological evidence of agriculture might itself provide a measure of control. Does the pollen of cultigen and weeds continue into what ought to be culturally sterile basal sediments below cultivated levels? Do assemblages within agricultural features contrast in the presence of agricultural markers with stratigraphically equivalent exterior assemblages? Well designed controls offer the means for refining the parameters of reliability in direct studies of agricultural and other terrestrial contexts.

Sampling in Gardens and Fields

A first step in coordinating pollen studies with the excavations of gardens and fields is the collection of modern analogue samples from the vicinity. One or several samples from the ground surface before excavation allow the analyst to relate present vegetation communities in both the site locale and the region with the modern pollen assemblage. This is essential information for interpreting the archaeological assemblages. It reveals the variety of present pollen types, their relative proportions, and establishes a baseline for evaluating departures from such distributions in the excavated samples. If resources permit the analysis of no more than a single analogue sample, about one-half cup of sediment should be collected as a series of ten or more pinches at widely scattered points on the uppermost soil surface, after removal of any plant litter. Plant debris is to be avoided because flowering parts produce highly localized and quantitatively significant bias from individual species, and thus obscure the distribution of pollen types representing the vegetation community as a whole. If multiple modern samples can be analyzed, several more localized pinch samples will provide guidelines for interpreting horizontal variability within archaeologically contemporary assemblages across a single stratigraphic unit.

A layer or stratum is the most realistic way to envision the sampling unit in an agricultural feature because cultivation mixes the soil to some depth below the planting surface. The uppermost part of an agricultural stratum may contain pollen that accumulated after cropping had ceased but before the stratum was sealed by further sedimentation. The excavator should ideally sample buried surfaces or layers that were exposed to airborne, waterborne, and locally dispersed pollen during the interval of agricultural activity, then sealed rapidly by subsequent sedimentation or other mechanisms, thereby excluding increments postdating cultivation. If chronological discrimination is possible, samples collected from strata closely predating and postdating the agricultural interval may reveal conditions just prior to feature construction and after final use. Such samples could shed light on site vegetation when farming was initiated, plant succession in the abandoned feature, and aspects of local and regional vegetation indicating earlier and later land use practices in the area.

Samples should be collected at the moment of excavation exposure or from a freshly cleaned surface or profile. Modern airborne pollen contaminates exposed surfaces in a matter of hours (Cully 1979). Clean implements and containers are necessary. As a rule of thumb, the more coarse grained or rapidly deposited the sediments, the larger the volume needed to extract adequate amounts of pollen. A half cup of sediment is usually sufficient to allow for a repetition of extraction procedures in the case of laboratory error or other mishaps. If sediments are even slightly damp, impermeable packaging such as plastic bags can promote the growth of fungus. Samples may be dried at controlled temperatures or placed in heavy paper envelopes that permit natural drying. Containers must be totally sealed against the entry of air in order to avoid contamination by modern pollen.

Agricultural Features

The structures and stratigraphy of each agricultural site determine the details of sampling strategy. To recognize fully all sampling opportunities, the archaeologist must consider feature construction, stratigraphic processes, and ethnographic or historic analogues for likely agricultural practices. If a single surface (or layer) was tilled repeatedly over time, its pollen content will reflect a compendium of extended land use, with heaviest representation of pollen from the latest episodes; portions of the previously incorporated pollen would have been sequentially oxidized as sediments were disturbed and overturned during each season of planting, cultivating, and harvesting.

Rebuildings of terraces, walls, and other features or details of stratigraphy sometimes indicate successive field surfaces that are vertically separable and therefore datable to different intervals of cultivation. Discrete successive surfaces are particularly likely where runoff in slope situations or sediments in irrigation water create progressive soil buildup (e.g., Dart 1986; Fish and Fish 1984). If horizontal divisions of garden and field complexes are apparent or suspected, they also should be sampled. Because many cultigens have very short ranges of pollen dispersal (Hall 1988; Raynor et al. 1970, 1972; Vuorela 1973), differential plantings within internal divisions (for example, seed beds, heavily manured strips, hand-watered specialty gardens, field sectors adjacent to canals and those at the edges of irrigable acreage) might be detected.

Appropriate sampling points for particular research questions are most readily identified when formal constructions or well defined stratigraphy indicate relevant levels and when the agricultural functioning of the features under investigation is well understood. Even durable and obvious features such as terraces, however, may present uncertainties for sampling and interpretation. Does the current ground surface in the terrace represent the surface of the prehistoric planting zone, or has subsequent sedimentation or erosion covered or removed it? Might crop pollen from uppermost terraces in a slope series be transported by runoff to lower terraces that supported different crops in a system of specialized production? Sampling coverage that encompasses all possibilities is the best hope for resolving such uncertainties.

A wide variety of agricultural remains have been investigated with palynology. Urban gardens and yards (Jashemski 1979), terraces (Fish et al. 1984; Martin and Byers 1965), check dams (Winter 1978), walled enclosures (O'Connell 1986), raised fields (Wiseman 1983), gridded fields (Winter 1978), and rockpile fields (Fish 1983) are among the features marked by formal and durable constructions. Additional possibilities for sampling can be sought in the less formal and substantial remains resulting from cultivation practices. Charcoal in cultivated sediments has been recovered from the fill of plow marks cut into compact strata underlying ancient fields (Vorren 1986), and it is likely that pollen could be obtained as well.

Even agricultural sediments preserved near the present ground surface in geomorphologically stable situations can yield clear pollen evidence for agriculture (Berlin et al. 1977). A field consisting of ridges of volcanic ash and alternating swales was discovered in northern Arizona through aerial photographs. Maize and squash pollen appeared only in near-surface levels of these well preserved remains and was absent from control samples outside the features. Pollen of beeweed (*Cleome serrulata*), a tolerated and utilized weed of historic Hopi Indian fields, had the same distribution as the cultigen types.

Arable Locales

Former fields that are associated with agricultural features, but not clearly delineated by them, can be investigated by interpolating the position of sampling points from the locational and elevational attributes of the related remains. Distinctive pollen content in test pits (O'Connell 1986) and in segments of sampling transects (Sergerstrom 1991) revealed the locations of exterior fields surrounding walled enclosures. Sampling transects in a radius about farmhouse foundations also directed the recovery of assemblages yielding the palynological signature of fields (Sergerstrom 1991). Assemblages of cultigen and weed pollen have been recovered from soil columns in trenches that intercepted the likely horizontal and vertical range of adjacent fields, as projected from well preserved stretches of canals and the probable path of irrigation outflow (Fish 1983).

Sampling to locate or confirm fields in locales lacking discernible agricultural features can be guided by environmental variables such as landforms, soil types, or water supplies that would have been particularly favorable for ancient farming technologies and crops. A program of this sort is most practical if the targeted variables are confined to a limited area. Analyses are thus not expended among many possible loci that prove totally or mostly negative. Palynologists have encountered diagnostic weed and cultigen pollen by sampling environmentally favorable locales without visible features in both forested and desert regions (Fish 1983; O'Connell 1986; Sergerstrom 1991; Winter 1978).

In the absence of agricultural features, it may be necessary to examine vertical columns of samples from test pits, trenches, or tube cores in order to locate the depth of levels corresponding to ancient cultivation. Suspected arable plots are most convincingly confirmed if a contiguous set of sampling points yield agricultural pollen and are surrounded by outlying points that do not. Even in those cases where nearby residential sites or agricultural pollen in lake and bog sequences suggest chronological and cultural associations for fields identified solely by pollen (O'Connell 1986; Sergerstrom 1991), affiliation of such fields may not be conclusive until direct determinations can be obtained.

Fieldside Facilities and Structures

Structures and facilities sometimes provide evidence for certain crops even more readily than field sediments because activities involving newly harvested plants dislodge and concentrate rare pollen types. Concentration increases the probability of detecting types that are produced in small quantities and dispersed only in the immediate vicinity of the source plant. Substantial structures for seasonal residence among fields, termed fieldhouses in North American archaeology, accumulated concentrations of cultigen pollen (Fish 1984). The contrast between a fieldhouse in southern Arizona and irrigated fields in the general vicinity illustrate these effects (Fish 1983, 1984). No cotton pollen was encountered in a series of samples from the fields, but six instances of this rare type were recovered in a single sample from the fieldhouse floor.

Farmers also built ephemeral shelters for rest during the work day, postharvest processing activities, or temporary storage of crops. Facilities for fieldside processing of crops include threshing floors for Old World cereals and pits or hearths for bulk roasting of corn to enhance storability in the southwestern United States. Granaries and other storage structures adjoining fields are additional kinds of features that could be sampled to independently identify or confirm field evidence for crops. Crops attributable to contiguous sets of fields or to an arable locale might be identified by pollen from storage structures of corresponding date in the vicinity, such as ones built in caves for climatic protection or secrecy.

Water Control Features

A broad class of agricultural features functions in the management of water, including features for storage and delivery such as reservoirs and canals, and features for removal of excessive amounts such as drainage ditches. In many cases, the fill of these features will contain cultigen pollen from associated fields and thus identify crops. If plantings are immediately adjacent, pollen may be introduced by wind and even by plant fragments that are scattered and blown about in the course of harvesting and transport. If tailwater is reintroduced into canals as a conservation measure in arid areas or if excess water from field surfaces is drained from damp soils, cultigen and weed pollen is even more likely to be incorporated into the water-laid fill of features. Agricultural pollen types have been recovered in repeated instances from archaeological canal and reservoir sediments (Fish 1987; Lytle-Webb 1981; McLauglin 1976; Nials and Fish 1988; Puleston 1977; Wiseman 1983, 1990).

A substantial fraction of the pollen in waterlaid sediment originates in the suspended load of soil, pollen, and other particles transported by flowing water to the locus of deposition (Bonny 1976, 1978; Peck 1973; Pennington 1979). If the incoming flow taps a large watershed, the pollen of distant vegetation zones will be carried to downstream locations. In arid regions, an outcome of this process is the transport of arboreal pollen from upland sectors of watersheds into downstream segments of drainages below the lower elevational limits of those trees (Fall 1987). Sorting of suspended particles by size and buoyancy during processes of transport and deposition differentially distributes particular upland pollen types among waterlaid strata. For example, concentrations of buoyant conifer pollen are correlated with layers of clay in channel deposits because deposition of both tends to occur when rates of flow decrease (Fall 1987).

Infusions of upland pollen types in canal water create potential palynological markers for agricultural practices in the form of anomalous quantities of those types for the downstream depositional location (Fish 1987; Gish 1991; Lytle-Webb 1978; McLaughlin 1976). Seasonal or annual deposits in canals are customarily removed to maintain capacity and flow, and the sediments are spread laterally or added to non-adjacent fields for enrichment. Upland pollen types could also be imparted directly to field surfaces by irrigation waters. As a result, assemblages from outlying sediments along downstream canals sometimes contain unusual amounts of upland tree pollen types (Fish 1981). This pattern could conceivably help to demarcate the limits of irrigated fields. Pollen content of channel fill might also discriminate between possible water sources for isolated canal segments and for reservoirs that could have been filled either from tributaries with lowland catchments or from drainages with upland watersheds.

In a manner similar to upland types, pollen of riparian plant communities along incoming drainages is transported into water control features. Species of damp habitats also grow along the perimeters of artificial impoundments that hold water for extended periods. The recovery of types such as cattail or sedge in man-made canals, ponds, and reservoirs or in sediments behind checkdams has been attributed both to the damp microhabitats created by these features (McLaughlin 1976; Winter 1978) and to long distance transport in the water of the drainages supplying them (Fish 1987; Gish 1991; Lytle-Webb 1978; Nials and Fish 1988). To correctly interpret the seasonal persistence of the water supply in an agricultural feature on the basis of pollen from permanently damp habitats, both possibilities would have to be considered.

Secondary Vegetation of Agrarian Landscapes

Gardens and fields are categories of intensively managed agricultural land, but they are set within more broadly modified agrarian landscapes. Archaeological pollen studies and sampling designs can be directed toward the secondary vegetational configurations of cultivated locales. Hedgerows are vegetational structures that emphasize useful plants, heighten biological diversity about fields, and provide opportunities for fuel collection, hunting, and gathering (Rea 1979, 1983; Wilken 1970). Willows and other trees outline and stabilize lake margin chinampa gardens in central Mexico. Willows and cottonwoods of "living hedgerows" reclaim and stabilize floodplain fields in northern Mexico (Nabhan and Sheridan 1977). These are examples of ancillary plantings with important structural functions in field layout and maintenance.

The weedy species of cultivated ground and pasture, as well as those of canals, ditches, reservoirs, other water control features, banked constructions, paths, and fallow land are members of specialized plant communities that respond to microhabitats of cultural origin. Each community furnishes varied resources in a mosaic of agrarian vegetation. Pollen analyses offer an opportunity to detect the presence or heightened abundance of these significant non-crop taxa.

For example, with large sets of samples from a number of sites in Arizona, it was possible to recognize differences among characteristic suites of weed pollen from residential areas, fields, and canal-side habitats (Fish 1984). Under optimal circumstances, the recovery of diagnostic and localized types should furnish information about the composition and locations of secondary agrarian plant communities.

Two Hypothetical Sampling Designs

Although sampling designs should be developed prior to excavation of agricultural remains and, most importantly, in active collaboration with the future pollen analyst, the ability to discriminate archaeologically meaningful units is a final determinant of sampling strategies and objectives. Two figures illustrate hypothetical cross-sections of excavated features. Suggested sampling points exemplify the variety of information that could be sought under ideal circumstances of pollen preservation, assemblage integrity, and stratigraphic intelligibility. Strategies and results from several excavation projects in southern Arizona are idealized in Figure 3.1 (P. Fish et al. 1986; S. Fish et al. 1984) and Figure 3.2 (Fish 1983).

In Figure 3.1, a trench exposes dual construction and use episodes for a hillside terrace. Sample 1, in the uppermost portion of the culturally sterile basal soil, records vegetation shortly before first use of the site locale, which may or may not correspond to earliest land use in the vicinity or region. If it appears that the terrace base was excavated into the original surface of the slope, the pollen in Sample 1 could represent vegetation predating the archaeological interval by centuries or more. Sample 2 intercepts a cultural stratum from a time preceding feature construction, when farming may or may not have occurred at the site. Contrasts between pollen contents of Samples 1 and 2 may clarify these alternative scenarios. Sample 3, at the upper contact of the pre-feature cultural stratum, represents vegetation conditions just before the initial terrace construction.

Samples 4, 5, and 6 are collected to detect any temporal change from bottom to top in the original terrace, although cultivation must have repeatedly mixed the fill to some depth below the terrace surface. Sample 7, at the level of the Stage 1 planting surface, provides a horizontal contrast with Sample 6. Comparison of these samples offers a remote possibility of detecting different crops at the front and back of the terrace, but minimally should confirm that horizontal variability in a single terrace layer is less than the variability among vertical strata. In this regard, stratigraphic replicates for each of the foregoing samples are desirable if funding permits.

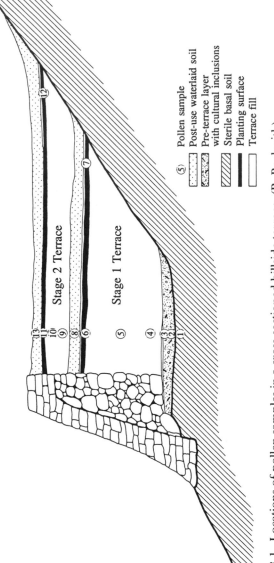

Stage 2 Terrace

Stage 1 Terrace

⑤ Pollen sample

Post-use waterlaid soil

Pre-terrace layer
with cultural inclusions

Sterile basal soil

Planting surface

Terrace fill

3.1. Locations of pollen samples in a cross-sectioned hillside terrace. (R. Beckwith)

Sample 8 is collected in a depositional layer accumulating between the final farming of the original terrace and a subsequent rebuilding to greater height and width. This sample might reveal a vegetational succession signaling temporary site abandonment or the continuing deposition of agricultural assemblages during disuse of this individual feature. Again, an internal temporal sequence is sought with Samples 9, 10, and 11. Sample 12 provides a contrast between front and back for the rebuilt terrace. Sample 13 characterizes vegetation between the final abandonment of this feature and the attainment of geomorphological equilibrium, at which time sedimentation ceased.

Figure 3.2 is the cross-section of a canal, adjoining agricultural land, and the preserved floor of a ramada or fieldside shelter that consisted of posts and a roof. The pre-canal ground surface (Sample 1) is preserved under the bank formed by the dirt removed in digging the channel. Samples 2, 3, and 4 are collected on successive bank surfaces that were covered in turn by sediments cleaned periodically from the interior. The bank surface of Sample 3 is covered by a thin layer of charred plant fragments, created when weeds growing in the canal were removed by burning. The three bank samples might yield information on irrigated crops, weeds of adjacent fields, the specialized flora along canal channels and banks, and the upland source of water as indicated by pollen types from a distant watershed.

The same range of information might be derived from Samples 5, 6, and 7 in channel fill. The lower fill strata are composed of sediments from a terminal period of waterlaid deposition which were never subjected to cleaning. The lowermost of these pertain to the time of last agricultural use. The uppermost waterlaid channel strata were deposited by the final canal flow or by natural floods just after abandonment. Pollen in the waterlaid strata exhibit a degree of sorting by size in tandem with the different sizes of deposited soil particles. Infilling of the abandoned canal by local sediments is monitored by Samples 8, 9, and 10, shedding light on vegetation and land use postdating this feature.

The floor of an adjacent ramada is present in the trench that exposes the cross-section of the canal. It is possible that the structure was built here for easy access to water. Sample 11, collected from the floor, likely contains greater concentrations of rare crop pollen types than the sediments of the fields where the crops were grown.

Samples intended to intercept field sediments are collected from trenches or test pits by reference to the canal and related stratigraphy. The projected water level in the canal and an elevational drop approximating gravity flow to an adjoining field surface are guides to

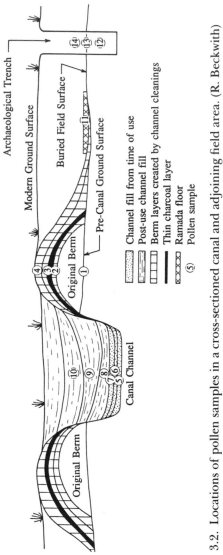

Archaeological Trench

Modern Ground Surface

Buried Field Surface

Pre-Canal Ground Surface

Original Berm

Canal Channel

Original Berm

Channel fill from time of use
Post-use channel fill
Berm layers created by channel cleanings
Thin charcoal layer
Ramada floor
⑤ Pollen sample

3.2. Locations of pollen samples in a cross-sectioned canal and adjoining field area. (R. Beckwith)

the positioning of samples in a vertical trench column (Samples 12–14). Vertical columns are necessary because the contact between the former field surface and post-agricultural sediments is not visually discernible in trench profiles. Samples in an appreciable segment of the column are likely to yield cultigen and field weed pollen because sediments from canal cleaning and irrigation continued to build up field surfaces over time.

Bases for Interpretation

The foregoing discussion has presented methodology, investigative opportunity, and results in a simplified manner. The interpretation of pollen from gardens and fields is highly complex, however. Different plant species disperse highly unequal amounts of pollen over varying distances because they accomplish pollination in different ways. Therefore, there is no simple correlation between the representation of species within a given radius about a point of deposition and their representation in the resulting pollen assemblage. The composition of vegetation producing an archaeological assemblage is inferred on the basis of the dynamics of modern pollen deposition within the same region. These dynamics vary with different combinations of undisturbed natural vegetation and culturally modified plant communities. A variety of modern vegetational situations approximating those expected in the past should be sampled in order to facilitate archaeological interpretation, particularly if there is little prior palynological research in the area to be studied.

A broad spectrum of knowledge is necessary apart from the mechanics of pollen dispersal and deposition, and the kinds and amounts of archaeologically recovered pollen. Equally critical is an understanding of the archaeological features and setting, the variety of likely farming practices, and the ecological attributes of crops and other species. Palynological analogues and controls reflecting the circumstances of agriculture are keys to the meaningful integration of pollen results with these other kinds of evidence. They necessitate an investment in the analysis of samples beyond those from archaeological proveniences, but are invaluable in deriving and supporting conclusions about the environmental and cultural parameters of cultivation.

The identification of crops is perhaps the most clear-cut research goal. Most crops are potentially detected through their pollen, but there are always exceptions. Agave, for instance, is harvested prior to flowering and pollen production. Secure linkage between a crop and a feature yielding the corresponding pollen depends upon the taxonomic specifity of the pollen type and the likelihood that it was deposited in some other way. For example, Old World cereals produce pollen of such similar morphology (Andersen 1979; Kohler and Lange 1979) that it is not always possible to distinguish between crops such as barley and wheat, particularly if the condition of pollen grains is less than excellent. In such cases, a few wild grasses can also be confused with cereals (e.g., Edwards 1988:259).

The probability of windblown crop pollen from local or regional sources outside the feature cannot be evaluated without knowledge of the dispersal mechanism of the plant and the transport characteristics of the pollen type. Fortunately for purposes of inferring archaeological association, many important crops do not disperse pollen copiously or over great distances as a result of the pollination characteristics of the wild progenitor or genetic changes accompanying domestication. Some produce large pollen grains that travel poorly by air (e.g., maize, pumpkin, or squash), produce comparatively small amounts of pollen (e.g., cotton), or primarily self-pollinate inside the flower in lieu of external dispersal (e.g., common beans). The pollen of such cultigens is seldom encountered in modern samples at any distance from source plants and almost never in appreciable quantities. For example, frequencies of maize pollen in samples from modern fields seldom exceed a few percent, and it is not observed in every sample (Berlin et al. 1977; Fish 1984:113; Martin and Schoenwetter 1965). Several strategies have been developed to increase the chances of detecting such cultigen types in spite of their rarity in archaeological pollen assemblages. These include the rapid microscope scanning of untabulated portions of samples and the selection of maximally productive sampling loci (Edwards et al. 1986; Edwards and McIntosh 1988; Gish 1991).

As guides to archaeological interpretation, analogue studies provide the best models for crop pollen recovery under varying agricultural circumstances. Modern situations, even experimental recreations of farms and gardens, seldom replicate prehistoric conditions in all details, but can suggest relative magnitudes and patterns of relationships among key variables. Analogue studies have demonstrated pollen dispersal and recovery rates for a number of domesticates (Berlin et al. 1977; Fish 1984; Martin and Schoenwetter 1965; O'Connell 1986; Raynor et al. 1970, 1972; Vuorela 1973), the circumstances under which agricultural activity might concentrate cultigen pollen (Hall 1988; Robinson and Hubbard 1977; Vuorela 1973) and the potential for spatial discrimination in agricultural contexts (O'Connell 1986; Vuorela 1973). Nevertheless, palynological analogues of any sort are presently available for no more than a tiny fraction of prehistoric crops, and predominantly for staples that are annuals rather than perennial crops or minor cultigens.

Agricultural information embodied by weeds is varied and valuable. Strong correlation with specialized microhabitats is the criterion for indicator species that serve as diagnostics for modes of land use such as cultivation and herding (Behre 1981, 1986; Lytle-Webb 1978), for physical conditions such as fertile or impoverished soils (Kvamme 1988:357), and for agricultural practices such as burning off fields in preparation for planting (Bohrer 1987, 1992). Because the weeds of different land use categories such as fields, pastures, fallow land, and habitations generally overlap to some degree, the overall configurations of pollen assemblages must be considered in addition to the presence of individual weedy types (Edwards 1988; Fish 1984). As with all other plants, pollen output, and thus detectability, differs among the constituent species of weedy agrarian plant communities. Valuable information is imparted by the pollen of one or a few weeds with narrow ecological ranges; the breadth of data in Europe (Behre 1986) has fostered the additional development of quantitative indices for commonly occurring weedy taxa (Behre 1981). The transferral of weeds between New and Old Worlds impedes modern acquisition of analogues fully duplicating the past conditions, as does the disappearance of old farming techniques in favor of technologies that modify the soil in new ways (Behre 1981; Fish 1985; O'Connell 1986).

The critical role of analogues, controls, and other contrastive or comparative measures is illustrated by the potential for confusion if additives were used to improve soil fertility, texture, and other qualities (see Miller and Gleason, this volume). Fertilizers are a troublesome element in evaluating the significance of cultigen and weed pollen (Dimbleby 1985:141–148), although this problem is of lesser magnitude in the New World where the prehistoric rarity of domestic livestock limited the use of animal manures. Animal wastes, which contain intact pollen, are applied by farmers or delivered by livestock while grazing on stubble. In either case, pollen of non-local cultigens and weeds in the animals' diet would be introduced. Where animals move to seasonal pastures, pollen from some distance could be involved. For example, traces of pollen types from lower elevations were probably transported into mountain lakes in Norway in this manner (Moe et al. 1988). The correct interpretation of such types is established by consideration of broader patterns and additional contexts. The use of human fertilizer is still more problematic in view of the wider range of diet and its greater isomorphism with cultivated products.

Both crop identity and fertilization techniques are of archaeological interest, but competing modes of pollen introduction into a feature must be distinguished in order to arrive at valid interpretations. A crop association might be strengthened by the consistent recovery of a cultigen type in one class of agricultural features and not in other classes or in contemporary non-field soils. However, this sort of approach requires multiple analyses from a variety of proveniences. In the case of animal dung, occasional well-preserved layers of manure in fields or the fill of archaeologically contemporary stables and corrals might aid in isolating its typical pollen content, and therefore the probable pollen contribution of fertilizer. Contrasts between samples from features that were unequivocally used to raise crops and those that delimited pastures are further possibilities for interpretive discrimination.

Carefully designed analogue studies help palynologists recognize the hallmarks of alternatives among complex sets of variables. Comprehensive controls further aid in reaching valid conclusions. Expanded development of such guidelines is the key to more fully understanding former agriculture through the study of its pollen.

Concluding Remarks

Compared to traditionally studied aquatic regimes, archaeological gardens and fields offer advantages for refining the history of plant husbandry in that a greater range of localities can be investigated and the plant taxa specific to the plot of land may be identified. The benefits justify continuing efforts to resolve methodological and interpretive issues posed by the analysis of pollen in these and other archaeological sediments. Details of time and place derived from the study of agricultural remains are the building blocks for questions concerning production and consumption at more inclusive scales. The most convincing arguments for such economic processes as agricultural intensification and specialization proceed from cumulative evidence for crops and production at particular times and places. Such data are also unsurpassed for determining the organization of farming with regard to environment, settlement, and social groups, and changes in these patterns over time. The archaeological pollen record of gardens and fields is a unique and valuable asset in reconstructing agricultural behavior and its implications for societies of the past.

Figures were drafted by Ron Beckwith. Paul Fish and Naomi F. Miller made useful comments on several drafts.

References

Andersen, S.Th. 1979. Identification of Wild Grasses and Cereal Pollen. *Danmarks Geologiske Undersogelse Arbog*. (1978): 69–70.

——. 1988. Changes in Agricultural Practices in the Holocene Indicated in a Pollen Diagram from a Small Hollow in Denmark. In *The Cultural Landscape: Past, Present, and Future*, ed. H.H. Birks, H.J.B. Birks, P. Kaland, and D. Moe, pp. 395–408. Cambridge University Press, Cambridge.

Anderson, R.Y. 1955. Pollen Analysis, a Research Tool for the Study of Cave Deposits. *American Antiquity* 21:84–85.

Behre, K.-E. 1981. The Interpretation of Anthropogenic Indicators in Pollen Diagrams. *Pollen et Spores* 23:225–245.

—— (editor). 1986. *Anthropogenic Indicators in Pollen Diagrams*. A.A. Balkema, Rotterdam.

Berlin, G.L., J.R. Ambler, R.H. Hevly, and G.G. Schaber. 1977. Identification of a Sinagua Agricultural Field by Aerial Thermography, Soil Chemistry, Pollen/Plant Analysis, and Archaeology. *American Antiquity* 42:588–600.

Bohrer, V.L. 1970. Ethnobotanical Aspects of Snaketown, a Hohokam Village in Southern Arizona. *American Antiquity* 35:413–430.

——. 1987. Tale of the Burnt Bush. *Desert Plants* 5:122–124.

——. 1992. New Life from Ashes II: A Tale of Burnt Brush. *Desert Plants* 10:122–125.

Bonny, A.P. 1976. Recruitment of Pollen to the Seston and Sediment of Some Lake District Lakes. *Journal of Geology* 64:859–887.

——. 1978. The Effect of Pollen Recruitment Processes on Pollen Distribution over the Sediment Surface of a Small Lake in Cumbria. *Journal of Ecology* 66:385–416.

Brugam, R.B. 1978. Pollen Indicators of Land-Use Change in Southern Connecticut. *Quaternary Research* 9:349–362.

Bryant, V.M. 1986. Review of "The Palynology of Archaeological Sites" by G.W. Dimbleby. *American Association of Stratigraphic Palynology Newsletter* 18:5–6.

Bryant, V.M. and R.G. Holloway. 1983. The Role of Palynology in Archaeology. In *Advances in Archaeological Method and Theory*, vol. 6, ed. M.B. Schiffer, pp. 191–223. Academic Press, Orlando, FL.

Cully, A.C. 1979. Some Aspects of Pollen Analysis in Relation to Archaeology. *The Kiva* 44:95–100.

Cushing, E.J. 1967. Evidence for Differential Pollen Preservation in Late Quaternary Sediments in Minnesota. *Review of Palaeobotany and Palynology* 4:87–101.

Dart, A. 1986. Sediment Accumulation Along Hohokam Canals. *The Kiva* 51:63–84.

Davis, O.K., R.H. Hevly, and R.D. Foust, Jr. 1985. Comparison of Historic and Prehistoric Vegetation Change Caused by Man in Central Arizona. In *Late Quaternary Vegetation and Climates of the American Southwest*, ed. B. Jacobs, P. Fall, and O. Davis, pp. 63–76. American Association of Stratigraphic Palynologists Contribution Series 16. American Association of Stratigraphic Palynologists Foundation, Houston.

Delcourt, P.A., H.R. Delcourt, P.A. Cridlebaugh, and J. Chapman. 1986. Holocene Ethnobotanical and Paleoecological Record of Human Impact on

Vegetation in the Little Tennessee River Valley, Tennessee. *Quaternary Research* 25:330–349.

Dimbleby, G.W. 1985. *The Palynology of Archaeological Sites.* Academic Press, New York.

Edwards, K.J. 1988. The Hunter-Gatherer/Agricultural Transition and the Pollen Record in the British Isles. In *The Cultural Landscape: Past, Present, and Future,* ed. H.H. Birks, H.J.B. Birks, P. Kaland, and D. Moe, pp. 255–266. Cambridge University Press, Cambridge.

Edwards, K.J. and C.J. McIntosh. 1988. Improving the Detection Rate of Cereal-Type Pollen Grains from *Ulmus* Decline in Earlier Deposits from Scotland. *Pollen et Spores* 30:179–188.

Edwards, K.J., C.J. McIntosh, and D.E. Robinson. 1986. Optimising the Detection of Cereal-type Pollen Grains in Pre-Elm Decline Deposits. *Circaea* 4:11–13.

Faegri, K. and J. Iversen. 1975. *Textbook of Pollen Analysis.* Blackwell, Oxford.

Fall, P. 1987. Pollen Taphonomy in a Canyon Stream. *Quaternary Research* 28:393–406.

Fish, P.R. and S.K. Fish. 1984. Agricultural Maximization in the Sacred Mountain Basin. In *Prehistoric Agricultural Strategies in the Southwest,* ed. S.K. Fish and P.R. Fish, pp. 147–160. Arizona State University Anthropological Research Papers 33. Tempe.

Fish, P.R., S.K. Fish, A. Long, and C. Miksicek. 1986. Early Corn Remains from Tumamoc Hill, Southern Arizona. *American Antiquity* 51:563–572.

Fish, S.K. 1981. Palynological Results from Las Colinas. In *Report of the Testing at Interstate 10 Corridor Prehistoric and Historic Archaeological Remains Between Interstate 17 and 30th Drive (Group II, Las Colinas),* ed. K.J. Schreiber, C.H. McCarthy, and B. Byrd, pp. 245–252. Arizona State Museum Archaeological Series 156. Tucson.

——. 1983. Pollen Studies from Agricultural Features. In *Hohokam Archaeology Along the Salt-Gila Aqueduct, Central Arizona Project, Volume III: Specialized Activity Sites,* ed. L. Teague and P. Crown, pp. 575–604. Arizona State Museum Archaeological Series 150. Tucson.

——. 1984. Agriculture and Subsistence Implications of the Salt-Gila Project Pollen Analyses. In *Hohokam Archaeology Along the Salt-Gila Aqueduct, Vol. VII, Environment and Subsistence,* ed. L. Teague and P. Crown, pp. 111–138. Arizona State Museum Archaeological Series 150. Tucson.

——. 1985. Prehistoric Disturbance Floras of the Lower Sonoran Desert and Their Implications. In *Late Quaternary Vegetation and Climates of the American Southwest,* ed. B. Jacobs, P. Fall, and O. Davis, pp. 77–88. American Association of Stratigraphic Palynogists Contribution Series 16. American Association of Stratigraphic Palynologists Foundation, Houston.

——. 1987. Pollen Results from the Las Acequias-Los Muertos Irrigation System and Related Features. In *Archaeological Investigations of Portions of the Las Acequias-Los Muertos Irrigation System,* ed. W.B. Masse, pp. 159–167. Arizona State Museum Archaeological Series 162. Tucson.

——. 1989. The Beidha Pollen Record. In B.F. Byrd, *The Natufian Encampment at Beidha,* pp. 91–96. Jutland Archaeological Society, Hojbjerg, Denmark.

Fish, S.K. and M. Donaldson. 1991. Production and Consumption in the Archaeological Record: A Hohokam example. *The Kiva* 56:255–276.

Fish, S.K., P.R. Fish, and C. Downum. 1984. Terraces and Hohokam Agricultural Production in the Tucson Basin, Arizona. In *Prehistoric Agricultural Strategies in the Southwest*, ed. S.K. Fish and P.R. Fish, pp. 55–72. Arizona State University Anthropological Research Papers 33. Tempe.

Gish, J.W. 1991. Current Perceptions, Recent Discoveries, and Future Directions in Hohokam Palynology. *The Kiva* 56:237–254.

Hall, V. 1988. The Role of Harvesting Techniques in the Dispersal of Pollen Grains of Cerealia. *Pollen et Spores* 30:265–270.

Hansen, B.C.S. 1990. Pollen Stratigraphy of Laguna de Cocos. In *Ancient Maya Wetland Agriculture: Excavations on Albion Island, Northern Belize*, ed. M.D. Pohl, pp. 155–186. Westview Press, Boulder, CO.

Havinga, A.J. 1967. Palynology and Pollen Preservation. *Review of Palaeobotany and Palynology* 2:81–98.

———. 1971. An Experimental Investigation into the Decay of Pollen and Spores in Various Soil Types. In *Sporopollenin*, ed. J. Brooks, P.R. Grant, M.D. Muir, P. van Gijzel, and G. Shaw, pp. 446–479. Academic Press, London.

Higham, C. and B. Maloney. 1989. Coastal Adaptation, Sedentism, and Domestication: A Model for Socio-Economic Intensification in Prehistoric Southeast Asia. In *Foraging and Farming: The Evolution of Plant Exploitation*, ed. D.R. Harris and G.C. Hillman, pp. 650–656. Unwin Hyman, London.

Jashemski, W.F. 1979. *The Gardens of Pompeii: Herculaneum and the Villas Destroyed by Vesuvius*. Caratzas Brothers, New Rochelle, NY.

Kautz, R.R. and Richard Keatinge. 1977. Determining Site Function: A North Peruvian Coastal Example. *American Antiquity* 42:86–97.

Kohler, E. and E. Lange. 1979. A Contribution to Distinguishing Cereal from Wild Grass Pollen Grains by LM and SEM. *Grama* 18:133–140.

Kvamme, M. 1988. Pollen Analytical Study of Mountain Summer-Farming in Western Norway. In *The Cultural Landscapes, Past, Present, and Future*, ed. H.H. Birks, H.J.B. Birks, P.E. Kaland, and D. Moe. Cambridge University Press, Cambridge.

Lytle-Webb, J. 1978. Pollen Analysis in Southwestern Archaeology. In *Discovering Past Behavior: Experiments in the Archaeology of the American Southwest*, ed. P. Grebinger, pp. 13–28. Gordon and Breach, New York.

———. 1981. Pollen Analysis of Irrigation Canals. In "Arizona U:9:46, a Dual Component Hohokam Site in Tempe, Arizona," by R.M. Herskovitts. *The Kiva* 47:83–90.

Martin, P.S. 1963. *The Last 10,000 Years: A Fossil Pollen Record of the American Southwest*. University of Arizona Press, Tucson.

Martin, P.S. and W. Byers. 1965. Pollen and Archaeology at Wetherill Mesa. *American Antiquity* 31:122–135.

Martin, P.S. and J. Schoenwetter. 1965. Arizona's Oldest Cornfield. *Science* 132:33–34.

McAndrews, J.H. 1976. Fossil History of Man's Impact on the Canadian Flora: An Example from Southern Ontario. *Canadian Botanical Association Bulletin Supplement* 9:1–6.

McLaughlin, D. 1976. Report on Analysis of Pollen Samples from Hohokam Irrigation Canal Sites AZ U:9:2, AZ U:9:28, and AZ U:9:26. In *The Hohokam Expressway Project*, ed. R. Masse, pp. 66–69. Arizona State Museum Contributions to Highway Salvage in Arizona 43. Tucson.

Mehringer, P.J., Jr. 1967. Pollen Analysis of the Tule Springs Area, Nevada. In *Pleistocene Studies in Southern Nevada*, ed. H.M. Wormington and D. Ellis, pp. 130–200. Nevada State Museum Anthropological Papers 13. Carson City.

Moe, D., S. Indrelid, and A. Fasteland. 1988. The Halne Area, Hardangarvidda: Use of a High Mountain Area During 5,000 Years—An Interdisciplinary Study. In *The Cultural Landscape: Past, Present, and Future*, ed. H.H. Birks, H.J.B. Birks, P.E. Kaland, and D. Moe, pp. 429–444. Cambridge University Press, Cambridge.

Nabhan, G.P. and T. Sheridan. 1977. Living Fencerows of the Rio San Miguel, Sonora, Mexico: Traditional Technology for Floodplain Management. *Human Ecology* 5:97–111.

Nials, F. and S.K. Fish. 1988. Canals and Related Features. In D. Gregory, W.L. Deaver, S.K. Fish, R. Gardiner, R. Layhe, F. Nials and L. Teague, *The 1982–1984 Excavations at Las Colinas, Volume 2, The Site and Its Features*, pp. 275–306. Arizona State Museum Archaeological Series 162. Tucson.

O'Connell, M. 1986. Reconstruction of Local Landscape Development in the Post-Atlantic Based on Palaeoecological Investigations at Carrownaglogh Prehistoric Field System, County Mayo, Ireland. *Review of Palaeobotany and Palynology* 49:117–176.

Pals, J.P. and M.C. van Dierendonck. 1988. Between Flax and Fabric: Cultivation and Processing of Flax in a Mediaeval Peat Reclamation Settlement near Midwoud (Prov. Noord Holland). *Journal of Archaeological Science* 15:237–251.

Peck, R.M. 1973. Pollen Budget Studies in a Small Yorkshire Catchment. In *Quaternary Plant Ecology*, ed. H.J.B. Birks and R.G. West, pp. 43–60. Blackwell, Oxford.

Pennington, W. 1979. The Origin of Pollen in Lake Sediments: An Enclosed Lake Compared with One Receiving Inflow Streams. *New Phytologist* 83:189–213.

Puleston, D.E. 1977. The Art and Archaeology of Hydraulic Agriculture in the Maya Lowlands. In *Social Process in Maya Prehistory*, ed. N. Hammond, pp. 445–467. Academic Press, London.

Raynor, G.S., J.V. Hayes, and E.C. Ogden. 1970. *Experimental Data on Dispersion and Deposition of Timothy and Corn Pollen from Known Sources*. Brookhaven National Laboratory 957 (T-398). Brookhaven National Laboratory, Upton, NY.

Raynor, G.S., E. Ogden, and J. Hayes. 1972. Dispersion and Deposition of Corn Pollen from Experimental Sources. *Agronomy Journal* 64:420–427.

Rea, A.M. 1979. The Ecology of Pima Fields. *Environment Southwest* 484:8–15.

———. 1983. *Once a River: Bird Life and Habitat Changes on the Middle Gila*. University of Arizona Press, Tucson.

Reynolds, K.S. and J.A. Catt. 1987. Soils and Vegetation History of Abandoned Enclosures in the New Forest, Hampshire, England. *Journal of Archaeological Science* 14:507–527.

Robinson, D.E. 1988. Neolithic Cultivation at Weier, Switzerland—Some New Evidence. In *The Cultural Landscape: Past, Present, and Future*, ed. H.H. Birks, H.J.B. Birks, P.E. Kaland, and D. Moe, p. 480. Cambridge University Press, Cambridge.

Robinson, M. and R.N.L.B. Hubbard. 1977. The Transport of Pollen in the Bracts of Hulled Cereals. *Journal of Archaeological Science* 4:197–199.

Sangster, A.G. and H.M. Dale. 1964. Pollen Grain Preservation of Under-

Represented Species in Forest Spectra. *Canadian Journal of Botany* 42: 347–499.

Schoenwetter, J.B. 1987. Review of "The Palynology of Archaeological Sites" by G.W. Dimbleby. *American Antiquity* 52: 204–206.

Sergerstrom, U. 1991. Soil Pollen Analysis—An Application for Tracing Ancient Arable Patches. *Journal of Archaeological Science* 18: 165–175.

Tsukada, M. 1966. The Pollen Sequence. In *The History of Laguna de Petenxil, U*, ed. G. Cowgill and G.E. Hutchinson, pp. 63–66. Memoirs of the Connecticut Academy of Arts and Sciences 17. New Haven.

Tsukada, M., S. Sugita and Y. Tsukada. 1986. Oldest Primitive Agriculture and Vegetational Environments in Japan. *Nature* 322: 632–634.

van Zant, K.L., T. Webb III, G. Peterson, and R. Baker. 1979. Increased *Cannabis/Humulus* Pollen as an Indicator of European Agriculture in Iowa. *Palynology* 3: 227–233.

Vaughn, H.H., E.S. Deevey, Jr., and S. Garrett-Jones. 1985. Pollen Stratigraphy of Two Cores from the Peten Lake District. In *Prehistoric Lowland Maya Environment and Subsistence Economy*, ed. M.D. Pohl, pp. 73–89. Harvard University Papers of the Peabody Museum, Vol. 77. Cambridge, MA.

Vorren, K.D. 1986. The Impact of Early Agriculture on the Vegetation of Northern Norway: A Discussion of Anthropogenic Indicators in Biostratigraphical Data. In *Anthropogenic Indicators in Pollen Diagrams*, ed. K.-E. Behre, pp. 1–18. A.A. Balkema, Rotterdam.

Vuorela, I. 1973. Relative Pollen Rain Around Cultivated Fields. *Acta Botanica Fennica* 87: 1–40.

Watts, W.A., and J.P. Bradbury. 1982. Paleoecological Studies at Lake Patzcuaro on the West-Central Mexican Planteau and at Chalco in the Basin of Mexico. *Quaternary Research* 17: 56–70.

Wilken, G.C. 1970. The Ecology of Gathering in a Mexican Farming Region. *Economic Botany* 24: 286–295.

Winter, J.C. 1978. Anasazi Agriculture at Hovenweep, I: Field Systems. In *Limited Activity and Occupation Sites: A Collection of Conference Papers*, ed. A.E. Ward, pp. 83–98. Center for Anthropological Studies Contributions to Anthropological Studies 1. Albuquerque, NM.

Wiseman, F.M. 1983. Analysis of Pollen from the Fields at Pulltrouser Swamp. In *Pulltrouser Swamp: Ancient Maya Habitat, Agriculture, and Settlement in Northern Belize*, ed. B.L. Turner II and P.D. Harrison, pp. 105–119. University of Texas, Austin.

———. 1990. San Antonio: A Late Holocene Record of Agricultural Activity in the Maya Lowlands. In *Ancient Maya Wetland Agriculture: Excavations on Albion Island, Northern Belize*, ed. M.D. Pohl, pp. 313–322. Westview Press, Boulder, CO.

Chapter 4
Remote Sensing of Gardens and Fields

Bruce Bevan

Remote sensing can be an economical and rapid method of searching the landscape for clues about former methods of cultivation. Aerial photography and ground-based geophysical exploration can aid the study of land use and cultivation practices. Remote sensing is also employed to detect canals, roads, causeways, paths, or farmhouses; these features can furnish indirect evidence of agriculture. While estimates of earlier practices of plowing or fertilization are possible, remains of ancient crops or garden plants probably cannot be located or identified.

The different techniques of remote sensing are summarized. Then, searches for specific features are described.

Tools of the Search

Remote sensing usually refers to aerial and satellite photography or non-photographic imagery of features visible at the earth's surface, but it also includes geophysical exploration, often a localized search for materials below ground. While these disciplines are concerned with discovery and mapping and with the analysis of spatial patterns, the instruments and analytical techniques of geophysics are quite different from those of aerial photography. In practice, therefore, the two realms of study are separate, and practitioners usually attend independent conferences and read different journals.

Aerial Photography

Every archaeologist with an interest in the landscape of a region should view it from the air in order to see the patterns and relationships of the features at the surface more clearly (see Bradford 1957). Often agricultural systems can be detected only from the air (see Erickson, this volume; Ford et al., this volume). If photographs of an area are made, a later and more leisurely study will also be possible. The techniques of oblique aerial photography are simple (Ebert and Lyons 1983; Wilson 1975) and normal practices of ground-level photography will usually work fine in the air. A small fixed wing aircraft can be chartered from nearby. It may be best to fly at a specific time of the day; the shadows from a low sun will emphasize slight topographic relief. If the flight is in the winter when the leaves are off the trees, the surface of the ground will be visible. A knowledge of the site on the ground will allow a prediction of the best time for aerial photography.

Aerial photographs taken by commercial firms or government agencies are available for many parts of the world. If the study area is very large, such photographs may be the only practical method of reconnaissance (Kruckman 1987). Bibliographies on the subject of aerial photography and archaeology have been published by Deuel (1969), Schorr (1974), and Lyons et al. (1980).

There are two general applications of aerial photography. The most important and easiest one is that of examining the surface for changes in topography, vegetation, or soil color. A rather different and more subtle search involves the exploration for hints of archaeological features that are completely underground. These clues are created almost entirely by the growth contrast of vegetation. The character of the soil (moisture, chemistry, and stoniness) sometimes causes changes in the above-ground parts of plants, frequently seen as differences in vegetation height or color. Different species of plants are sometimes associated with buried features as well (see Brooks and Johannes 1990 for many examples).

These patterns are usually called crop marks, for the growth of cultivated plants can be sensitive to soil conditions and the fields provide a uniform canvas in which subtle changes can be detected. Archaeological reconnaissance for crop marks has been particularly successful in Europe (Wilson 1975). Aerial photography in North America (Ebert and Lyons 1980) has had more disappointing results; the most distinct examples of crop marks appear to be prehistoric fortifications on the upper Missouri River (Lehmer 1971:11; Strandberg 1967).

There are several explanations for the success of aerial photography in Europe. One is that some of the soils there are more sharply stratified; a rather thin topsoil is sometimes underlain by gravel or chalk. Another might be that the earlier cultures in Europe built larger, more geometrical structures that are now easier to detect. Possibly the archaeological sites in Europe are more likely to be covered by uniform crops of small grains (i.e., wheat and barley rather than maize).

Aerial surveys can utilize the invisible part of the optical spectrum. For example, viewed through special imaging instruments, vegetation can be very bright in the near-infrared spectrum and limestone can be bright in the ultraviolet. Further into the infrared spectrum, temperatures at the surface of the earth can be estimated with thermography; for this thermal infrared spectrum, photographic film is not adequate; electronic sensors are required and so this technique can be called non-photographic imagery. These more esoteric parts of the optical spectrum may aid an aerial search, but the visible spectrum and normal photographic film often yield the most information.

A major advantage of satellite images is that they are usually available for different seasons of the year; this can aid in discerning vegetation patterns. While satellite imagery now has a lower resolution than aerial photography, it can be adequate for the study of fields and regional topography (Southworth 1985). For some areas, satellite images are readily available while aerial photographs are not.

In one experiment, satellite images were taken of southern England in an attempt to determine the best time for photography of crop marks from aircraft (Rainey et al. 1976). While the archaeological crop marks in the area were not visible from space, the appearance of large patterns in the fields, caused by buried traces of former river meanders, was found to be synchronized with the time during which the small archaeological crop marks were visible on the ground or from aircraft. Cloud cover resulted in infrequent images from the spacecraft, however, and this experiment was not successful.

Geophysical Exploration

Geophysical measurements are essentially a form of extrasensory perception; this is what makes the subject more complex than aerial photography. While we can see the direction of a magnetic field with a compass, we do not normally sense how strong the field is. While we sense our own weight, we cannot perceive that we weigh less when walking over an underground cavity. Scientific instruments, however, readily measure these subtle effects.

They do so, though, with very low resolution. The "visual acuity" of a geophysical survey, searching for objects only a meter underground, is comparable to that of human eyesight for objects at a distance of 3 km. Since the eye cannot see through even 1 mm of soil, we accept the poor "vision" of geophysical exploration, even though it is legally blind.

Geophysical instruments can be operated from aircraft and even spacecraft, but this lowers their resolution even further. In the search for large archaeologically-related features, such as the course of an ancient river, airborne geophysics could be tried. Geophysical instruments also can be operated in boreholes in order to define more sharply buried strata. Except for simple electrical resistance measurements, this is seldom practical. Geochemical tests on soil samples can be very helpful in the study of ancient gardens and fields (Custer et al. 1986; Eidt 1977; Hassan 1981; Lippi 1988; Schwarz 1967; Stein 1984; Woods 1977). Since this is not remote sensing, it is not discussed here. However, wind-lofted soil has been collected from aircraft; Barringer Research Ltd. (Toronto) has developed a rapid system for the sampling and chemical analysis of airborne soil.

Remote sensing is one of the tools of geoarchaeology (Davidson and Shackley 1976; Gladfelter 1977; Lasca and Donahue 1990; Stein and Farrand 1985). Introductions to archaeological geophysics have been given by Tite (1972), Aitken (1974), Weymouth and Huggins (1985), Clark (1990), Scollar et al. (1990), and Heimmer (1992). A recent review of geophysical surveying for archaeology has been given by Wynn (1986). Dobrin and Savit (1988) have given an up to date discussion of the general principles of geophysical exploration.

One of the simplest of the geophysical instruments, the resistivity meter (Carr 1982; Clark 1969), can provide much information to the archaeologist. It measures the electrical resistivity of the earth and can readily distinguish clay, which is low in resistivity, from sand or rock, which are high. Fertilization or manuring sometimes decreases the resistivity of the soil, thereby enabling the extent of fertilization to be mapped. If the boundaries between fields were never plowed or if they contain buried stones, these might sometimes be detectable.

Besides mapping lateral contrasts, a resistivity survey also can estimate how the soil changes with increasing depth. This procedure, called a resistivity sounding, can detect the stratification and approximate thickness of the soil. Strata must have a thickness that is greater than their depth in order to be clearly distinguished by the sounding. Thin strata can be sought with one of the agricultural probes for measuring soil moisture; farmers use these rod-like instruments to determine the need for irrigation, and they simply measure the electrical resistance of the earth at the tip of the probe.

While resistivity instruments are inexpensive, surveys are time-consuming. Lateral changes in the resistivity of the earth can be more quickly mapped with an earth conductivity meter (Frohlich and

Lancaster 1986; Tabbagh 1986). This is also called an electromagnetic induction meter and is similar to one type of metal detector.

A magnetometer detects iron, and magnetic surveys are ideal for locating iron artifacts and magnetite-containing rocks (Gibson 1986; Martin et al. 1991; von Frese and Noble 1984; Weymouth 1986). This instrument can aid the search for field boundaries. Segments of old wire fence might be buried at the boundaries; there could also be an accumulation of iron trash or igneous rock underground there. Magnetic surveys are fast; in a wooded area, they are much easier to perform than a resistivity survey (Mason 1984).

For the most detailed look at soil stratigraphy, a ground-penetrating radar can be considered (Imai et al. 1987; Vaughan 1986). This elaborate instrument sends short radio pulses into the earth that can reflect from stratification boundaries and objects in the soil. By pulling a radar antenna along a line of interest, the approximate soil profile will be determined. This can suggest the two-dimensional form of interfaces in the earth.

Radar has major limitations. Its profiling depth in conductive soils, such as clay, will be less than 1 m; in sand, however, the radar can generate profiles to a depth greater than 10 m. It generally cannot be employed where there is heavy brush at the surface, for the antenna needs to follow the surface of the ground. While ground-penetrating radar surveys can be done from the air, the lower resolution is a disadvantage for archaeological surveys.

Radar probably can detect a greater variety of underground features than any other type of geophysical instrument. By making closely-spaced parallel profiles, one can get a rough idea of the three-dimensional form of buried features. Radar is good for estimating shapes, but it is not particularly good at identifying the materials that are underground.

Goals of the Search

The following sections will describe some of the applications of remote sensing to several specific searches. While the references illustrate sites from a wide range in time and location, they are far from complete.

Field Boundaries

Derelict field boundaries can be suggested by a wall or fence, an uncultivated strip of land, or a change in the detectable crop or tillage pattern.

Aerial photography has been particularly successful at revealing the cultivation contrasts of former fields, even where they cross the boundaries of modern fields (Beresford and St. Joseph 1979; Moore 1988). Ordinary visible light photography can be quite suitable for this search (Gumerman and Lyons 1971).

Stones might have been placed at the field boundaries either to mark them or to clear them from the cultivated area. Even if covered by soil, they might be detected by geophysics; either resistivity or magnetic surveys could be tried. Metallic trash and old bits of fence wire also might have accumulated along the field boundary; a magnetic survey might delineate these boundaries. During a search for an early farm house on a battlefield of the American Civil War, the line of an abandoned fence was readily traced with magnetic and conductivity surveys;[1] segments of wire at a shallow depth were detected by both surveys. At Chaco Canyon, New Mexico, a magnetic survey appears to have mapped the boundary of a prehistoric field; abnormally low readings were found at the raised earth border (Loose and Lyons 1976).

In the recent past, property corners have been sometimes marked with iron pipes or rods driven into the earth; these can be readily located with a magnetic survey; a simple, inexpensive audio-indicating fluxgate magnetometer is all that is needed; surveyors use these instruments for just this purpose.

Plants

It is difficult to detect traces of former crops or vegetation with remote sensing. Most plant remains are generally too small to be detected by geophysics. However, some large roots can be found by geophysical surveys, and the filled-in pits of uprooted trees are detectable in principle.

Small or vertical roots will generally be invisible. For example, the root cavities found by excavation at a Pompeii vineyard (Jashemski 1973) could probably not be found by a geophysical survey.

The roots of standing trees can cause distinctly high readings on a resistivity survey. It is possible that the undecayed roots of former trees may sometimes be detected by such a survey. At Effigy Mounds National Monument in Ohio, a ground-penetrating radar survey[2] was

1. The survey was a search for the Widow Tapp farm house, within the area of the Battle of the Wilderness, near Fredericksburg, Virginia. This survey was done in May 1989, for Wilson Greene and David Orr of the National Park Service.
2. This survey of mound 52 was done for Robert Nickel of the National Park Service in November 1981. The high resolution radar antenna had a spectral peak of about 315 MHz.

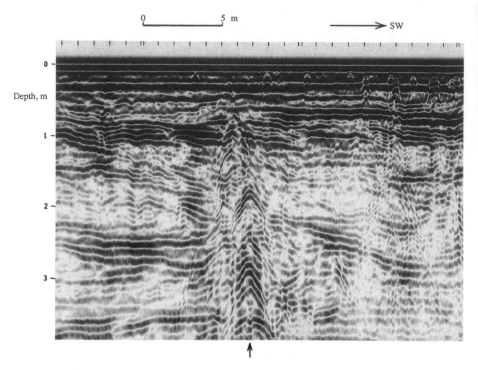

0 ⌞_____⌟ 5 m   ⟶ SW

4.1. Arc-shaped radar echoes at depths of 1–3 m are marked with an arrow on this profile. They could be caused by a tree trunk buried in beach sand.[3]

done over the Little Bear earthen mound; it detected lines of echoes radiating from an area where there is nothing but grass at the surface. An earlier photograph of the mound shows a tree at that point; its roots were traced by the radar. However, a geophysical survey at the historical house of Morven in New Jersey (Yentsch et al. 1987) failed to locate a former line of trees.

A tree that has blown over and been uprooted can leave a crater at the surface. While this can become refilled with soil, it can be detectable by many of the techniques of geophysics. A ground-penetrating radar survey at the Pictured Rocks National Lakeshore in Michigan detected irregular lines of echoes from depths of 2–5 m. These appear to be the trunks of trees buried in the beach sand of Lake Michigan (Figure 4.1).

3. A SIR System-7 radar (Geophysical Survey Systems) and model 3102 (315 MHz) antenna generated this profile on June 20, 1987, in an area about 100 m southwest of the Lakeshore headquarters. It is line Y = 0, and this part of the profile goes from X = −5 (on the left) to X = 20. The depth scale assumes a pulse velocity of 13.3 cm/ns.

Cultivation

The ridges, mounds, and furrows of fields are sometimes encountered during archaeological excavations (Gallagher et al. 1985; Riley and Freimuth 1979; Sheets 1979); aerial photography has recorded them around the world (Armillas 1971; Baker 1975; Denevan 1970; Evenari et al. 1966; Fowler 1969; Parry 1978; Siemens 1983). If these field patterns are visible at the surface as undulations, it is best to take aerial photographs with a low sun angle; at some places, differential snow accumulation or partial flooding would enhance these patterns. Aerial thermography delineated prehistoric field ridges in Arizona (Berlin et al. 1977; Schaber and Gumerman 1969).

At Valley Forge National Park in Pennsylvania, a ground-penetrating radar survey[4] detected shallow echoes that fell along ten parallel lines that were spaced by about 0.7 m. It is possible that these mark the line of plow scars on the subsoil interface.

If soil particles have been aligned by plowing, measurements of the changes in electrical resistivity with direction can be tried in order to determine the direction of the plowing (Taylor and Fleming 1988).

Fertilization

A thin scatter of artifacts in an area can suggest that manure or compost might have been placed on a garden or field there (Roberts and Barrett 1984; Wilkinson 1982; Miller and Gleason, this volume); these artifacts would generally not be detectable by remote sensing. While it is possible that the manure might make the soil more electrically conductive, the conductive components will most probably have leached from the soil in the intervening years. Still, the physical structure of the soil might change, possibly increasing its moisture retention, and this effect might persist indefinitely and be detectable with geophysics (Semple 1971:406).

Landscaping

Geophysical and aerial surveys (Davis 1979) can sometimes detect fields or gardens that were leveled by deposition or removal of soil

---

The electrical resistivity of the sand soil was 8000–20,000 ohm-m. The shallow echoes at a depth of 0.2 m appear to be caused by tree roots. This survey was done for Robert Nickel at the Midwest Archaeological Center of the National Park Service in Lincoln, Nebraska.

4. This was part of a large remote sensing survey of Valley Forge directed by Elizabeth Ralph of the University of Pennsylvania Museum. The survey was done for the National Park Service in 1978.

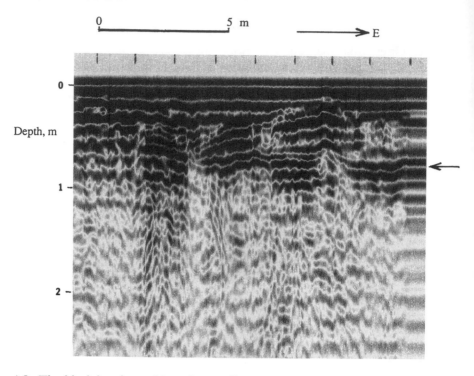

0 ————————————— 5 m   ——————→ E

Depth, m

0 –

1 –

2 –

4.2. The black bands on this radar profile, at a depth of about 0.6 m, are echoes from topsoil buried beneath landscaping fill earth.[5]

from a plot of ground. Natural processes of soil alteration can have similar effects that will also be picked up by these methods (Turnbaugh 1978).

The removal of soil is generally more difficult to detect than its deposition. However, topsoil can be much more magnetic than subsoil, due to organic activity or fires (Le Borgne 1965, Graham 1976). A magnetic survey might therefore detect the loss of topsoil.

The deposition of soil can best be detected by the two techniques used to determine stratification: resistivity (Martinaud and Colmont 1971) and ground-penetrating radar (Imai et al. 1987). At the Theodorus van Wyck house in East Fishkill, New York, ground-penetrating radar mapped rather flat soil interfaces. Figure 4.2 illustrates these by

5. The depth scale on the radar profile assumes a pulse velocity of 11.9 cm/ns; the radar was a SIR System-7 with a model 3102 (315 MHz) antenna. Tick marks at the top of the profile are at 5 ft intervals. This profile is line N50, from W20 to E20 (the southwest corner of the house is the reference N0E0 point). The survey was done on

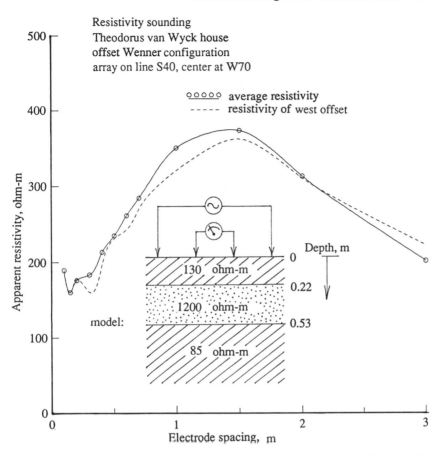

4.3. This resistivity sounding estimates the stratification of the soil. The middle layer has a high electrical resistivity and probably contains more sand or gravel than the layers above and below it.[6]

black bands at a depth of about 0.6 m. Excavation in this area discovered a buried layer of topsoil. A resistivity sounding made in another part of the yard revealed three soil strata, progressing from low to high to low resistivity with increasing depth (see Figure 4.3). That

May 15, 1984, for Roberta Wingerson and Gary Zern (Cultural Resource Surveys, Verbank, NY) and sponsored by IBM.

6. This was the same site and date as the above figure. The resistivity meter was a Gossen Geohm 3, having a source frequency of 108 Hz and a maximum voltage of 30 V. The offset Wenner configuration (Barker 1981) has the two offsets averaged here for the solid line on the graph. The model has been determined by curve match-

figure also gives an estimate of the thickness and resistivity of each layer as determined from a calculated model that assumes that the interfaces are horizontal and abrupt.

Terraces and Walls

Terraces or retaining walls can be readily visible from the air (Turner 1974; see also Treacy and Denevan, this volume). Even if the walls have crumbled, the change in soil thickness above and below them could sometimes result in markedly different vegetation.

If a wall or "ha-ha" wall (i.e., ditch) is completely buried, a geophysical survey might locate it; a resistivity survey would be the first priority. At an Early Bronze Age site in Sicily, it appears that terraces were located with an earth conductivity meter.[7]

Canals and Causeways

Because of the large area these features can cover, aerial photography is frequently the only economical way of searching for them. These searches have been quite successful (Adams et al. 1981; Masse 1981; Nichols 1988; Pope and Dahlin 1989; Showalter 1993). Normal panchromatic and infrared films have both been found suitable. Satellite-borne radar located river channels below the dry sands of north Africa (McHugh et al. 1988). In certain situations, an airborne optical profiler would be ideal for detecting the subtle topographic traces of canals and causeways; these profilers typically employ pulsed lasers and have been called lidars (Thyer et al. 1989). Where the vegetation is too dense for sporadic detection of the ground surface with a beam of light, an airborne, low frequency, surface-profiling radar could be substituted.

Since canals and causeways are typically linear, ground-based geophysics could sometimes be considered for tracing them. At some locations, resistivity or conductivity surveys might be able to locate the fill soil within a canal. While ground-penetrating radar can profile the stratification of the fill, canals with clayey or conductive soil severely limit the profiling depth of the radar.

---

ing (Orellana and Mooney 1966), supplemented with calculations from a computer program (Mooney 1980). Many other, quite different, models also approximate the measurements.

7. This survey, for Brian McConnell of Brown University, was done with a Geonics EM38 electromagnetic induction meter in June, 1990, at the site of La Muculufa (McConnell 1992).

4.4. Prehistoric roads at Chaco Canyon are delineated as darker lines in this photograph, which shows an area of about 600 m on a side. The dark tone is partly caused by a greater density of brush in the shallow depressions of the roads.[8]

Roads and Paths

These features are only indirectly associated with gardens and fields, but it can be valuable to locate them because they can lead to or define the edges of these fields.

8. The photo area is about 1 km northwest of Pueblo Alto. It was taken at about 9:30 am on April 27, 1982, for Thomas Lyons of the National Park Service. The camera was a Hasselblad 500EL with a 40 mm lens (Whittlesey 1975) and 1/500 s exposure; it was borrowed from Julian Whittlesey. This is a vertical photograph, with the 2.25 inch Ektachrome film converted to this black and white print. The project was funded by the National Park Service.

4.5. The dark, curved band that crosses this photo from left to right appears to mark a former road.[9]

Traces of old roads can sometimes be detected readily from the air (Newton and Raphael 1971). The prehistoric roadways at Chaco Canyon, New Mexico were partly mapped from the air (Obenauf 1980); Figure 4.4 is an illustration. The scene of Figure 4.5 is at Odessa, Delaware; a former road appears to have been delineated.

Developed areas are difficult for aerial photography because many false patterns are visible there. Figure 4.6 illustrates some of them. The turf grass between the two roads shows patterns caused by recent and natural events. The straight dark line may mark a trench of a buried pipe or wire. The dark blotches are caused by low vines in the

9. This is about a 45° oblique photo taken from an elevation of about 500 ft at 1:10 pm on May 21, 1974. The camera was a Rollei 35 with a 40 mm lens and an exposure of 1/250 s; 35 mm black and white film was combined with a Wratten #92 filter (deep red). The photo was taken for Horace Hodgkiss of Winterthur Museum and the work was sponsored by the National Science Foundation.

4.6. Many false patterns are evident in this photograph of Valley Forge, Pennsylvania.[10]

grass. The dark circular lines are caused by fairy rings: fungus-enhanced growth of the grass. It appears likely that vehicles have made a short cut between the two roads.

In Costa Rica, the erosional trenches of 1000-year-old paths were located with infrared aerial photographs (Sheets and Sever 1988).

Geophysical surveys can sometimes locate roads and paths; magnetic and resistivity methods have both been successful at this (Aitken 1974:233; Chevallier 1976:107; Goodyear 1971:232; Linington 1972; Tagg 1964:80). If the thickness of a path or road is sufficient, ground-penetrating radar can trace it. The pattern shown in Figure 4.7 is almost surely a path buried at a depth of roughly 10 cm.

10. This oblique photo was taken at an elevation of about 1000 ft of the area between Outer Line Drive and Baptist Road. It was taken at 12:37 pm on April 23, 1976. The camera was a Canon FTb with a 50 mm lens and the film was Tri-X with an exposure of 1/500 s and a Wratten #25 filter. There is roughly a 50 ft elevation difference between the two roads. The project was funded by the National Science Foundation. This photograph and the previous one were taken with dark red filters over the camera's lens; this increases the contrast of patterns in the green vegetation.

0   5 m

⟶ W

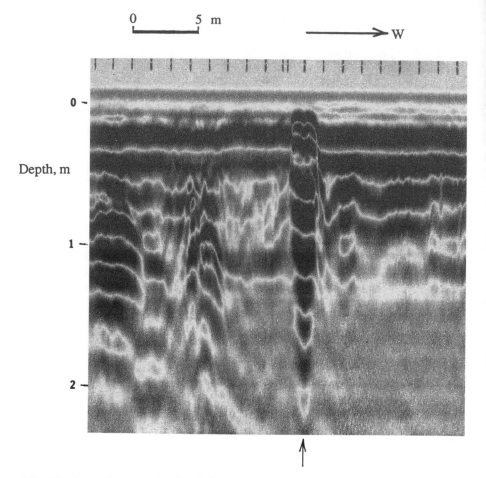

Depth, m

0 –

1 –

2 –

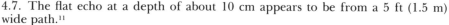

4.7. The flat echo at a depth of about 10 cm appears to be from a 5 ft (1.5 m) wide path.[11]

Somewhat similar echoes detected at Mount Vernon in Virginia and Morven in New Jersey have resulted from either recent excavations or gravel in a soil-draining trench. Radar can similarly map buried

11. The site is the Eppes Mansion in City Point, Virginia. This profile is line N3255, from E700 to E605; this is north of the present mansion. Tick marks at the top of the profile mark 5 ft intervals. For the model 3105 (180 MHz) antenna, a pulse velocity of 10.1 cm/ns has been assumed. The survey was done on May 3, 1983 for David Orr, of the Mid-Atlantic Region of the National Park Service. The electrical resistivity of the soil here is about 100 ohm-m.

roads. At Friendship Hill in Pennsylvania a radar survey[12] suggested that a former gravel road was offset by about 3 m from the present road.

Farm Houses and Implements

Farm buildings can be sought with aerial photography (Heichelheim 1956:171; Wainwright 1977) or geophysics (Linington 1974). Agricultural tools made of iron can readily be located with a magnetic survey. It is possible that other structures, such as threshing floors, can also be detected with geophysical surveys.

Conclusion

Remote sensing might speed or economize the search for dispersed or buried features of the landscape. However, success in these surveys is never sure; the illustrations in this chapter are distinctly clearer than the average for these types of survey. It is often not possible to identify a feature with remote sensing only; after a feature has been detected by remote sensing, it is usually necessary to identify it by examining it on the ground and by making test excavations. Remote sensing can then be excellent for extrapolating the results of those ground checks to other areas.

References

Adams, R.E.W., W.E. Brown, Jr., and T.P. Culbert. 1981. Radar Mapping, Archeology, and Ancient Maya Land Use. *Science* 213:1457–1463.
Aitken, M.J. 1974. *Physics and Archaeology*. Second edition. Clarendon Press, Oxford.
Armillas, P. 1971. Gardens on Swamps. *Science* 174:653–661.
Baker, W.A. 1975. Infra-red Techniques. In *Aerial Reconnaissance for Archaeology*, ed. D.R. Wilson, pp. 46–51. Research Report 12. Council for British Archaeology, London.
Barker, R.D. 1981. The Offset System of Electrical Resistivity Sounding and Its Use with a Multicore Cable. *Geophysical Prospecting* 29:128–143.
Beresford, M.W. and J.K.S. St. Joseph. 1979. *Medieval England*. Second edition. Cambridge University Press, Cambridge.
Berlin, G.L., J.R. Ambler, R.H. Hevly, and G.G. Schaber. 1977. Identification of a Sinagua Agricultural Field by Aerial Thermography, Soil Chemistry, Pollen/Plant Analysis, and Archaeology. *American Antiquity* 42:588–600.

12. This site, near Uniontown, Pennsylvania, was surveyed in September 1984, for David Orr of the National Park Service.

Bradford, J.S.P. 1957. *Ancient Landscapes.* G. Bell and Sons, London.

Brooks, R.R. and D. Johannes. 1990. *Phytoarchaeology.* Dioscorides Press, Portland, OR.

Carr, C. 1982. *Handbook on Soil Resistivity Surveying.* Center for American Archeology Press, Evanston, IL.

Chevallier, R. 1976. *Roman Roads.* University of California Press, Berkeley.

Clark, A. 1969. Resistivity Surveying. In *Science in Archaeology* (revised edition), ed. D. Brothwell and E. Higgs, pp. 695–707. Thames and Hudson, Bristol.

———. 1990. *Seeing Beneath the Soil.* B.T. Batsford, London.

Custer, J.F., E.C. Coleman, W.P. Catts, and K.W. Cunningham. 1986. Soil Chemistry and Historic Archaeological Site Activity Areas: A Test Case from Northern Delaware. *Historical Archaeology* 20(2):89–94.

Davidson, D.A. and M.L. Shackley (editors). 1976. *Geoarchaeology.* Westview Press, Boulder, CO.

Davis, E.L. 1979. The Geoarcheology and Remote Sensing of PaleoAmerican Sites. *Pacific Coast Archaeological Society Quarterly* 15:1–19.

Denevan, W.M. 1970. Aboriginal Drained-Field Cultivation in the Americas. *Science* 169:647–654.

Deuel, L. 1969. *Flights into Yesterday.* St. Martin's Press, New York.

Dobrin, M.B., and C.H. Savit. 1988. *Introduction to Geophysical Prospecting.* Fourth edition. McGraw-Hill, New York.

Ebert, J.I. and T.R. Lyons. 1980. Remote Sensing in Archaeology, Cultural Resources Treatment and Anthropology: The United States of America in 1979. *Aerial Archaeology* 5:1–19.

———. 1983. Archaeology, Anthropology, and Cultural Resources Management. In *Manual of Remote Sensing* (second edition), volume 2, ed. Robert N. Colwell, pp. 1233–1304. American Society of Photogrammetry, Falls Church, VA.

Eidt, R.C. 1977. Detection and Examination of Anthrosols by Phosphate Analysis. *Science* 197:1327–1333.

Evenari, M., L. Shanan, N. Tadmor, and Y. Aharoni. 1966. Ancient Agriculture in the Negev. In *New Roads to Yesterday*, ed. J.R. Caldwell, pp. 480–514. Basic Books, New York.

Fowler, M.L. 1969. Middle Mississippian Agricultural Fields. *American Antiquity* 34:365–375.

Frohlich, B. and W.J. Lancaster. 1986. Electromagnetic Surveying in Current Middle Eastern Archaeology: Application and Evaluation. *Geophysics* 51:1414–1425.

Gallagher, J.P., R.F. Boszhardt, R.F. Sasso, and K. Stevenson. 1985. Oneota Ridged Field Agriculture in Southwestern Wisconsin. *American Antiquity* 50:605–612.

Gibson, T.H. 1986. Magnetic Prospection on Prehistoric Sites in Western Canada. *Geophysics* 51:553–560.

Gladfelter, B.G. 1977. Geoarchaeology: The Geomorphologist and Archaeology. *American Antiquity* 42:519–538.

Goodyear, F.H. 1971. *Archaeological Site Science.* American Elsevier, New York.

Graham, I. 1976. The Investigation of the Magnetic Properties of Archaeological Sediments. In *Geoarchaeology*, ed. D.A. Davidson and M.L. Shackley, pp. 49–63. Westview Press, Boulder, CO.

Gumerman, G.J. and T.R. Lyons. 1971. Archeological Methodology and Remote Sensing. *Science* 172:126–132.

Hassan, F.A. 1981. Rapid Quantitative Determination of Phosphate in Archaeological Sediments. *Journal of Field Archaeology* 8:384–387.

Heichelheim, F.M. 1956. Effects of Classical Antiquity on the Land. In *Man's Role in Changing the Face of the Earth*, vol. 1, ed. W.L. Thomas, Jr., pp. 165–182. University of Chicago Press, Chicago.

Heimmer, D.H. 1992. Near-Surface, High Resolution Methods for Cultural Resource Management and Archaeological Applications. Interagency Archeological Services, National Park Service, Denver, CO.

Imai, T., T. Sakayama, and T. Kanemori. 1987. Use of Ground-Probing Radar and Resistivity Surveys for Archaeological Investigations. *Geophysics* 52:137–150.

Jashemski, W.F. 1973. Large Vineyard Discovered in Ancient Pompeii. *Science* 180:821–830.

Kruckman, L. 1987. The Role of Remote Sensing in Ethnohistorical Research. *Journal of Field Archaeology* 14:343–351.

Lasca, N.P. and J. Donahue. 1990. *Archaeological Geology of North America*. Geological Society of America, Boulder, CO.

Le Borgne, E. 1965. Les propriétés magnétiques du sol. Application à la prospection des sites archéologiques. *Archaeo-Physika* 15:1–20. Böhlau Verlag, Köln.

Lehmer, D.J. 1971. Introduction to Middle Missouri Archeology. *Anthropological Papers* 1, National Park Service, Washington, DC.

Linington, R.E. 1972. The Magnetic Survey at Metapontum, Italy. *Prospezioni Archeologiche* 7–8:135–149.

———. 1974. Magnetic, Electrical and Coring Surveys at Colle del Forno, Montelibretti, 1970–1973. *Prospezioni Archeologiche* 9:47–59.

Lippi, R.D. 1988. Paleotopography and Phosphate Analysis of a Buried Jungle Site in Ecuador. *Journal of Field Archaeology* 15:85–97.

Loose, R.W. and T.R. Lyons. 1976. The Chetro Ketl Field: A Planned Water Control System in Chaco Canyon. In Remote Sensing Experiments in Cultural Resource Studies, assembled by T.R. Lyons. *Reports of the Chaco Center* 1:133–156. Chaco Center, National Park Service, Albuquerque, NM.

Lyons, T.R., R.K. Hitchcock, and W.H. Wills. 1980. A Bibliography of Remote Sensing in Cultural Resource Studies. *Remote Sensing: A Handbook for Archeologists and Cultural Resource Managers*, supplement no. 3, National Park Service, Washington, DC.

Martin, W.A., J.E. Bruseth, and R.J. Huggins. 1991. Assessing Feature Function and Spatial Patterning of Artifacts with Geophysical Remote-Sensing Data. *American Antiquity* 56:701–720.

Martinaud, M. and G. Colmont. 1971. Interêt de l'étude des sols par mésure de résistivité et carottages mécaniques. *Prospezioni Archeologiche* 6:53–60.

Masse, W. 1981. Prehistoric Irrigation Systems in the Salt River Valley, Arizona. *Science* 214:408–415.

Mason, R.J. 1984. An Unorthodox Magnetic Survey of a Large Forested Historic Site. *Historical Archaeology* 18(2):54–63.

McConnell, B.E. 1992. The Early Bronze Age Village of La Maculufa and Prehistoric Hut Architecture in Sicily. *American Journal of Archaeology* 94:23–44.

McHugh, W.P., C.S. Breed, G.G. Schaber, J.F. McCauley, and B.J. Szabo. 1988. Acheulian Sites Along the "Radar Rivers," Southern Egyptian Sahara. *Journal of Field Archaeology* 15:361–379.

Mooney, H.M. 1980. *Handbook of Engineering Geophysics.* Vol. 2, *Electrical Resistivity,* Bison Instruments, Minneapolis, MN.

Moore, J.D. 1988. Prehistoric Raised Field Agriculture in the Casma Valley, Peru. *Journal of Field Archaeology* 15:265–276.

Newton, M.B., Jr. and C.N. Raphael. 1971. Relic Roads of East Feliciana Parish, Louisiana. *Geographical Review* 61:250–264.

Nichols, D.L. 1988. Infrared Aerial Photography and Prehispanic Irrigation at Teotihuacán: The Tlajinga Canals. *Journal of Field Archaeology* 15:17–27.

Obenauf, M.S. 1980. A History of Research on the Chacoan Roadway System. In *Cultural Resources Remote Sensing,* ed. T.R. Lyons and F.J. Mathien, pp. 123–168. National Park Service, Washington, DC.

Orellana, E. and H.M. Mooney. 1966. Master Tables and Curves for Vertical Electrical Sounding over Layered Structures. Interciencia, Madrid.

Parry, J.T. 1978. Ring-Ditch Fortifications in the Rewa Delta, Fiji: Archaeology from the Air Using Panchromatic, Infrared, and Color Photography. *Proceedings of the Twelfth International Symposium on Remote Sensing of the Environment,* pp. 1573–1582. Environmental Research Institute of Michigan, Ann Arbor.

Pope, K.O. and B.H. Dahlin. 1989. Ancient Maya Wetland Agriculture: New Insights from Ecological and Remote Sensing Research. *Journal of Field Archaeology* 16:87–106.

Rainey, F.G., J.N. Hampton, and B.W. Bevan. 1976. Detection of Crop Mark Contrast for Archaeological Surveys. National Aeronautics and Space Administration, ERTS Investigation no. 23220, contract NAS5–20792 final report.

Riley, T.J. and G. Freimuth. 1979. Field Systems and Frost Drainage in the Prehistoric Agriculture of the Upper Great Lakes. *American Antiquity* 44:271–285.

Roberts, D.G. and D. Barrett. 1984. Nightsoil Disposal Practices of the 19th Century and the Origin of Artifacts in Plowzone Proveniences. *Historical Archaeology* 18(1):108–115.

Schaber, G.G. and G.J. Gumerman. 1969. Infrared Scanning Images: An Archeological Application. *Science* 164:712–713.

Schorr, T.S. 1974. A Bibliography, with Historical Sketch. In *Aerial Photography in Anthropological Field Research,* ed. E.Z. Vogt, pp. 163–188. Harvard University Press, Cambridge, MA.

Schwarz, G.T. 1967. A Simplified Chemical Test for Archaeological Field Work. *Archaeometry* 10:57–63.

Scollar, I., A. Tabbagh, A. Hesse, and I. Herzog. 1990. *Archaeological Prospecting and Remote Sensing.* Cambridge University Press, Cambridge.

Semple, E.C. 1971. *The Geography of the Mediterranean Region.* AMS Press, New York.

Sheets, P.D. 1979. Maya Recovery from Volcanic Disasters. Ilopango and Ceren. *Archaeology* 32(3):32–42.

Sheets, P.D. and T. Sever. 1988. High-Tech Wizardry. *Archaeology* 41(6):28–35.

Showalter, P.S. 1993. A Thematic Mapper Analysis of the Prehistoric Hohokam Canal System, Phoenix, Arizona. *Journal of Field Archaeology* 20: 77–90.

Siemens, A.H. 1983. Oriented Raised Fields in Central Veracruz. *American Antiquity* 48:85–102.

Southworth, C.S. 1985. Characteristics and Availability of Data from Earth-Imaging Satellites. *U.S. Geological Survey Bulletin* 1631. U.S. Government Printing Office, Washington DC.

Stein, J.K. 1984. Organic Matter and Carbonates in Archaeological Sites. *Journal of Field Archaeology* 11:239–246.

Stein, J.K. and W.R. Farrand (editors). 1985. *Archaeological Sediments in Context*. Peopling of the Americas 1. Center for the Study of Early Man, University of Maine, Orono.

Strandberg, C.H. 1967. Photoarchaeology. *Photogrammetric Engineering* 33: 1152–1157.

Tabbagh, A. 1986. Applications and Advantages of the Slingram Electromagnetic Method for Archaeological Prospecting. *Geophysics* 51:576–584.

Tagg, G.F. 1964. *Earth Resistances*. Pitman Publishing, New York.

Taylor, R.W. and A.H. Fleming. 1988. Characterizing Jointed Systems by Azimuthal Resistivity Surveys. *Ground Water* 26:464–474.

Thyer, N.H., J.A.R. Blais, and M.A. Chapman. 1989. High Altitude Laser Ranging over Rugged Terrain. *Photogrammetric Engineering and Remote Sensing* 55:559–565.

Tite, M.S. 1972. *Methods of Physical Examination in Archaeology*. Seminar Press, London.

Turnbaugh, W.A. 1978. Floods and Archaeology. *American Antiquity* 43: 593–607.

Turner, B.L., II. 1974. Prehistoric Intensive Agriculture in the Mayan lowlands. *Science* 185:118–124.

Vaughan, C.J. 1986. Ground-Penetrating Radar Surveys used in Archaeological Investigations. *Geophysics* 51:595–604.

von Frese, R.R.B. and V.E. Noble. 1984. Magnetometry for Archaeological Exploration of Historical Sites. *Historical Archaeology* 18(2):38–53.

Wainwright, G. 1977. A Celtic Farmstead in Southern Britain. *Scientific American* 237:157–169.

Weymouth, J.W. 1986. Archaeological Site Surveying Program at the University of Nebraska. *Geophysics* 51:538–552.

Weymouth, J.W. and R. Huggins. 1985. Geophysical Surveying of Archaeological Sites. In *Archaeological Geology*, ed. G. Rapp, Jr. and J.A. Gifford, pp. 191–235. Yale University Press, New Haven, CT.

Whittlesey, J.H. 1975. Elevated and Airborne Photogrammetry and Stereo Photography. In *Photography in Archaeological Research*, ed. E. Harp, Jr., pp. 223–263. University of New Mexico Press, Albuquerque.

Wilkinson, T.J. 1982. The Definition of Ancient Manured Zones by Means of Extensive Sherd-Sampling Techniques. *Journal of Field Archaeology* 9: 323–333.

Wilson, D.R. 1975. Photographic Techniques in the Air. In *Aerial Reconnaissance for Archaeology*, ed. D.R. Wilson, pp. 12–31. Research Report 12. Council for British Archaeology, London.

Woods, W.I. 1977. The Quantitative Analysis of Soil Phosphate. *American Antiquity* 42:248–252.

Wynn, J.C. 1986. A Review of Geophysical Methods used in Archaeology. *Geoarchaeology* 1:245–257.

Yentsch, A.E., N.F. Miller, B. Paca, and D. Piperno. 1987. Archaeologically Defining the Earlier Garden Landscapes at Morven: Preliminary Results. *Northeast Historical Archaeology* 16:1–29.

Chapter 5
The Creation of Cultivable Land Through Terracing

John M. Treacy and William M. Denevan

Agricultural terraces are impressive human landscape features distributed throughout much of the world. Terracing is widespread in the Old World, especially in the Mediterranean region, the Far East, the Near East (Vogel 1988), the Himalayas (Johnson et al. 1982), and Southeast Asia (Conklin 1980). In the New World, agricultural terraces occur from the southwest United States to northwest Argentina (Donkin 1979). Terracing evokes images of rock-walled and visually pleasing "staircase farms" (Cook 1916) imposed upon steep slopes; notable examples of these fields occur in Peru, the Philippines, and China. Most of the world's terraces, however, are more humble features on gently sloping terrain where soils are retained by stone lines, low earthen ridges, vegetation or logs, as well as by stone walls.

Since agricultural terracing is a widespread and ancient phenomenon, the study of terraces has long been within the purview of both cultural geography and archaeology. Geographers tend to envision terracing as a major landscape modification that is worthy of attention in its own right. Geographic inquiry focuses upon the environmental matrices of slope, soil, and climate that have encouraged terrace farming, and on field typologies and the distribution of terracing (cf. Denevan 1980; Knapp 1991; Spencer and Hale 1961; Treacy 1989a). Geographers, however, also share with archaeologists an interest in broader issues such as environmental adaptation and land use history, population dynamics and agricultural intensification, settlement strategies, and cultural/historical origins of land forms. The analysis of relict, or ancient but still functioning, terrace systems may shed light on these questions, not only by clarifying agronomic functions of terraces, but by providing data on construction labor inputs, productivity, and by dating the fields.

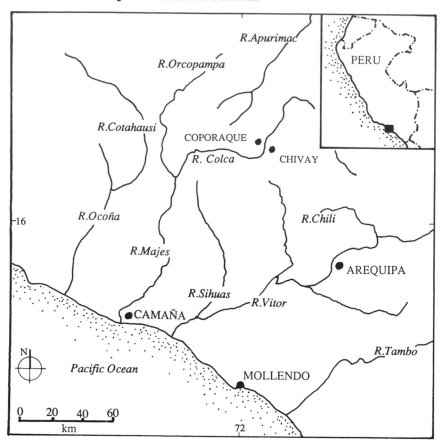

5.1. Map of the Río Colca region, Peru. (T. Hoffman, after original by
J. Treacy)

There is also interest in terrace systems from an applied aspect,
especially in developing countries where soil loss on sloped cultivated
land is lowering agricultural productivity (Blaikie and Brookfield
1987). How can long-abandoned terraces be brought back into productivity? Knowledge of how terracing may combat land degradation
and how terrace systems function may be gleaned from the study of
ancient sites.

This essay is a general consideration of terrace forms, agronomic
functions, and construction procedures, drawing largely on venerable
literature in cultural geography, especially for the New World. Some
information is specifically from our research on prehistoric and current terracing and irrigation in the village of Coporaque in the Colca
Valley of the southern Peruvian Andes (Figure 5.1).

Terrace Definitions and Environmental Considerations

A definition of an agricultural terrace is that by Spencer and Hale (1961:3): "any artificially flattened surface on which crops are grown subsequent to the flattening, no matter how small, how crude, or how purposeful." This notion of a terrace is necessarily broad since there are a wide variety of terrace types. The presence of a retaining wall is not a definitive component of a terrace since contour plowing may be considered terracing. However, many geographers (Denevan 1980; Field 1966) suggest that terraces in the traditional sense consist of a retaining wall (sometimes termed a riser) that holds back or accumulates soil to create a planting platform (or tread). The question of whether slope flattening precedes wall construction or is a consequence of walling depends upon construction techniques, as is discussed below.

Agricultural terraces are found upon steeply sloping terrain (to 70%) as well as upon very gentle slopes (less than 5%). On vertiginous slopes, terracing creates agricultural space (see Pulsipher, this volume); on less steep land terracing improves crop land but does not necessarily create it. In many regions of the world, land that is terraced could be cropped easily without terracing, implying that farmers have other motivations for building terraces. These may include (1) soil deepening, (2) erosion control, (3) moisture management, and (4) microclimate modification. Any of these could be a prime cause for terracing, or a secondary one, or even an epiphenomenal one.

Soil Deepening

Embanking soil behind retaining walls obviously produces soils deeper than the original soils. However, soil deepening may be a secondary reason for terracing except in cases where cropping surfaces are created on thin or non-existent soils. Soil deepening has been mentioned as an occasional prime reason by Spencer and Hale (1961: 5), Denevan (1980:622), and Donkin (1979:34). Wright (1962:99) adds the proviso that soil deepening is usually linked to irrigation opportunities.

Erosion Control

Terracing halts or drastically reduces soil erosion, and it seems intuitive that one of the major reasons farmers build terraces is to counter gradual soil loss (Denevan 1980:622; Field 1966:8; Hopkins 1968:5;

Maldonado and Gamarra 1978:164; Sanders et al. 1979:383; Turner 1983:93). However, Donkin (1979:34) stresses that erosion control is merely an epiphenomenal advantage of most terracing, while Spencer and Hale (1961:26–27) emphatically dismiss erosion as a prime reason, stating that ancient farmers generally lacked the acumen to take preventive action against the long term hazards of soil loss.

The argument that terraces are not specifically erosion control devices rests in part on the existence of alternative prime functions, such as irrigation. It also makes sense to discount erosion control in reference to slopes uncultivated prior to terracing. Simple terraces made of stone lines or vegetation may, however, be responses to sheet erosion. Terraces constructed accretionally by slope processes (soil build-up by controlled erosion) indicate that farmers are aware that soils may be highly subject to erosion.

Microclimatic Control

Terraced fields may have favorable microclimates for crops due to frost avoidance (Donkin 1979:25; Field 1966:9). Wind turbulence on terraces inhibits cold air from descending on terraced slopes (Denevan 1980:623; Donkin 1979:26; Patrick 1980:763); terraces can control slope aspect and sun angle (Earls 1986:100–124; Fejos 1944:33); and the re-radiation from terrace walls warms planting platforms (Denevan 1980:623; Field 1966:430; Patrick 1980:763).

Frosts occur in mountainous areas because of night time radiational cooling under clear skies, and katabatic (downslope) movements of cold air toward valley floors. Plants within the thermal belt of a slope (above the point where cold air collects at night), and below the point where temperatures begin to fall according to the normal lapse rate, often avoid frosts since cold air glides over the hillslope. The effect of thermal zones was surely understood by early farmers. Therefore frost avoidance may have been an important function of initial terracing, especially in the case of terracing for frost-sensitive plants such as maize. The fact that terrace-induced wind turbulence disrupts falling layers of cold air may not constitute a prime function of terraces, but rather may be a by-product of the act of terracing.

The role of slope aspect (direction faced) may depend upon local conditions. Other considerations—soils, access to irrigation water, proximity to settlements—may have been more important than slope aspect. In areas of droughty soils, slopes with abundant insolation may be avoided to decrease evaporation; in other cases, sunny slopes may be preferred to hasten plant development.

Moisture Control

A preponderance of theory and data on agricultural terracing supports the position that moisture retention and irrigation were extremely common prime functions. Perry (1916) was perhaps the first scholar to associate terracing with irrigation, and certainly the first to produce a world map of irrigated "terraced cultivation." The spatial distribution of Andean terracing strongly suggests that moisture control was a prime function, prompting Donkin (1979:22) to suggest that New World terraces are primarily moisture retention and management features. The importance of water control was highlighted by Spencer and Hale (1961:4–5), who noted that the creation of spreading or impounding surfaces for water, whether from canals, springs, or rainfall, is a fundamental aim of many terraces worldwide. Soil moisture retention figures highly among the agronomic functions described by Denevan (1980:622), Maldonado and Gamarra (1978: 165), Field (1966:9), Hopkins (1968:6), Donkin (1979:34), and Sanders et al. (1979:231).

There are other water management advantages of terracing besides moisture retention: (1) a reduced slope allows water percolation into the soil to minimize runoff; (2) leveled and deepened soils allow plant roots to seek stored moisture from depth, thus improving drought resistance; and (3) flattened surfaces allow irrigation water to flow evenly over soils. This last point is of particular interest for Colca Valley terraces.

A corollary of moisture retention is adequate drainage. Terraces with permeable stone walls and/or cobble-fill horizons allow excess moisture to drain freely and thus soil waterlogging is avoided (Bonavia 1967/68:232; Field 1966:10; Maldonado and Gamarra 1978:165; Turner 1983:94).

Agronomic Features Summary

The focus on agronomic functions largely reflects a utilitarian perspective. Functions tell us what terraces accomplish as artificial habitats for crops under the assumption that farmers are aware of all the unique agronomic properties of terraces. Yet the tendency to assign prime function status to terraces may ignore the probability that the reasons why farmers build terraces are multiple, intertwined, and analytically inseparable from each other. Breaking down terrace purposes into discrete functions fails to capture the sense of overall agronomic advantage that terracing provides and that farmers recognize as necessary for adequate harvests. The apparent paucity of native language names for terraces in the Andes and the general acceptance of the Spanish term *andenes* for terraces suggest that terraces are simply considered "agricultural fields" with little unique conceptualization differentiating them from other types of fields.

Terrace Typology

The taxonomy used by geographers is well suited for interpreting terrace landscapes, and a review will be useful for those not acquainted with the literature on the topic. Terrace typologies are based primarily on field morphology. Form, in turn, is largely a function of degree of slope, both of the original soil surface and the terrace platform, the type of wall and wall materials, and the degree of horizontal or vertical contiguity of the terraces. In general, steeper slopes imply the need for higher retaining walls. Shallower slopes result in lower terrace walls, but such terracing requires more labor to level soil behind the walls since the distance soil must be transferred is greater.

An additional definitional element is temporal; that is, whether a field is self-filling (accretional; wall building precedes field flattening), or whether it is hand filled (wall building concurrent with field flattening). Accretional fields have been noted for many regions of the New World (for Mexico, see Doolittle 1984; Guzmán 1962; Sanders et al. 1979:247–248). A historical model of accretional terrace building that attempts to explain terrace formation has been formulated by Williams (1990).

Agronomic functions of terraces may be deduced from a study of field morphology. The variables of slope, wall type, contiguity, and time create the basis for most terrace typologies (summarized in Table 5.1).

Weir Terraces

This terrace type is usually short, made of stone piles or plant material placed at right angles to narrow or low-discharge intermittent streams. The function of this form of terrace is either to trap sediment to deepen the soil, or to capture and impound water for wet-field cultivation. Weir terraces also control erosion, control downstream flooding, and may essentially destroy intermittent streams if terrace construction continues upstream (Doolittle 1985). These fields are rudimentary and are found in many parts of the world. Other

TABLE 5.1. A General Terrace Typology[a]

Type	Platform	Wall	Fill process	Contiguity[b]
Weir	Usually sloping	Stone, logs, earth	Accretional by water-borne sediment	Segmented
Barrage	Sloping	Stone	Accretional by erosion	Segmented or serial rows
Sloping, dry-field	Sloping	Stone, earth, adobe, vegetation	Accretional and/or hand fill	Segmented or dry-serial rows
Bench	Horizontal to gently sloping	Stone	Accretional and/or hand fill	Serial rows
Valley floor	Horizontal to gently sloping	Stone, earth blocks	Hand fill	Serial rows
Wet-field	Horizontal	Stone, earth	Accretional and/or hand fill	Serial rows

[a] Adapted from Spencer and Hale (1961); Denevan (1980); Treacy (1989a: 74–100).
[b] Segmented refers to fields not horizontally contiguous; serial means contiguous vertically and horizontally, although there may be some space with sloping-field and barrage terraces (open rows).

terms for weir terraces include cross-channel terraces, check dams, and silt-trap terraces.

Barrage Terraces

This category was singled out by Spencer and Hale (1961) to describe the unique cross-channel drainage terraces of the Negev in southern Israel (Evenari et al. 1982). Stone lines trap sediments from large catchments, often 20 to 30 times the size of the slightly levelled planting platform. The purpose of these fields is to harvest water from occasional heavy rains by intercepting sheetwash. Similar kinds of fields have also been reported in Peru (Benfer et al. 1987) and in New Mexico (Sandor et al. 1986: 53–59).

Sloping, Dry-field Terraces

Dry-field terraces (Figure 5.2) are an extremely common form of field worldwide. They often slope slightly toward their retaining walls

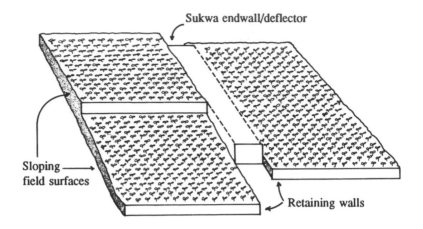

Sukwa endwall/deflector

Sloping → field surfaces

Retaining walls

Wall length: 30-50m
Platform width: 13-16m
Wall height: 1.3-2m
Sukwa dimensions: 1.4m high, 1.3m wide, 30m long
Slope positions: on slopes up to 50%,
planting surfaces slope up to 20%
Construction method: some hand filling,
accretionary filling by slope processes

5.2. Schematic view of sloping, dry-field terraces, Colca Valley.
(E. Brescia, after original by J. Treacy)

and are made either by slow soil build-up behind walls (accretionary
method) or by digging and backfilling. Some are backed by planted
vegetation, such as the *metepantli* (maguey) terraces of Mexico (Patrick
1977; West 1970). Sloping-field terraces appear to be most common
in regions of moderate precipitation and function to conserve soil
moisture, control erosion, and deepen the soil for cropping. The sloping platforms of dry-field terraces usually do not permit irrigation.

Bench, Linear Contour Terraces

These fields (Figures 5.3 and 5.4), usually irrigated, may not be the
most common variant, but they are the best known. In the Andes the
type is often labeled "Inca terrace," although many predate the Inca
period. The fundamental characteristics of bench terraces are (1) high

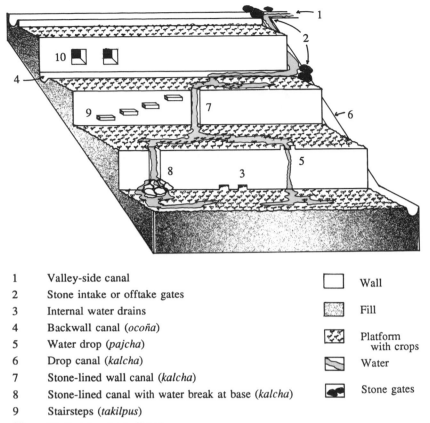

1	Valley-side canal
2	Stone intake or offtake gates
3	Internal water drains
4	Backwall canal (*ocoña*)
5	Water drop (*pajcha*)
6	Drop canal (*kalcha*)
7	Stone-lined wall canal (*kalcha*)
8	Stone-lined canal with water break at base (*kalcha*)
9	Stairsteps (*takilpus*)
10	Wall niches (*pukullutas*)

☐ Wall

▨ Fill

▨ Platform with crops

◩ Water

◪ Stone gates

5.3. Schematic view of bench terraces and associated features at Coporaque, Colca Valley. (E. Brescia, after original by J. Treacy)

(from 1 m to ca. 4 or 5 m) retaining walls made of stacked stones; (2) level platform surfaces; (3) valley-side positions closely following slope contours; (4) arrangement in closed vertical serial rows; (5) cut-and-fill construction methods (see below); (6) inward sloping walls (batter); and (7) built-in irrigation and other devices, such as side walls, water drops, canals, drains, intakes and offtakes, steps, and niches (Figure 5.3).

A variation of bench terraces is the tree crop terrace, narrow platforms which provide space for permanent shrub or tree crops. A good example is the *grada* in Bolivia, a stone or earthen embanked

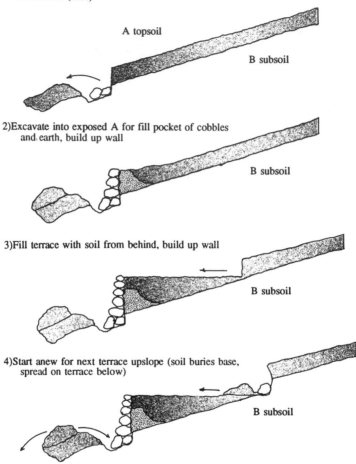

1)Excavate A horizon topsoil 30-50cm into B set first
wall stones (base)

A topsoil

B subsoil

2)Excavate into exposed A for fill pocket of cobbles
and earth, build up wall

B subsoil

3)Fill terrace with soil from behind, build up wall

B subsoil

4)Start anew for next terrace upslope (soil buries base,
spread on terrace below)

B subsoil

5.4. Bench terrace construction procedures at Coporaque, Colca
Valley. (E. Brescia, after original by J. Treacy)

terrace wherein coca shrubs are planted in trenches between the
raised *gradas* (Donkin 1979: 122–125).

Valley-Floor Terraces

These fields (Figure 5.5) are in many respects similar to bench terraces, but they are much wider, have lower walls, and are found on

Wall length: up to 60m
Platform width: 20-30m
Wall height: 0.20-1m
Slope positions: on slopes from 5-20%˙
Construction method: accretionary filling
by plowing, leveling, and slope processes

footslope positions or perpendicular to stream channels on valley-floor areas.

Wet-Field Terraces

In China and Southeast Asia, wet-field or pond terraces are used primarily for padi rice cultivation (e.g., Conklin 1980). Field platforms are invariably horizontal, and earthen bunds extend along the retaining wall edges to pond water. Walls are of stone or earth, and the fields often have elaborate mechanisms for moving and controlling water.

There are, without doubt, other categories of terraces that could be advanced; however, most would fall within the parameters of the above typology.

The typology, modified from Spencer and Hale (1961), suggests a possible evolutionary scheme whereby farmers learn to transform a simple terrace type into more complex ones (e.g., sloping, dry-field into irrigated bench). More likely involved, however, is a change in function. Changes in terrace type have been recorded, as the Colca data indicate.

Terraces in the Colca Valley

The valley of the Colca River is located in the Department of Arequipa in southern Peru on the western slope of the Andean *cordill-*

era. It is but one of a series of valleys incised into the southwestern Andean flanks, most of which had been terraced in pre-Hispanic times. The cultivable portion of the valley is approximately 50 km long. Almost the entire valley, with the exception of steep and eroded slopes, is terraced to an upslope elevation of approximately 4000 m (Figure 5.1). Farmers today grow maize, barley, alfalfa, broad beans, quinoa, potatoes, and other minor crops. Maize is planted only on terraces, while the other crops appear both on terraces and elsewhere.

The valley's arid climate may have strongly influenced terrace construction. The agricultural core has a semi-arid montane steppe climate (Holdridge system; see Treacy 1989a:52−62), receiving an annual average of 385 mm of precipitation measured at the main valley village of Chivay (3633 m). Rains are highly seasonal, peaking in December and abating sharply during late May to early August. For this reason, almost all cultivable land is irrigated by canals bringing water either from natural springs or from streams flowing from mountains topped by permanent snow. The roles of irrigation are thus: (1) to extend the growing season by one to two months, allowing farmers to plant in August and harvest in May; and (2) to provide supplementary water in case rains slacken during the growing season.

The valley has been the site of a multi-disciplinary study to discover why large areas of terracing are abandoned there even while farmers struggle to reclaim lost land (see Denevan 1987; Treacy 1989a; also see Guillet 1987, 1992). Reputed causes for abandonment have included post-Conquest depopulation, the introduction of European crops and livestock leading to shifts in land use, climatic change that dried up water sources, tectonic uplift distorting canal trajectories, and soil exhaustion (Denevan 1987). Another explanation is that some terrace abandonment in the valley was due to pre-Hispanic terrace reconstruction which replaced unirrigated fields with irrigated ones. Large areas of abandoned fields are obsolete unirrigated terraces beyond the reach of newly-constructed irrigation canals.

Colca Terrace Construction

The Colca Valley features a variety of terrace types that may be keyed into the terrace typology presented above. The common and visually impressive type is the linear contour or bench terrace on valley-side slopes (Figure 5.3). Bench terraces measure between 1 and 3 m in wall height, between 3 and 7 m in width depending upon degree of hillside slope, and from 40 to 60 m in length. Practically all Colca Valley bench terraces are irrigated by gravity fed canals, and terraces often have built-in water drops and channels ensconced in walls or upon the terrace platform. The disposition of vertical irrigation channels running down terraced slopes determines terrace length. Bench terraces are essentially irrigation platforms on steep slopes; their microclimatic virtues allow intensive maize cultivation.

Builders used cut-and-bench methods to construct bench terraces (Figure 5.4). They excavated through A horizon topsoil into an indurated B horizon to emplace wall base stones ranging in size from 30 to 60 cm in diameter. Stability and interlocking fit were more important than the size of wall stones; base stones may be smaller than stones placed on top of them. Next, soil was removed from the exposed vertical soil face in order to make the cobble and earthen drainage horizon which all Colca Valley bench terraces have. Builders then moved soil down from the slope behind the wall, while stone masons built the wall higher to retain the soil. Mineralogical examination shows that terrace fill soil is composed of in situ slope soil; no exogenous soils were used. In extensively terraced regions such as the Colca Valley, the costs in labor would preclude transport of soil fill from elsewhere.

Often, a bench terrace is damaged when waterlogged soil bursts the retaining wall and spills forth. Careless wall repair hastens further wall failure. Builders blame poor masonry techniques or dry soil construction for broken walls. Builders prefer to terrace with wet soil since dry soil is porous and will quickly become saturated following heavy rains, thus provoking sudden, early bursting. Common mistakes cited include not fitting wall stones together tightly, or failure to press stones against the earthen fill behind. In the latter case, a gap forms between the wall and fill causing the wall to collapse.

Bench terrace reconstruction duplicates the labor techniques of construction, except that soil spilled from ruptured walls has to be thrown back upslope and re-walled. Workers trench down to the original base to remove the fallen and buried stones from the original wall. The wall is rebuilt and the fill stones and soil are carefully repacked in behind the wall and tamped down. When reconstructing fields, masons replace up to 80 percent of the ancient walls, and must laboriously throw spilled soils upslope, which demands more effort than moving soils downslope for new terraces.

Sloping, dry-field terraces are found upon higher slopes (above bench terraces) beyond the limits of irrigation canals (Figure 5.2). Their staggered and segmented slope dispositions distinguish them from bench terraces. Sloping-field terraces tend to measure between 1.3 and 2 m in wall height, 13 to 16 m in width, and between 30 and 50 m in wall length. The broad, sloping catchments of these terraces suggest that they were in part accretional or self-filling fields, although some cut-and-bench building techniques may have been used because the terraces also feature cobble drainage horizons. Fields of this type are invariably now abandoned in the Colca Valley since they are not irrigable.

Simple weir terraces, some no more than a rough line of stacked stones, are scattered thinly through parts of the valley. They generally cross gullies or intermittent stream channels. Examination of aerial photographs shows that barrage-like terraces—stone walls flanked by long, perpendicular water diversion walls—may have been constructed in some areas of the Colca Valley, but field ground checks are still needed to confirm them. Weir and barrage terraces, like sloping-field terraces, are today unfarmed. Valley-floor terraces (Figure 5.5) are common on gentle, lower slopes and alluvial flats.

Non-terraced fields in the valley include level or slightly sloping fields on the valley floor, house and garden plots, and very recent (since the 1970s) unterraced valley-side sloping fields. The latter fields were made following new canal construction, and it would appear that such fields would have been unthinkable in pre-Columbian times.

Colca Terrace Functions

The contrasting morphologies of bench terraces and sloping field terraces underscore their contrasting agronomic functions. Bench terraces are leveled or slightly sloping fields; they are invariably vertically contiguous; and they are irrigated. Sloping fields are not vertically contiguous, have large moisture-contributing areas, and do not have irrigation facilities. If the sloping fields *predate* irrigated fields, it suggests that climatic conditions may have been wetter in the pre-bench-terrace past, or that farmers designed the sloping fields to harvest sheetwash; thereby they could charge fields with moisture following the kinds of heavy rains that characterize present climatic conditions. If the sloping fields *postdate* the bench terraces, or are coeval with them, it would then suggest they represent agricultural expansion into marginal (unirrigated) slope lands. Results from surface collections of archaeological material and from excavations, however, provided data to establish the greater antiquity of the sloping-field terraces (see Treacy 1989a:105–138).

The Archaeology of Terracing

There are relatively few archaeological studies of New World terraces based upon excavations and stratigraphic analysis. The few studies done to date highlight the need for adequate field drainage in terrace construction. Bonavia (1967/68) excavated pre-Inca sloping-field terraces in the Mantaro region of central Peru, uncovering evidence of carefully made drainage horizons. Builders placed a cobble fill layer below the topsoil, presumably to speed internal (through the wall) drainage when the topsoil filled to capacity and moisture seeped into the subsoil. Similar artificial cobble fills have been noted in the Urubamba valley region near Cuzco (Keeley 1985), on the coast of Peru (Maldonado and Gamarra 1978:165), and most notably in the Colca Valley of Peru (Treacy 1989a:191–192).

In Chile, terraces may have been drained internally by compacting the subsurface clayey soil into an inward and sideways-sloping platform so that water percolates out of the terrace solum (Wright 1963:71). Maya sloping-field terraces in Belize feature cobble or rubble fill perhaps designed to play a drainage function similar to Peruvian fill pockets, although Maya terrace builders also placed walls at slight downsloping angles to drain away excess overland flow (Turner 1983:94).

Soil studies to determine terrace construction methods should reveal whether ancient terraces were self-filling or accretional fields, or back-filled by hand. Accretional fields should display a finely layered stratigraphy indicating episodic soil deposition by controlled erosion. In some cases accretional fields have soil horizons similar to alluvial depositions (Guzmán 1962:403). In cases of relict terraces, however, post-abandonment erosion may erase evidence of building methods, or it may create horizontal strata resembling original controlled erosion fill. Distinguishing between accretional and hand-filled terraces is important for understanding terrace functions and history. Controlled erosion terraces cannot be easily irrigated, at least not until they are eventually leveled; therefore they are most often found in dry-farmed regions.

Dating of New World terraces is often done by site association. Field (1966:321) reports stone-walled terraces at Tafi del Valle (northwest Argentina) that date to possibly as early as 265–405 B.C. based upon radiocarbon samples from nearby sites. Earthen ridges and swales at Chachapoyas (northern Peru) have been dated to A.D. 900 by associated radiocarbon dates from burial sites near the fields (Schjellerup 1985:118). Dating by ceramic seriation revealed ages of A.D. 700 in Ayacucho, Peru (Lumbreras 1974:133–135), while ceramics excavated from terraces at Chala (Arequipa, Peru) suggest an early building period at A.D. 200 (Engel 1973:278). Colca terraces may date to A.D. 500–600 (several calibrated C-14 dates; Malpass 1987:60–62).

Dating terraces by archaeological methods presents some difficulties. Sequent occupation and the reconstruction of sites may hide the true antiquity of terraces. Dates obtained for agricultural landforms could refer to the most intensive phase of use or to remodeling rather than to the epoch of initial construction (Smith 1987:41). On the other hand, recovered dates may well refer to the earliest dates of construction. The interpretive problem of dating terraces arises in the Colca Valley study where radiocarbon dates, ceramic material, and field morphologies indicate several episodes of occupation and farming in the region. Also, terraces are by nature disturbed sites, and soils and datable residues may be mixed by erosion or churned by farming thus confounding stratigraphic clarity.

Social Functions of Terracing

Agricultural landform investigations have gone beyond a pure agronomic focus to elucidate the social and political dimensions of terracing (see Yentsch, this volume). Terracing in some instances may have embodied expressions of political and economic might, engineering prowess, aesthetic preferences, and cosmological beliefs. There have been tentative probes into the symbolic content of Andean terracing. Donkin (1979:132) observed that the stupendous royal terraces such as those at Yucay (Urubamba, Peru) appear to be conscious and intimidating demonstrations of imperial power. Niles (1982) has differentiated between relatively commonplace Inca production terraces and more elaborate high-prestige terraces dedicated to the state religion. Finally, Nickel (1982) writes that Incaic terracing in part reflects deep-seated cultural and aesthetic preferences for geometric structuring, and thus terraces functioned as visual metaphors for social, environmental, and cosmological order.

Conclusions

This review indicates that geographical, archaeological, and ethnographic field research are all essential for understanding agricultural terracing. Functions vary with environmental conditions. Most terraces in the world were initially constructed hundreds or even thousands of years ago, so that excavation is necessary to determine original construction and function. Current practices, in turn, can provide insights into past agroecology.

We find that there are several functions of terraces, which vary from place to place as to whether they are primary, secondary, or not important at all. Erosion control, often considered to be a primary function, is more likely to be a secondary function, whereas water management is frequently the primary function. There are only a few basic types of terraces—cross channel, sloping field, and bench—but there are numerous variations of each. Construction procedures vary considerably. Those described here for the Colca Valley are common in the Central Andes.

Terraces are ubiquitous in the world, creating impressive human landscapes involving massive movement of earth and stone, thereby altering ecological conditions in order to facilitate crop production. Nevertheless, terraces have been little studied in either their prehistoric or current traditional form. There are several general surveys (e.g., Donkin 1979; Field 1966; Spencer and Hale 1961), and there are some specific regional studies (e.g., Conklin 1980; Earls 1989; Patrick 1977; Sandor et al. 1986; Treacy 1989a; Turner 1983). However, these are relatively few. The opportunities for archaeological, historical, agroecological, and applied research are exciting, as nations with mountain lands seek knowledge about the origin and abandonment of terraces and the possibilities for their restoration and expansion.

Note. This essay by John Treacy was in draft form and still in progress at the moment of his untimely death on October 24, 1989. It has been revised and edited, with some additions and a Conclusion and Bibliography by William Denevan. Treacy had intended to include a case study on the terrace archaeology of the Colca Valley in Peru, but this was not completed; only one section is provided here. For aspects of his Colca research, see Treacy (1987a, 1987b, 1989a, 1989b, 1994, and in press); also Denevan (1987). Useful suggestions were made by Blenda Femenias.

References

Benfer, R.A., G.H. Weir, and B. Ojeda Enriquez. 1987. Early Water Management Technology on the Peruvian Coast. In *Arid Land Use Strategies and Risk Management in the Andes*, ed. D.L. Browman, pp. 195–206. Westview Press, Boulder, CO.

Blaikie, P. and H. Brookfield. 1987. *Land Degradation and Society*. Methuen, New York.

Bonavia,. D. 1967/68. Investigaciones arqueológicas en el Mantaro medio. *Revista del Museo Nacional* 35:211–294. Lima.

Conklin, H.C. 1980. *Ethnographic Atlas of Ifugao*. Yale University Press, New Haven, CT.

Cook, O.F. 1916. Staircase Farms of the Ancients. *National Geographic Magazine* 29:474–534.

Denevan, W.M. 1980. Tipología de configuraciones agrícolas prehispánicas. *América Indígena* 40:619–652.

————. 1987. Terrace Abandonment in the Colca Valley. In *Pre-Hispanic Agricultural Fields in the Andean Region*, ed. W.M. Denevan, K. Mathewson, and G. Knapp, pp. 1–43. British Archaeological Reports, International Series 359. Oxford.

Donkin, R.A. 1979. *Agricultural Terracing in the Aboriginal New World*. Viking Fund Publications in Anthropology 56. University of Arizona Press, Tucson.

Doolittle, W.E. 1984. Agricultural Change as an Incremental Process. *Annals of the Association of American Geographers* 74:124–137.

————. 1985. The Use of Check Dams for Protecting Downstream Agricultural Lands in the Prehistoric Southwest: A Contextual Analysis. *Journal of Anthropological Research* 41:279–305.

Earls, J. 1986. Experimentación agrícola en el Perú precolombino y su factibilidad de reempleo. In *Andenes y camellones en el Perú andino*, ed. C. de la Torre and M. Burga, pp. 301–330. CONCYTEC, Lima.

————. 1989. *Planificación agrícola andina: Bases para un manejo cibernético de sistemas de andenes*. COFIDE, Lima.

Engel, F. 1973. New Facts About Pre-Columbian Life in the Andean Lomas. *Current Anthropology* 14:271–280.

Evenari, M., L. Shanan, and N. Tadmore. 1982. *The Negev: The Challenge of a Desert*. Harvard University Press, Cambridge, MA.

Fejos, P. 1944. *Archaeological Explorations in the Cordillera Vilcabamba, Southeastern Peru*. Viking Fund Publications in Anthropology 3. Viking Fund, New York.

Field, C. 1966. *A Reconnaissance of Southern Andean Agricultural Terracing*. Ph.D. dissertation. University of California, Los Angeles.

Guillet, D. 1987. Terracing and Irrigation in the Peruvian Highlands. *Current Anthropology* 28:409–430.

————. 1992. *Covering Ground: Communal Water Management and the State in the Peruvian Highlands*. University of Michigan Press, Ann Arbor.

Guzmán, L.E. 1962. Las terrazas de los antiguos Mayas montañeses, Chiapas, México. *Revista Interamericana de Ciencias Sociales* 1:398–406.

Hopkins, J.W. III. 1968. *Prehispanic Agricultural Terraces in Mexico*. Master's thesis. University of Chicago, Chicago.

Johnson, K., E.A. Olson, and S. Manandhar. 1982. Environmental Knowledge and Response to Natural Hazards in Mountainous Nepal. *Mountain Research and Development* 2:175–188.

Keeley, H.C.M. 1985. Soils of Prehispanic Terrace Systems in the Cusichaca Valley, Peru. In *Prehistoric Intensive Agriculture in the Tropics*, ed. I.S. Farrington, pp. 547–586. British Archaeological Reports, International Series 232. Oxford.

Knapp, G. 1991. *Andean Ecology: Adaptive Dynamics in Ecuador*. Dellplain Latin American Studies 27. Westview Press, Boulder, CO.

Lumbreras, L.G. 1974. *The Peoples and Cultures of Ancient Peru*. Smithsonian Institution Press, Washington, DC.

Maldonado, A. and L. Gamarra Dulanto. 1978. Significado arqueológico, agrológico, y geográfico de los andenes abandonados de Santa Inés y Chosica en el valle del Rímac. In *Tecnología andina*, ed. R. Ravines, pp. 157–171. Instituto de Estudios Peruanos, Lima.

Malpass, M.A. 1987. Prehistoric Agricultural Terracing at Chijra in the Colca Valley, Peru: Preliminary Report II. In *Pre-Hispanic Agricultural Fields in the*

Andean Region, ed. W.M. Denevan, K. Mathewson, and G. Knapp, pp. 45–66. British Archaeological Reports, International Series 359. Oxford.

Nickel, C. 1982. The Semiotics of Andean Terracing. *Art Journal* 42:200–204.

Niles, S. 1982. Style and Function in Inca Agricultural Works near Cuzco. *Ñawpa Pacha* 20:163–182.

Patrick, L.L. 1977. *A Cultural Geography of the Use of Seasonally Dry, Sloping Terrain: The Metepantli Crop Terraces of Central Mexico*. Ph.D. dissertation. University of Pittsburgh, Pittsburgh.

———. 1980. Los orígenes de las terrazas de cultivo. *América Indígena* 40:757–772.

Perry, W.J. 1916. The Geographical Distribution of Terraced Cultivation and Irrigation. *Proceedings of the Manchester Literary and Philosophical Society* 60:1–25.

Sanders, W.T., J.R. Parsons, and R.S. Santley. 1979. *The Basin of Mexico*. Academic Press, New York.

Sandor, J. 1987. Initial Investigation of Soils in Agricultural Terraces in the Colca Valley, Peru. In *Pre-Hispanic Agricultural Fields in the Andean Region*, ed. W.M. Denevan, K. Mathewson, and G. Knapp, pp. 163–192. British Archaeological Reports, International Series 359. Oxford.

Sandor, J.A., P.L. Gersper, and J.W. Hawley. 1986. Soils at Prehistoric Agricultural Terracing Sites in New Mexico. *Soil Science Society of America Journal* 50:166–180.

Schjellerup, I. 1985. Observations of Ridged Fields and Terracing Systems in the Northern Highlands of Peru. *Tools and Tillage* 5:101–120.

Smith, R. 1987. Indigenous Agriculture in the Americas: Origins, Techniques, and Contemporary Relevance. In *Latin American Development: Geographical Perspectives*, ed. D. Preston, pp. 34–69. Longman, London.

Spencer, J.E. and G.A. Hale. 1961. The Origin, Nature, and Distribution of Agricultural Terracing. *Pacific Viewpoint* 2:1–40.

Treacy, J.M. 1987a. Building and Rebuilding Agricultural Terraces in the Colca Valley of Peru *Yearbook, Conference of Latin Americanist Geographers* 13:51–57.

———. 1987b. An Ecological Model for Estimating Prehistoric Population at Coporaque, Colca Valley, Peru. In *Pre-Hispanic Agricultural Fields in the Andean Region*, ed. W.M. Denevan, K. Mathewson, and G. Knapp, pp. 147–162. British Archaeological Reports, International Series 359. Oxford.

———. 1989a. *The Fields of Coporaque: Agricultural Terracing and Water Management in the Colca Valley, Arequipa, Peru*. Ph.D. dissertation. University of Wisconsin, Madison.

———. 1989b. Agricultural Terraces in Peru's Colca Valley: Promises and Problems of an Ancient Technology. In *Fragile Lands of Latin America: Strategies for Sustainable Development*, ed. J.O. Browder, pp. 209–229. Westview Press, Boulder, CO.

———. 1994. The Construction of Agricultural Terraces in the Colca Valley. In *Achoma Archaeology: A Study of Terrace Irrigation in Peru*, ed. D.E. Shea. Occasional Papers of the Beloit College Museums, Beloit, WI. (forthcoming)

———. In press. Teaching Water: Hydraulic Management and Terracing in Coporaque, the Colca Valley, Peru. In *Irrigation at High Altitudes*, ed. D. Guillet and W. Mitchell. American Anthropological Association, Washington, DC.

Turner, B.L. II. 1983. *Once Beneath the Forest: Prehistoric Terracing in the Río Bec Region of the Maya Lowlands.* Dellplain Latin American Studies 13. Westview Press, Boulder, CO.

Vogel, H. 1988. Impoundment-Type Bench Terracing with Underground Conduits in Jibal Haraz, Yemen Arab Republic. *Transactions of the Institute of British Geographers* 13:29–38.

West, R.C. 1970. Population Densities and Agricultural Practices in Pre-Columbian Mexico, with Special Emphasis on Semi-Terracing. *Verhandlungen des XXXVIII internationalen Amerikanistenkongresses (1968)* 2:361–369. München.

Williams, L.S. 1990. Agricultural Terrace Evolution in Latin America. *Yearbook, Conference of Latin Americanist Geographers* 16:82–93.

Wright, A.S.C. 1962. Some Terrace Systems of the Western Hemisphere and Pacific Islands. *Pacific Viewpoint* 3:97–105.

———. 1963. The Soil Process and the Evolution of Agriculture in Northern Chile. *Pacific Viewpoint* 4:65–74.

Chapter 6
Methodological Considerations in the Study of Ancient Andean Field Systems

Clark L. Erickson

Raised field agriculture is a pre-Hispanic intensive crop production system used in the Andean region of highland Peru and Bolivia around the Lake Titicaca Basin (Figure 6.1). The system combines the use of large raised earthen planting platforms with complex networks of intervening canals and ditches. These features are evidence of massive earthmoving and landscape modification covering an area of over 82,000 ha of seasonally waterlogged land surface.

The methods for studying raised field agriculture discussed in this paper were employed by the Raised Field Agricultural Project, a long term (over 7 years) multidisciplinary study of ancient Andean agriculture. The research focused on the determination of original raised field morphology, origins and evolution of the system, carrying capacity and population dynamics, field functions, and crops cultivated. Key research problems included an assessment of the labor input necessary for construction and maintenance and a study of the field productivity and potential carrying capacity. This information was used to evaluate the efficiency of raised field farming in comparison to other past and present systems. The project also included an applied dimension, in that raised field technology was reintroduced to several communities and actively included the participation of local farmers in the agricultural experiments and fieldwork.

Archaeological techniques including analysis of aerial photographs, trenching, chronology development based on stratigraphic, ceramic thermoluminescence and radiocarbon dating, flotation and pollen analysis, settlement analysis and experimental archaeology established a basic outline of the extinct agricultural system. Agricultural experimentation created new possibilities for understanding the pro-

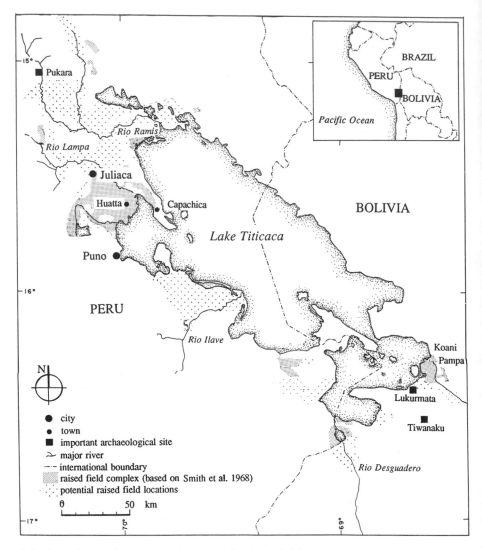

6.1. Locations of known and potential raised field remains in the Lake Titicaca Basin (after Smith et al. 1968)

ductive and social aspects of the ancient agricultural system. Finally, the data provided by these techniques form the basis for the design and implementation of an experimental program of raised field construction and use within the context of indigenous farming communities in the Lake Titicaca Basin.

Raised Field Agriculture in the Andean Landscape

The Andean landscape is truly anthropogenic. Where any agriculture was possible, the natural land features have been totally transformed into cultural features by prehistoric farmers. The remains of these human transformations, such as terraces, raised fields, sunken fields, reservoirs, irrigation canals, aqueducts, channelized rivers, and road-ways, are abundant throughout the Central Andean Highlands of Peru and Bolivia (Burga and de la Torre 1986; Denevan 1980; Denevan et al. 1987; Erickson 1992). Ironically, much of this once productive landscape now lies abandoned and much of the traditional technological knowledge base and resources have been lost. These prehistoric remains of agricultural systems can tell us a great deal about the people who made them. Even more important is how this knowledge can potentially be used in solving contemporary problems in rural development.

Raised fields are large, artificially elevated planting platforms. The excavation of soil to create adjacent platforms creates "canals," "swales," or "ditches" (Denevan and Turner 1974; Erickson 1985, 1986, 1988a, 1988b, 1992). Evidence of these fields has been found throughout the Americas in Colombia, Ecuador, Peru, Bolivia, Venezuela, Surinam, Guatemala, Belize, Mexico, Florida, Wisconsin, and Michigan (Denevan 1970, 1982; Parsons and Denevan 1967).[1] In the Lake Titicaca region, raised fields are highly variable in form and size. Most common forms are long straight linear platforms arranged in "bundles" of five to seven fields (for some of the field forms, see Figure 6.2). Commonly, fields range from 4 to 10 m wide, 10 to 100 m long and 1 m in elevation (see Erickson 1986, 1988a; Lennon 1982, 1983; Smith et al. 1968 for commonly used classifications). Remains of raised fields are estimated to cover at least 82,000 ha of the extensive flat plains (pampas) around Lake Titicaca (Smith et al. 1968), although this figure is probably very conservative (Erickson 1988a).

All prehistoric raised fields in the Lake Titicaca Basin of Peru and Bolivia are abandoned.[2] Archaeological evidence indicates that this probably happened before the arrival of the Spanish, and no early historical records mention the field systems (Erickson 1988a). Because

1. Raised fields are found throughout much of the tropical and some of the temperate zones of both the New World and the Old World (e.g., Denevan 1982; Denevan and Turner 1974; Farrington 1985).

2. Large "lazy beds" for potatoes are used in the Lake Titicaca Basin and these are considered by some to be a small form of raised fields. I find that size of canal and platform is critical in the functioning of a true raised field and that most, if not all, of the currently used beds are not of sufficient size to be classified as true raised fields (Erickson 1988a).

of the lack of written records referring to raised field farming or local ethnographic analogy, the only direct means by which to investigate prehistoric raised field farming in the Lake Titicaca Basin were through the application of archaeological techniques and raised field experimentation.

The Archaeological Study of Raised Field Systems

The Lake Titicaca raised fields were first investigated by geographers in the late 1960s (Smith et al. 1968) and later by an archaeologist in the late 1970s (Lennon 1982, 1983). The research on which this paper is based was done between 1981 and 1986. A similar program of excavation and experimentation has recently begun in highland Bolivia (Kolata 1989). In 1981, the Raised Field Agricultural Project began a detailed multidisciplinary investigation in the northern Lake Titicaca Basin, where the largest known block of prehistoric raised fields (some 56,000 ha) is located. Results of this project have been presented in various publications and monographs (Brinkmeier 1985; Erickson 1985, 1986, 1987, 1988a, 1988b, 1989, 1992, 1993; Erickson and Brinkmeier 1990, 1993; Erickson and Candler 1989; Garaycochea 1986a, 1986b).[3]

The archaeological techniques employed in this study provide information regarding the original morphology, chronology, crops cultivated, and site formation processes of raised field agriculture. These data are then used to reconstruct the fields accurately for agronomic experimentation to address field function, crop productivity, labor investment and organization, and sustainability.

Aerial Photographic Analysis

The raised fields of the Lake Titicaca Basin were first discovered in the 1960s through the use of aerial photographs, despite having been walked over by scholars for over a hundred years (Smith et al. 1968). Most fields and canals in the Lake Titicaca Basin can easily be dis-

3. There is an extensive bibliography on the subject of archaeological techniques employed for the study of raised fields (including Bray et al. 1987; Broadbent 1987; Culbert et al. 1991; Eidt 1984; Evenari et al. 1971; Farrington 1983; Freidel and Scarborough 1982; Gliessman et al. 1985; Golson 1977; Graffam 1990; Hammond et al. 1987; Knapp and Ryder 1983; Kolata and Graffam 1989; Kus 1972; Moore 1988; Moseley 1983; Muse and Quintero 1987; Ortloff 1988; Ortloff et al. 1985; Parsons et al. 1985; Pohl 1989; Puleston 1976, 1977a, 1978; Siemens 1989; Stemper 1987; Turner and Harrison 1983b; Zucchi and Denevan 1979). These techniques have also been employed in studies of terracing (e.g., Malpass 1987) and irrigation (e.g., Farrington 1983; Moseley 1983).

cerned in aerial photographs because of contrasting vegetation and soil conditions and because of the lack of dense ground cover (see Figures 6.2, 6.3, 6.4, 6.5). Aerial photograph interpretation proved very useful in locating and mapping field patterns, their areal distribution (Erickson 1988a; Kolata 1986; Lennon 1982, 1983; Smith et al. 1968), and associated archaeological occupation sites (Erickson 1988a, in prep. a). The aerial photographic record is also very useful in guiding the experimental reconstruction of raised fields discussed below.

Throughout the raised field system in the pampas are isolated and clustered occupation mounds (Figure 6.4). Most of these mounds are unoccupied, although some have permanent and seasonal residences of families who use the pampa for pasture. We know from excavation and surface collections that the occupation of most of these mounds is multicomponent and continuous. One of the advantages of working in the Lake Titicaca Basin is that prehistoric occupation sites of raised field farmers are easy to locate with stereo pairs of aerial photographs. The slight topographic relief (0.5 to 1.0 m in elevation) of these mounds stands out against the relatively flat lake plain surface. Even the smallest individual house mounds can usually be distinguished (Figure 6.4). Many mounds are also surrounded by water during the rainy season when the pampa is inundated.

The patterns of field shape, size, and orientation provide many kinds of information on the organization of raised field farming. In spite of the great degree of variation, most raised field blocks were carefully designed to the point of approaching a form of standardization. Discrete rectangular or square "bundles" of five to ten parallel fields are very common (Erickson 1988a; Lennon 1983) (Figures 6.2, 6.4, 6.5). Many of these are bordered by canals or earthen embankments. These appear to have been family or extended family holdings (land that could be worked and maintained by a group of five or more people). These in turn are nestled within larger blocks of fields defined by large straight canals which radiate outward from certain points (usually higher ground). These larger units probably represent *ayllus* or the local Andean land holding units. These, in turn, combine at a higher level unit, the local community or *llacta* (Figure 6.5). Since we know that most of the fields visible on the surface in the Huatta area date to the Late Intermediate Period and thus are probably contemporary, the differences between field patterns in larger areal extent may reflect ethnic differences and social boundaries.

Farmer aesthetics and basic cognitive structures may also be represented in the formal patterning of the earthworks. The majority of raised fields in the Lake Titicaca Basin are oriented to the cardinal directions. The most common type of general patterning, the

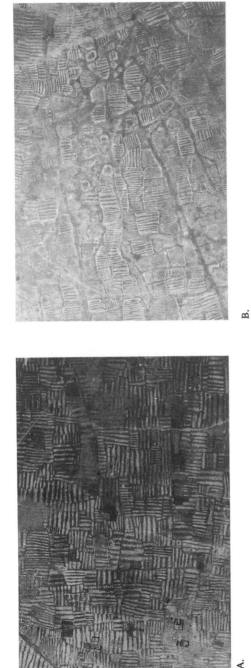
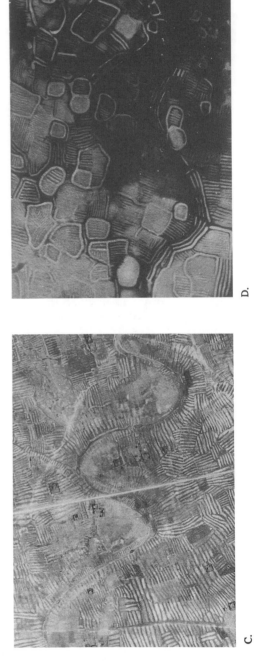

6.2. Variations in the forms of raised fields in the Huatta area of Peru.

6.3. Prehispanic raised fields in Viscachani Pampa, Huatta. The darker fields in the center are reconstructed raised fields, part of the experimental program.

6.4. Raised field platforms (light colored strips) and prehispanic occupation mounds (upper right and lower left) in the shallows of Lake Titicaca.

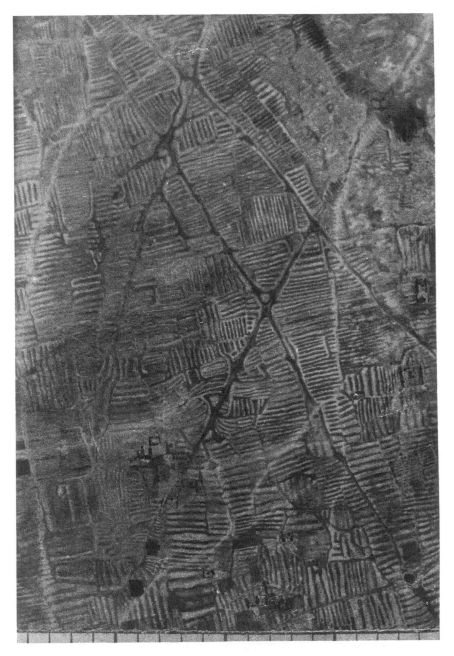

6.5. Highly patterned raised fields in Viscachani Pampa. The long dark linear features are large canals which divide up the blocks of raised fields into larger units.

"checkerboard" form (Smith et al. 1968) clearly has structural similarities to textile patterning (Erickson in prep. b), something that has been argued for by archaeologists working with pre-Hispanic Andean architectural patterning. While it is expected that some aspects of the form of raised fields were specific to their function and efficiency, the majority of decisions regarding patterning of fields probably was culturally based. In several locations, whimsical or cultural metaphors appear to have been expressed in the visible spatial patterning (complex spirals, circles, and other possible shapes).

Trenching

The trenching of earthworks and architectural features has been a very useful tool in archaeology throughout its history (see Yentsch and Kratzer, this volume). Excavation trenches provide long stratigraphic profiles of complex features which allow the definition of construction stages and internal chronology, original morphology and extent of cultural disturbance of the original land surface, and the effects of natural and cultural site formation processes during use and after abandonment. In the case of the raised fields of the Lake Titicaca Basin, the topographic features are heavily eroded and sometimes buried. Sediments have filled the once deep canals and the field platform surfaces have been planed off by wind and water erosion, human disturbances through agricultural and pastoral activities, road building, urbanization, and sod removal for construction. In this context, surface remains will only provide a limited amount of information and thus excavation of deep trenches is necessary.

In order to determine original morphology, numerous trenches were excavated within raised field complexes. The most effective placement of a trench is *perpendicular* to the principal axis of a block of fields and canals (Figures 6.6, 6.7, 6.8, 6.9). The ideal length of a trench extends from the center of one raised field surface to the center of the adjacent raised field surface across the intervening canal (see Figure 6.6). Long trench excavations are much more efficient than small test units or soil coring for raised field investigation. Small units that do not span the distance between raised field and canal do not provide adequate information for the interpretation of the complex stratigraphy. The changes which occur over a short horizontal and vertical distance within raised fields would be missed or misinterpreted without the long profile perspective provided by trenches. On exceptionally large fields, trenches were excavated from canal center to adjacent field center and the unexcavated half extrapolated from

6.6. Excavation of Unit A at Viscachani Pampa, Huatta. The trench extends from the center of one raised field across a canal to the center of field.

6.7. Excavations of trenches in raised fields.

the known strata. The trenches were 1 or 2 m wide to allow sufficient space and light for mapping profiles and to detect complex horizontal stratigraphy. Trenches were excavated to a depth below the boundary between subsoil and cultural levels (normally between 1 and 2 m below the present pampa surface; see Figure 6.8).

In trenches with very complex stratigraphy, a second 1 m wide trench was excavated alongside the original one (Figure 6.6). This excavation used the first profile as a guide, so that each cultural stratum

6.8. Unit NOPQ at the site of Pancha showing portions of two small wavelength Phase I raised field plat-forms under larger wavelength Phase II raised fields (visible at the surface). The meter scale is at the center of the Phase II canal.

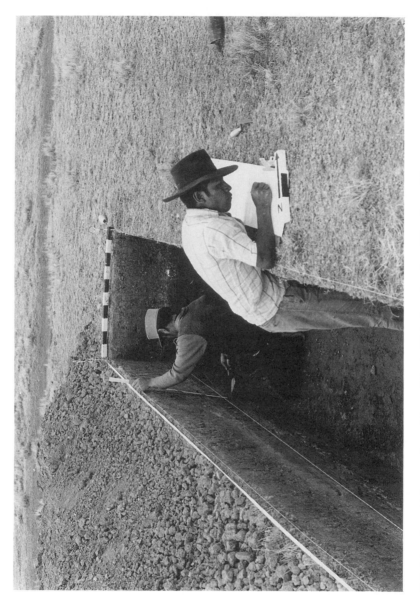

6.9. Mapping of the stratigraphic profiles in Unit A at the site of Jucchata, Huatta.

of the second trench could be "peeled back." This technique permitted very precise control of micro-strata and permitted accurate recording and recovery of in situ artifacts useful in dating and interpreting field function.

The canal stratigraphy and canal boundaries are clearest because they were originally cut into the lighter-colored B and C Horizons and later were filled with dark organic sediments, leaving a sharp stratigraphic contrast. The platform boundaries are often indistinct, since they generally have eroded into the canals. Canal depth and volume provided indirect information from which to extrapolate the original field surface height and fill volume dimensions (Erickson 1988a).

The internal stratigraphic complexity of the raised field construction fill and sediment-filled canals was surprising (Figure 6.10). Clear superposition of discrete periods of raised fields separated by periods of field abandonment was documented in five of the nine trenches excavated. All trenches showed evidence of distinct construction fill stages and field disuse and abandonment. This demonstrates the importance of trenching in order to determine complex field history. The study of surface features alone cannot provide any information on the evolution of field form or distinct building and use periods. Analysis of vertical stratigraphy demonstrated that all field systems were constructed over a long period of time, rather than all at once, as was formerly believed.

Large scale horizontal excavations to uncover and expose buried canals and field surfaces over large areas could be useful for documenting the horizontal morphology of superimposed field systems. Unfortunately, our project did not have the resources to do this. Depending on the issues to be resolved, the effort necessary for large scale horizontal excavation may be worthwhile, although it is certainly much less efficient than trenching operations. Golson (1977) and Gorecki (1982) found that horizontal excavations were productive in their investigations of raised fields and canals in highland New Guinea.

The Chronology and Evolution of Field Systems

Ancient field systems are often assigned to the period of nearby dated occupation sites (for example, see Denevan 1970; Kolata 1986; Smith et al. 1968; Turner and Harrison 1983). In many cases, associated sites are dated by surface artifactual remains. The sites located in our archaeological survey of raised field zones and those that were excavated are *multicomponent* sites, many with occupations that span a period of 3000 years. The abundance of late prehistoric remains on site surfaces gives no hint of the actual buried remains of earlier occupations. The only accurate way to determine when the fields were built, used, and abandoned is to directly date the field systems themselves. This can be done either through radiocarbon dating of organic remains within fields or the recovery of in situ diagnostic or datable artifacts.

As expected in non-occupational, agricultural features, absolute dating of construction phases, use, and abandonment proved difficult due to the paucity of in situ stylistically diagnostic or datable artifacts. Many trenches yielded few or no artifacts except the ubiquitous broken stone hoe flakes incorporated into the earthworks during use or resharpening of tools. Pottery fragments and organic materials were more plentiful in fields located near occupation sites, where garbage (bone, ash, lithics, and ceramics) had been incorporated intentionally or unintentionally into the field platform fill and canal sediments. Unfortunately, most ceramics recovered in situ were body sherds of utilitarian wares which could not be used for accurate stylistic dating. There was insufficient charcoal within canal and field strata for radiocarbon dating.[4] A number of pottery sherds recovered in situ were submitted for thermoluminescence (TL) dating. Nine TL dates provided the basis for the establishment of an evolutionary chronology of raised field construction, use, and abandonment (see Erickson 1987, 1988a).

An example of the results of trenching, stratigraphic analysis, and TL dating of in situ ceramics within a complex stratigraphic profile (Trench NOPQ) of two raised fields and a canal at the site of Pancha Pampa is presented in Figures 6.10 and 6.11. These agricultural features are directly associated with a large occupation mound in the pampa southwest of Huatta. Surface collections and test excavations at the residential site of Pancha indicate nearly continuous occupation dating to as early as 1500 B.C. Without excavation, there was no way to determine if the fields also were constructed and used over this considerable time span or if they were associated with particular periods of occupation at the site. Stratigraphic analysis of the raised field profile indicated that there were two major periods of construction and use of the raised fields at this location. During Phase I, small

---

4. In some cases of raised field investigation, it has been possible to date canal sediments and in situ organic artifacts directly using radiocarbon analysis. Dates were obtained from raised field canals in Belize (Puleston 1978, Pohl 1989, Turner and Harrison 1983a, 1983b), the Guayas Basin (Parsons 1978), the San Jorge Basin (Eidt 1984), and the Llanos de Mojos (Erickson et al. 1991). Recently, accelerator mass spectrometric technique has been applied to dating raised fields in Cobweb Swamp, Belize (J. Jacob, pers. comm.).

PANCHA

PPu7-28

UNIT NOPQ

WEST PROFILE

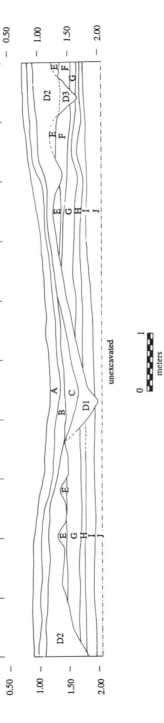

6.10. Stratigraphic profile of Unit NOPQ, Pancha.

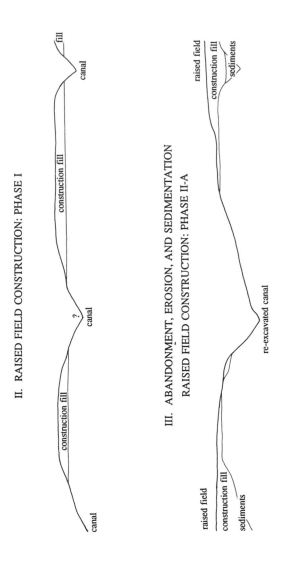

PANCHA UNIT NOPQ

I. ORIGINAL LANDSURFACE

II. RAISED FIELD CONSTRUCTION: PHASE I

construction fill

fill

canal

construction fill

canal

?

construction fill

canal

III. ABANDONMENT, EROSION, AND SEDIMENTATION
RAISED FIELD CONSTRUCTION: PHASE II-A

raised field

construction fill

sediments

re-excavated canal

raised field

construction fill

sediments

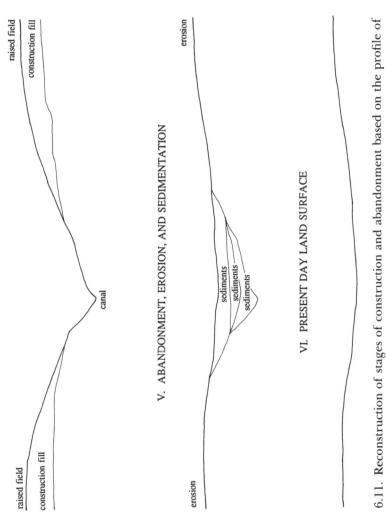

IV. RAISED FIELD CONSTRUCTION: PHASE II-B

raised field

construction fill

raised field

construction fill

canal

V. ABANDONMENT, EROSION, AND SEDIMENTATION

erosion

sediments

sediments

sediments

erosion

VI. PRESENT DAY LAND SURFACE

6.11. Reconstruction of stages of construction and abandonment based on the profile of Unit NOPQ, Pancha.

1–2 m wide raised fields were constructed with wavelengths of approximately 5 m between one canal and an adjacent canal and an elevation of 1–2 m between canal floor and field surface. At a later Phase II construction, the dimensions of the fields were expanded by closing every other Phase I canal with fill and constructing platforms of 5 m wide and up to 1 m tall. During this time, the canals were widened (up to 5 m) and excavated deep into the subsoil erasing the evidence of some of the earlier Phase I canals. The result produced raised fields with 10 m wavelengths of canal to canal. In addition, minor construction and maintenance activities could be detected in the microstrata of the raised field platform fill within both phases.

Thermoluminescence dating of ceramics recovered from various key contexts within the stratigraphic trench provided a means of direct dating of the relative chronology based on stratigraphy presented above.[5] A date of 400 B.C. ± 500 years (DUR TL 26-1as) was recovered from the base of the Phase I raised field fill and is interpreted as dating the initial construction of the raised field. Another date of A.D. 440 ± 310 years (DUR TL 8as) was obtained from ceramic pottery sherd in the sediments of the Phase I canal, probably deposited during a hiatus of raised field construction and use. Two overlapping dates of A.D. 1325 ± 120 years (DUR TL 26-3as) and A.D. 1540 ± 90 (DUR TL 35-7as) years on ceramics were recovered from samples in sediments of a Phase II canal. These are interpreted as dating the period after final abandonment of the fields as canals were gradually filled with sediments and occasional occupation midden.

Based on analysis of stratigraphic profiles, additional TL dates and stylistic dating of in situ ceramics from a total of 11 stratigraphic trenches in raised fields, we developed a tentative chronology of raised field construction, use, and abandonment (Erickson 1987, 1988a). The dating of ceramics within fields is internally consistent with the stratigraphy of the profiles and correlates closely with radiocarbon dating of the major occupations of associated sites within the pampa. There appear to have been two distinct periods of construction and use. The first period begins sometime around 1000 B.C. and lasted until A.D. 300 and is characterized by small raised fields. A second construction and use period probably began after a period of several hundred years of abandonment around A.D. 1000 and

---

5. Thermoluminescence (TL) dating is a relatively inexpensive and accurate technique for absolute dating. For TL dating, ceramic samples must be at least 2.5 cm in diameter and 0.6 cm thick. To prevent contamination by cosmic radiation, the samples must be sherds that were buried relatively quickly after deposition (preferably to a depth of at least 0.5 m). The context of raised fields helps insure that sherds recovered in raised field fill meet this criterion of rapid and deep burial.

lasted until the Inca conquest of the region around A.D. 1450. The complex internal stratigraphy and cycles of construction, use, and abandonment could never be accurately determined through study of eroded surface remains or associated occupation sites, only through careful analysis of long trenches excavated within the fields themselves.

Because agricultural fields are likely to have been regularly disturbed to a certain depth during the annual cultivation and harvest when in use, care must be taken in the interpretation of single dates. Because of this factor and the uncertainties inherent in TL dating, dates should be checked against independent data sets such as relative stratigraphy and ceramic stylistic dating. In our case, all TL dates were internally consistent with the relative dating of the stratigraphy within each TL date context and stylistic dating of the sherds. Despite potential problems, these methods are preferable to the common establishment of agricultural system chronology through dating of associated occupation sites.

Ethnobotanical Analysis

Flotation and pollen samples collected from raised field contexts and associated occupation sites were analyzed. In situ botanical remains helped to determine some of the original food crops cultivated on the raised fields in the past, in addition to providing data on past local environments and other non-cultivated resources used by the farmers.

Pollen preservation was poor in the raised field and canal contexts, probably because of the annual alternation of wet and dry conditions of the soils (Wiseman 1984). Although hampered by a lack of comparative collection of local pollen, many weedy species of plants not common to the wet conditions of the pampa were identified, strongly suggesting intensive agriculture, and pollen grains of *Solanum* and *Chenopodium* may represent cultivated potatoes and quinoa or cañihua. Unfortunately, many important highland Andean crops leave little pollen signature because they are reproduced vegetatively. Pollen of several aquatic species were recovered from raised field canals indicating that raised field canals supported permanent aquatic communities. Floral evidence of year round moisture conservation in many canals supports our hypothesis that the features served important functions to minimize droughts and provide protection against frosts. The evidence of aquatic plants also indicates that the canals were important for the production and cycling of organic nutrients to sustain continuous raised field crop production.

Standard flotation recovery of small animal and plant remains was also employed. A simple flotation rig consisting of a 55-gallon barrel and heavy fraction inset screen was used to recover carbonized macro-botanical remains (cf. Pearsall 1989). Flotation samples taken from raised field profiles did not yield any preserved macrobotanical remains. Soils from archaeological occupation sites associated with the raised fields did yield substantial quantities of identifiable remains of plants, some of which were potential cultigens. Among these were considerable numbers of seeds of *Chenopodium* (possibly the domestic quinoa and cañihua), *Lupinus* sp. (possibly the domestic crop tarwi), tuber fragments (presumably of domesticated potatoes and other Andean tuber crops), various wild pampa grasses, aquatic plants, and weedy species. Surprisingly, the majority of carbonized seeds and other plant parts identified in the samples from occupation sites are not of crop species, but represent wild or weedy species. This bias may be due to the Andean practice of using camelid dung as household cooking fuel (cf. Miller and Smart 1984). The llama and alpacas may have ingested many of the seeds which were carbonized during dung burning and later recovered in flotation.

This botanical information, in addition to lists of important crops cultivated during the early Colonial Period and those still cultivated today in the region, provided a basic inventory of cultigens (and economically important weedy species) that may have been grown on raised fields in the past. This data base was used in the planning of raised field experiments (discussed below).

Settlement Survey and Occupation Site Excavations

Large sections of the pampa and hillside around the community of Huatta were surveyed on foot. Of particular interest to this research were occupation sites on the pampa. Sites discovered using the aerial photographs were verified on the ground. It was relatively easy to locate sites and their boundaries in the pampa because of the elevation of sites, invariably located on low mounds, and because of the sparseness of vegetation on the overgrazed pampa. Sites were elevated both intentionally by the addition of fill and unintentionally by the collapse of adobe and sod structures and the accumulation of midden. Mounds tend to be spaced at regular intervals across the pampa. Several large sites have non-local cut stone on their surfaces and one large site has a substantial stone retaining wall suggesting important public architecture. At the other end of the spectrum are the temporary camps on small mounds within blocks of raised fields.

Sites were measured and diagnostic materials were surface collected for dating and determining site function. In addition to occupation sites, several special function sites (quarries, kilns, and field huts) were located.

Two settlements were excavated (Figure 6.12). Because of the problems mentioned above, these sites were dated independently of the raised fields using radiocarbon dating and stylistic analysis of diagnostic ceramics. These excavations documented the long occupation sequence, beginning around 1000 B.C. There was clear overlap of occupation of these sites in the lower levels and the construction and use of raised fields (both Phase I and Phase II mentioned above). In addition to chronology, the test excavations recovered information on households, domesticated and collected foods (both plant and animal), local environments and farm economy, agricultural tools, and household ceramic inventories (Erickson in prep. a). Subsistence was primarily based on crops produced by raised field farming, in addition to the collection and hunting of wild lacustrine floral and faunal resources.

The two mound sites, Kaminaqa (3.5 m high) and Pancha 3.0 m high), were excavated using limited horizontal excavation and deep probing. Excavations demonstrated that the mounds were totally artificial, yet very little of the mound area appeared to be made up of intentional fill. Most of the mound matrix was a gradual accumulation of a continual series of occupation floors, possibly houses, patios, and other structures. Alternating with floors were bands of what appeared to be "melted" adobe and adobe debris and sometimes midden debris. It is quite possible that many of the structures were also made of sod building material cut from the pampa, a practice still used today. These mounds represent the gradual build-up of household collapse and intentional leveling, and garbage accumulations of numerous generations of raised field farmers. House structures appear to have been densely packed on the mound surface. As the mounds increased in elevation, their value as ideal occupation sites for farmers increased. These mounds prevented inundation of households and provided a vantage point from which to view the vast agricultural plain. Today, the larger mounds such as Coata and Pojsin Karata are densely occupied population centers for the area.

Experiments in Raised Field Agriculture

Experimental archaeology (including simulations and replicative studies) has been a useful approach in a number of archaeological interpretations (Coles 1973). Although it is impossible to control all the experimental variables and to create the social and environmental

6.12. Excavations in households at the site of Viscachani Pampa (above) and Pancha (facing page).

conditions of prehistory, experiments can provide insights to how ancient technology functioned and how it was organized. Experimental archaeology has great potential for interpreting past agricultural systems (Coles 1973; Evenari et al. 1971; Puleston 1977a, 1977b; Steensberg 1980). Because raised fields, like many other prehistoric agricultural systems, are not currently used in the Andean region, direct ethnographic analogy can not be applied. Indirect analogy based on ethnographic situations in other parts of the world is of more limited use.[6] For example, a form of raised fields (the so-called "floating gardens" or *chinampas*) are still used on a limited scale in Central Highland Mexico (Coe 1964; Gomez-Pompa et al. 1982; Jiménez-Osornio and del Amo 1988). The inhabitants of the Wahgi and Baliem Valleys and Frederick-Hendrick Island of Papua and Indonesian New Guinea still farm using raised fields (Golson 1977; Heider 1970; Serpenti 1965; Steensberg 1980).

In Belize, Puleston (1977a, 1977b, 1978) conducted the earliest raised field archaeological experiments. He collected information on labor and maintenance costs, functions, and the crops potentially cultivated by the lowland Maya. The construction of the experimental fields was based on his archaeological research on pre-Hispanic Maya raised fields. Puleston's labor figures provided the basis for most raised field interpretations for the next decade. Other raised field reconstructions by archaeologists include small scale experimental work in Ecuador (Denevan and Mathewson 1983; Muse and Quintero 1987), Mexico (Gomez-Pompa et al. 1982), and the United States (Riley and Freimuth 1979). Unfortunately these projects did not extend beyond one year. New raised field experimental research is being conducted in Bolivia (Kolata 1991; Rivera 1989), although little of this work has been completed.

Most of the systems studied ethnographically and archaeologically are not directly analogous to Andean raised fields because they have very different cultural, historical, and environmental contexts. Local

6. Labor costs (construction and maintenance) and production (crop yields and sustainability) are very difficult to calculate without actual agricultural experimentation. Figures such as Erasmus's (1967) labor calculations for experimental construction of earthworks in Mesoamerica have been frequently applied to raised field construction (Denevan 1982). I argue that this application is inappropriate because different techniques are used and because of environmental differences. Investigations by Puleston (1977b) and Steensberg (1980) have also addressed the labor input of raised fields in their experiments. Estimates for raised field crop production have commonly relied on the regional production estimates for traditional agricultural systems (Denevan 1982, Harrison and Turner 1978, Turner and Harrison 1983b). These figures can only be considered indirect estimates of potential crop yield and may have little to do with the actual raised field production in functioning field systems.

raised field experimentation, based on the information obtained from direct archaeological investigation of prehistoric raised fields, is the most appropriate means of understanding the Lake Titicaca Basin field systems.

In our experiments, we rebuilt ancient abandoned raised fields as accurately as possible and planted them with traditional Andean crops. The original forms of raised fields were determined through the study of aerial photographs, topographic mapping, and excavation of stratigraphic trenches (Figure 6.13).

The experiments were conducted in collaboration with Quechua-speaking farmers of the communities of Huatta and Coata. Participant groups varied from single families farming privately owned lands to communities of up to 150 families farming communal lands. The family or community donated their land and labor in return for free seed (potato and other Andean crops) provided by the project, and the participants received all of the harvest. After our project ended in 1986, many farmers continued to experiment with raised field farming encouraged by various development projects that adopted raised field agriculture as part of their rural aid programs (Erickson and Brinkmeier 1991).

Traditional Andean tools (*chakitaqlla* [footplow], *rawkana* [hoe], *waqtana* [wooden clod breaker], and *manta* [carrying cloth for soils]) were used to construct the raised fields, in addition to shovels and picks (Figure 6.15). The area to be reconstructed was carefully marked off to delineate the canals and raised field boundaries. The area of the canal was approximately the same as the field platforms, as determined in the stratigraphic profile trenches. The *chakitaqlla* was used to cut rectangular sod blocks from the canals (Figure 6.16). The blocks were used to build a low 1–3 course wall, depending on the site's elevation and distance from the lake. The remaining soil from the canal (both as sod blocks and loose soil) was used for the platform fill, tossed between the sod retaining walls and broken up with clod breakers. A cambered planting surface was created to facilitate drainage (see Figures 6.14, 6.15, 6.16, 6.17). The fields were constructed most efficiently during the dry season when water levels are low.

Several forms of labor mobilization and organization were compared. The first two experimental fields were constructed in 1981 on private land worked by the owner and his family. The following year, experimental fields were also constructed with community labor. Communities of 35 to 150 families constructed raised fields on lands they control and farm communally. Group labor was first organized using *minka* (or *faena* in Spanish), a traditional practice whereby each family must send one able-bodied member to work on a community project

HYPOTHETICAL PROFILE OF RAISED FIELDS IN HUATTA, PERU

BASED ON EXCAVATION OF STRATIGRAPHIC PROFILES
AND RAISED FILED EXPERIMENTATION

aquatic vegetation:
llachu, totora, and laqo

Andean crops:
potato, quinua, canihua,
oca, isanu, ollucu,
maize, and tarwi

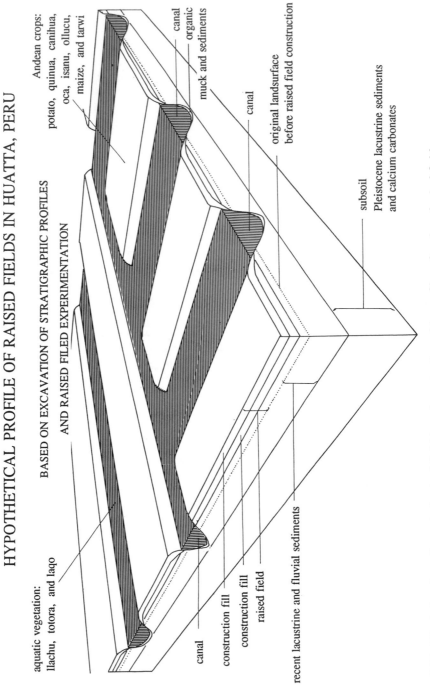

canal
organic
muck and sediments

canal

original landsurface
before raised field construction

subsoil
Pleistocene lacustrine sediments
and calcium carbonates

canal
construction fill
construction fill
raised field

recent lacustrine and fluvial sediments

6.13. Block drawing of a typical raised field based on stratigraphic profiles of archaeological fields.

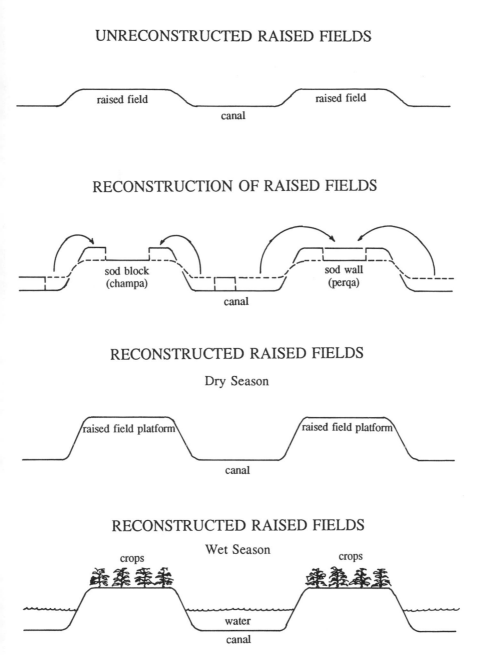

UNRECONSTRUCTED RAISED FIELDS

raised field

canal

raised field

RECONSTRUCTION OF RAISED FIELDS

sod block
(champa)

sod wall
(perqa)

canal

RECONSTRUCTED RAISED FIELDS

Dry Season

raised field platform

raised field platform

canal

RECONSTRUCTED RAISED FIELDS

Wet Season

crops

crops

water

canal

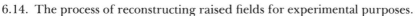

6.14. The process of reconstructing raised fields for experimental purposes.

6.15. The indigenous tools used in raised field construction (rawkana, hoe [right]; chakitaqlla, footplow [center]; waqtana; clod breaker [left]).

6.16. The use of chakitaqllas for construction of the retaining walls of experimental raised fields.

6.17. Raised field construction in Chojñocoto by the Community of Yasin.

on a specified day. These are often festive occasions. In the second year some communities decided to try another local form of labor organization, the *tarea* ("role"). In the *tarea* system, each family is responsible for the construction of a specified area of raised field, and it is up to each family to decide how to organize the labor and time needed to complete the work.

All the major Andean crops that would have been available to the prehistoric farmers of the Lake Titicaca Basin were planted on the reconstructed raised fields (Figure 6.18), including plants documented through our excavation. In addition to many varieties of potatoes (*Solanum* sp.), isañu (*Tropaeoleum tuberosum* R. & P.), ocas (*Oxalis tuberosa* Mol.), ollucu (*Ullucus tuberosus* Caldas), quinoa (*Chenopodium quinoa* Willd.), cañihua (*Chenopodium pallidicaule* Allen), tarwi (*Lupinus mutabilis* Sweet), and maize (*Zea mays* Linn.), some introduced crops from the Old World were also planted. The crops were monitored throughout the growing season and weather stations were set up on several blocks of fields to record temperature readings.

We confirmed many of the various functions proposed for raised field agriculture (Erickson 1986, 1988a, 1992; Garaycochea 1987). The platforms raised above the pampa increased the rich topsoil depth and protected the crops from seasonal inundation. The canals between them collected and stored water that provided irrigation for the fields. This water also protected crops against radiation frosts by storing heat from the sun and releasing it at night, creating a more favorable microclimate. Aquatic plants, organic detritus, and rich sediments collected in the canals were periodically put on the fields to renew soil fertility for continuous cropping. The canals also produced locally important economic plants and animals which could easily be harvested. We found that aquaculture (fish and plants) could be practiced.

There were many advantages to working directly with indigenous communities on raised field rehabilitation and experimentation. This situation provided a more natural setting for a traditional agriculture study than would be possible in a laboratory or a governmental experimental station location. In addition, the number of groups and individual farmers participating permitted experimentation in a wide variety of environmental conditions. The community setting also provided a long term context for the experiments (as long as raised field technology is considered beneficial to the community). The traditional Andean tools used by the local farmers are probably similar to those used by the original raised field farmers, with the exception of metal blades of *chakitaqllas* and *rawkanas* replacing the stone and wooden blades of the past. Some of the traditional social organization

6.18. Raised fields planted in quinoa (*Chenopodium quinoa*) in the Community of Sanganacachi, Capachica (1989).

(*ayllu*) is still present and functioning. Most important, this context provided a rich source of hypotheses and alternative approaches. The Quechua farmers continually suggested both traditional and innovative ways to do raised field farming, and many of these were better approaches than the original hypotheses posed by the investigators (Erickson and Brinkmeier 1990). Each community group and individual family participating in the experiments developed its own ways of building and maintaining the raised fields, and of farming them. Their expertise in local farming methods and their interest in the project contributed greatly to its success.

Several problems were encountered in the experiments. The original crops specifically adapted for the cultivation conditions on raised fields have been lost since the abandonment of the fields, and the only traditional crops available were those developed for the very different conditions on the slopes surrounding the pampa. The small scattered experimental field blocks reconstructed during the early years of the project experienced an "edge effect" whereby their small size could not produce the desired microclimate and hydraulic effects of the original larger field systems. This was corrected with the reconstruction of larger field blocks in the later years. A few fields were not sufficiently elevated to survive the massive floods of 1985–86. During the severe drought of 1982–83, most canals had not been excavated deeply enough to reach the water table and some crops were lost. It was found that small wells could be dug into the canal floors for access to irrigation water. The advantage of long term experiments was that these problems were addressed and resolved over time.

Discussion of the Raised Field Project

Our investigations show that raised field agriculture has a remarkably long history in the Lake Titicaca Basin of southern Peru and northern Bolivia, much longer than previously believed. The system had its beginnings around 1000 B.C. and underwent two periods of major expansion, once around 600 B.C.–A.D. 200/300 and another period around A.D. 1000 (Erickson 1987, 1988). The fields were apparently abandoned after A.D. 300 and again after A.D. 1400. A similar evolutionary history has been recorded for fields in the southern basin although apparently different in chronological details (Kolata 1986, 1991; Kolata and Graffam 1989; Graffam, pers. comm. 1990). Although raised fields certainly provided much of the food surplus necessary for supporting the series of complex societies that developed within the basin (Pukara, Tiwanaku, and Late Intermediate Period

Aymara Kingdoms), fields were constructed and managed at the local level (Erickson 1987, 1988a; Erickson and Candler 1989).

The agricultural experiments using raised fields provided several surprises in regard to pre-Hispanic labor, crop production, and social organization of the technology. The labor expended involved in the construction and maintenance of raised field systems is initially high, but over the long run, raised field systems are very efficient in terms of labor and energy. Crop yield on raised fields was remarkable, some two to three times higher than on fields farmed with traditional local methods. Raised fields are not as "labor intensive" as commonly believed and the efficiency of this system in terms of labor input for production output is very high. There was probably no population pressure or stress involved in the initial (and quite early) adoption of raised field agriculture. Another surprise related to the level of social organization necessary for construction and maintenance of the fields. It was found that small communal groups, organized in the traditional manner of the Andean region today, and even individual families are able to carry out raised field farming successfully. There is no need to invoke the centralized organization commonly believed responsible for the agricultural works.[7] The archaeological and experimental research indicate that the raised fields were constructed in an incremental process by many generations of farmers.

Archaeology and Experimentation in Field and Garden Studies

Due to the impossibility of direct observation, the interpretation of abandoned raised field remains is usually based on analogy to other agricultural systems (complex irrigation systems or raised field systems in very different historical or environmental settings), known both from contemporary ethnographic and historical accounts. This paper demonstrates how useful it is to apply direct archaeological and experimental techniques to the interpretation of raised field agriculture.

The methods described here are basic and relatively inexpensive techniques that generate substantial data and interpretations about past agricultural systems. I believe these archaeological and experimental methods have great potential in other field and garden systems where direct historical and ethnographic analogy is not available.

Another contribution of archaeological and experimental research in gardens and fields is its potential for demonstrating the effective-

7. For an alternative opinion, see Kolata (1986, 1991).

ness of ancient techniques (Erickson 1988a, 1988b, in prep. b). Abandoned farming systems such as raised fields have provided alternative models for rural development in the zones where their remains are found (Erickson 1992; Erickson and Brinkmeier 1990). In many cases, archaeological and traditional systems may be more sophisticated, more environmentally sound, more culturally appropriate, and more productive than those introduced from the outside. The methods utilized here allow us to determine the evolutionary trajectory of land use systems, information that should be useful for the planning of future sustainable land use strategies.

The most appropriate and productive approach to ancient agriculture is to combine archaeological investigation of fields with agricultural experimentation. Only archaeological research can provide the basis for the accurate reconstruction of the technology such as field form and structure, field maintenance, and the crops cultivated in cases where direct ethnographic and historical analogy are not available. In turn, the agricultural experimental models based on this basic archaeological research can address issues that cannot be examined archaeologically such as field function, crop yields, nutrient recycling, microclimate management, labor input and maintenance costs, tool efficiency, and system sustainability.

Archaeologists have long utilized multidisciplinary approaches to study complex phenomena. The study of archaeological gardens and fields is one such phenomenon that benefits greatly from collaboration of scholars from various backgrounds. Basic archaeological and agronomic field techniques adapted to a specific case of prehistoric raised field systems were successfully combined with extensive experimental studies to address basic anthropological questions of past human cultures. As a long term case study, the experience of the Raised Field Agicultural Project and its successors may be useful for investigations of ancient garden and field systems in other parts of the world. An approach that combines basic archaeological techniques with agricultural experimentation not only can yield many insights on now-abandoned agricultural features, but may also provide models for present day rural development in landscapes where archaeological remains of cultivation systems are found.

The research for this paper was supported by a National Science Foundation Dissertation Improvement Grant and a Social Science Research Council Fellowship. I would also like to thank Ing. Ignacio Garaycochea Z., Dr. Kay Candler, and Dan Brinkmeier. Permission for this research was granted by the Comisión Técnica of the Instituto Nacional de Cultura of Peru. The Proyecto de Investigación de Sistemas Agrícolas, the Convenio Perú-Canada, the Ministerio de Agricultura del Perú, and CARE of Peru also provided support. My deepest thanks goes to our friends in Huatta, Peru, who permitted us to conduct the archaeological research in their community and who played an important role in the experimental and applied aspects of the investigation.

References

Bray, W., L. Herrera, M. Cardale Schrimpff, P. Botero, and J.G. Monsalve. 1987. The Ancient Agricultural Landscape of Calima, Colombia. In *Pre-Hispanic Agricultural Fields in the Andean Region*, ed. W. Denevan, K. Mathewson, and G. Knapp, pp. 443–481. British Archaeological Reports, International Series 359. Oxford.

Brinkmeier, D.A. 1985. *A Plan for Disseminating Information about Traditional Agriculture to Indigenous Farmers in the Department of Puno, Peru*, Master's thesis, Department of Journalism and Mass Communication, Iowa State University, Ames.

Broadbent, S. 1987. The Chibcha Raised-Field System in the Sabana de Bogota, Colombia: Further Investigations. In *Pre- Hispanic Agricultural Fields in the Andean Region*, ed. W. Denevan, K. Mathewson, and G. Knapp, pp. 425–442. British Archaeological Reports, International Series 359. Oxford.

Burga, M. and C. de la Torre (editors). 1986. *Andenes y camellones en el Perú Andino: Historia Presente y Futuro*. Consejo Nacional de Ciéncia y Tecnología, Lima.

Coe, M. 1964. The Chinampas of Mexico. *Scientific American* 211:90–98.

Coles, J.M. 1973. *Archaeology by Experiment*. Heinemann, London.

Culbert, T.P., L. Levi, and L. Cruz. 1991. Lowland Maya Wetland Agriculture. In *Vision and Revision in Maya Studies*, ed. F. Clancy and P. Harrison. University of New Mexico Press, Albuquerque.

Denevan, W.M. 1970. Aboriginal Drained Field Cultivation in the Americas. *Science* 169:647–654.

———. 1980. Latin America. In *World Systems of Traditional Resource Management*, ed. G. Klee, pp. 217–244. Wiley, New York.

———. 1982. Hydraulic Agriculture in the American Tropics: Forms, Measures, and Recent Research. In *Maya Subsistence*, ed. K.V. Flannery, pp. 181–203. Academic Press, New York.

Denevan, W.M. and K. Mathewson. 1983. Preliminary Results of the Samborondon Raised Field Projet, Guayas Basin, Ecuador In *Drained Field Agriculture in Central and South America*, ed. J.P. Darch, pp. 167–182. British Archaeological Reports, International Series 189. Oxford.

Denevan, W.M., K. Mathewson, and G. Knapp (editors). 1987. *Pre-Hispanic Agricultural Fields in the Andean Region*. British Archaeological Reports, International Series 359. Oxford.

Denevan, W.M. and B.L. Turner II. 1974. Forms, Functions, and Associations of Raised Fields in the Old World Tropics. *Journal of Tropical Geography* 39:24–33.

Eidt, R.C. 1984. *Advances in Abandoned Settlement Analysis: Application of Prehis-*

toric Anthrosols in Colombia, South America. Center for Latin America, University of Wisconsin, Milwaukee.

Erasmus, C.J. 1965. Monument Building: Some Field Experiments. *Southwestern Journal of Anthropology* 21(4):277–301.

Erickson, C.L. 1985. Applications of Prehistoric Andean Technology: Experiments in Raised Field Agriculture, Huatta, Lake Titicaca, 1982–1983. In *Prehistoric Intensive Agriculture in the Tropics*, ed. I. Farrington, pp. 209–232. British Archaeological Reports, International Series 232. Oxford.

————. 1986 Agricultura en camellones en la cuenca del Lago Titicaca: aspectos técnicos y su futuro. In *Andenes y camellones en el Perú Andino: historia presente y futuro*, ed. M. Burga and C. de la Torre, pp. 331–350. CONCYTEC, Lima.

————. 1987. The Dating of Raised-Field Agriculture in the Lake Titicaca Basin, Peru. In *Pre-Hispanic Agricultural Fields in the Andean Region*, ed. W.M. Denevan, K. Mathewson, and G. Knapp, pp. 373–384. British Archaeological Reports, International Series 359. Oxford.

————. 1988a. *An Archaeological Investigation of Raised Field Agriculture in the Lake Titicaca Basin of Peru*, Unpublished Ph.D. dissertation. Department of Anthropology, University of Illinois, Urbana-Champaign.

————. 1988b. Raised Field Agriculture in the Lake Titicaca Basin: Putting Ancient Andean Agriculture back to Work. *Expedition* 30(3):8–16.

————. 1992. Prehistoric Landscape Management in the Andean Highlands: Raised Field Agriculture and Its Environmental Impact. *Population and Environment* 13(4):285–300.

————. 1993. The Social Organization of Prehispanic Raised Field Agriculture in the Lake Titicaca Basin of Peru. In *Aspects of Water Management in the Prehistoric New World*, ed. V. Scarborough and B. Isaac, 367–424. Research in Economic Anthropology, Supplement 7. JAI Press, Greenwich, CT.

————. In prep. a. *The Archaeology of Early Farming Communities in the Lake Titicaca Basin*. Manuscript in preparation, University Museum, University of Pennsylvania, Philadelphia.

————. In prep. b. *Waru Waru: Ancient Andean Agriculture.*. Manuscript in preparation, University Museum, University of Pennsylvania, Philadelphia.

Erickson, C.L. and D.A. Brinkmeier. 1991. *Raised Field Rehabilitation Projects in the Lake Titicaca Basin of Peru*. Unpublished manuscipt submitted to the Interamerican Foundation, Washington, DC.

Erickson, C.L. and K.L. Candler. 1989. Raised Fields and Sustainable Agriculture in the Lake Titicaca Basin of Peru. In *Fragile Lands in Latin America: Strategies for Sustainable Development*, ed. J.O. Browder, pp. 230–248. Westview Press, Boulder, CO.

Erickson, C.L., J. Esteves, M. Michel, and W. Winkler. 1991. *Estudio preliminar de los sistemas agrícolas precolombinos en el departamento del Beni, Bolivia*. Unpublished manuscript.

Evenari, M., L. Shanan, and N. Tadmore. 1971. *The Negev: The Challenge of a Desert*. Harvard University Press, Cambridge, MA.

Farrington, I. 1983. Prehistoric Land Reclamation Schemes: Preliminary Notes on River Canalization in the Sacred Valley of the Incas. In *Drained Field Agriculture in Central and South America*, ed. J.P. Darch, pp. 221–235. British Archaeological Reports, International Series 189. Oxford.

———— (editor). 1985. *Prehistoric Intensive Agriculture in the Tropics.* British Archaeological Reports, International Series 232. Oxford.

Friedel, D. and V. Scarborough. 1982. Subsistence, Trade and Development of the Coastal Maya. In *Maya Subsistence: Studies in Memory of Dennis E. Puleston,* ed. K.V. Flannery, pp. 131–155. Academic Press, New York.

Garaycochea Z., I. 1986a. *Rehabilitación de camellones en la Comunidad Campesina de Huatta, Puno.* Unpublished thesis, Department of Agronomy, Universidad Nacional del Altiplano, Puno.

————. 1986b. Potencial agrícola de los camellones en el altiplano Puneño. In *Andenes y camellones en el Perú Andino: historia presente y futuro,* ed. C. de la Torre and M. Burga, pp. 241–251. CONCYTEC, Lima.

————. 1987. Agricultural Experiments in Raised Fields in the Titicaca Basin, Peru: Preliminary Considerations. In *Pre-Hispanic Agricultural Fields in the Andean Region,* ed. W.M. Denevan, K. Mathewson, and G. Knapp, pp.385–398. British Archaeological Reports, International Series 359. Oxford.

Gliessman, S.R., B.L. Turner II, F.J. Rosado May, and M.F. Amador. 1985. Ancient Raised Field Agriculture in the Maya Lowlands of Southeastern Mexico. In *Prehistoric Intensive Agriculture in the Tropics,* ed. I. Farrington, pp. 97–112. British Archaeological Reports, International Series 232. Oxford.

Golson, J. 1977. No Room at the Top: Agricultural Intensification in the New Guinea Highlands. In *Sunda and Sahul,* ed. J. Allen, J. Golson, and R. Jones, pp. 602–638. Academic Press, New York.

Gomez-Pompa, A., H. Morales, E. Jiménez, and J. Jiménez. 1982. Experiences in Traditional Hydraulic Agriculture. In *Maya Subsistence,* ed. K.V. Flannery, pp. 327–342. Academic Press, New York.

Gorecki, P.P. 1982. *Ethnoarchaeology at Kuk: Problems in Site Formation Processes.* Unpublished PhD. dissertation, Department of Anthropology, University of Sydney.

Graffam, G. 1989. Back across the Great Divide: The Pakaq Señorio and Raised Field Agriculture. In *Multidisciplinary Studies in Andean Anthropology,* ed. V.J. Vitzthum. Michigan Discussions in Anthropology 8:33–50. Ann Arbor, MI.

————. 1990. *Raised Fields Without Bureaucracy: An Archaeological Examination of Intensive Wetland Cultivation in the Pampa Koani Zone, Lake Titicaca, Bolivia.* Unpublished Ph.D. dissertation, Department of Anthropology, University of Toronto, Toronto.

Hammond, N.S.D., C. Gleason, J. Staneko, D. Tuerenhout, and L. Kosakowsky. 1987. Excavations at Nohmul, Belize, 1985. *Journal of Field Archaeology* 14(3):257–282.

Harrison, P.D. and B.L. Turner II (editors). 1978. *Pre-Hispanic Maya Agriculture.* University of New Mexico Press, Albuquerque.

Heider, K. 1970 *The Dugam Dani: A Papuan Culture in the Highlands of West New Guinea.* Viking Fund Publications in Anthropology 49, Wenner-Gren Foundation for Anthropological Research, New York.

Jimenéz-Osornio, J. and S. del Amo. 1988. An Intensive Mexican Traditional Agroecosystem. In *Proceedings of the Sixth International Scientific Conference of the International Federation of Organic Agriculture Movements,* vol. II, pp. 451–456. University of California, Santa Cruz.

Knapp, G. and R. Ryder. 1983. Aspects of the Origin, Morphology, and

Function of Ridged Fields in the Quito Altiplano, Ecuador. In *Drained Fields of the Americas*, ed. J.P. Darch, pp. 201–220. British Archaeological Reports, International Series 189. Oxford.

Kolata, A.L. 1986. The Agricultural Foundations of the Tiwanaku State: A View from the Heartland. *American Antiquity* 51:748–762.

———. 1991. The Technology and Organization of Agricultural Production in the Tiwanaku State. *Latin American Antiquity* 2(2):99–125.

Kolata, A. (editor). 1989. *Arqueología en Lukurmata*, vol. 2. Instituto Nacional de Arqueología y Ediciones Puma Punku, La Paz.

Kolata, A. and G. Graffam. 1989. Los campos elevados de Lukurmata, Bolivia. In *Arqueología en Lukurmata*, vol. 2, ed. A. Kolata, pp. 173–212. Instituto Nacional de Arqueología y Ediciones Puma Punku, La Paz.

Kus, J. 1972. *Selected Aspects of Irrigated Agriculture in the Chimu Heartland, Peru.* Unpublished Ph.D. dissertation, Department of Geography, University of California, Los Angeles.

Lennon, T.J. 1982. *Raised Fields of Lake Titicaca, Peru: A Pre-Hispanic Water Management System.* Unpublished PhD. dissertation, Department of Anthropology, University of Colorado, Boulder.

———. 1983. Pattern Analysis of Prehispanic Raised Fields of Lake Titicaca, Peru. In *Drained Fields of the Americas*, ed. J.P. Darch, pp. 183–200. British Archaeological Reports, International Series 189. Oxford.

Malpass, M. 1987. Prehistoric Agricultural Terracing at Chijra in the Colca Valley, Peru: Preliminary Report II. In *Pre-hispanic Agricultural Fields in the Andean Region*, ed. W. Denevan, K. Mathewson, and G. Knapp, pp. 45–66. British Archaeological Reports, International Series 359. Oxford.

Miller, N.F. and T. L. Smart. 1984. Intentional Burning of Dung as Fuel: A Mechanism for the Incorporation of Charred Seeds into the Archeological Record. *Journal of Ethnobiology* 4:15–28.

Moore, J. 1988. Prehispanic Raised Field Agriculture in the Casma Valley: Recent Data, New Hypotheses. *Journal of Field Archaeology* 15:265–276.

Moseley, M.E. 1983. The Good Old Days Were Better: Agrarian Collapse and Tectonics. *American Anthropologist* 85:775–799.

Muse, M. and F. Quintero. 1987. Experimentos de reactivación de campos elevados de Peon del Rio, Guayas, Ecuador. In *Pre-Hispanic Agricultural Fields in the Andean Region*, ed. W.M. Denevan, K. Mathewson, and G. Knapp, pp. 249–266. British Archaeological Reports, International Series 359. Oxford.

Ortloff, C. 1988. Canal Builders of Pre-Inca Peru. *Scientific American* 259(6):100–107.

Ortloff, C.R., R.A. Feldman, M.E. Moseley. 1985. Hydraulic Engineering Aspects of the Chimu Chicama-Moche Intervalley Canal. *American Antiquity* 47:572–595.

Parsons, J. 1978. More on Pre-Columbian Raised Fields (Camellones) in the Bajo Rio San Jorge and Bajo Cauca, Colombia. In *The Role of Geographical Research in Latin America*, ed. W.M. Denevan, pp. 117–124. Conference of Latin American Geographers Publication 7. Muncie, IN.

Parsons, J. and W.M. Denevan. 1967. Pre-Columbian Ridged Fields in New World Archaeology. *Scientific American* 217(1):92–100.

Parsons, J.R., M.H. Parsons, V. Popper, and M. Taft. 1985. Chinampa Agriculture and Aztec Urbanization in the Valley of Mexico. In *Prehistoric In-*

tensive Agriculture in the Tropics, ed. I. Farrington, pp. 49–96. British Archaeological Reports, International Series 232. Oxford.

Pearsall, D.M. 1989. *Paleoethnobotany, A Handbook of Procedures*. Academic Press, San Diego.

Pohl, M. (editor). 1989. *Ancient Maya Agriculture: Excavations on Albion Island, Northern Belize*. Westview Press, Boulder, CO.

Puleston, D. 1976. The People of the Cayman/Crocodile: Riparian Agriculture and the Origin of Aquatic Motifs in Ancient Maya Iconography. In *Aspects of Ancient Maya Civilization*, ed. F.-A. de Montequin, pp. 1–26. Hamline University, St. Paul, MN.

———. 1977a. The Art and Archaeology of Hydraulic Agriculture in the Maya Lowlands. In *Social Processes in Maya Prehistory*, ed. N. Hammond, pp. 449–467. Academic Press, New York.

———. 1977b. Experiments in Prehistoric Raised Field Agriculture: Learning from the Past. *Journal of Belizan Affairs* 5:36–43.

———. 1978. Terracing, Raised Fields, and Tree Cropping in the Maya Lowlands: A Few Perspectives on the Geography of Power. In *Pre-Hispanic Maya Agriculture*, ed. P.D. Harrison and B.L. Turner II, pp. 225–246. University of New Mexico Press, Albuquerque.

Ramos, C. 1986. Evaluación y rehabilitación de camellones o "kurus" en Asillo. *Allpanchis* 27, año 18:239–284. Cuzco.

Riley, T.J. and G. Freimuth. 1979. Field Systems and Frost Drainage in the Prehistoric Agriculture of the Upper Great Lakes. *American Antiquity* 44:271–285.

Rivera Sundt, O. 1989. Una tecnologia que viene del pasado. *Anales del seminario de desarollo rural*, Serie Documentos 4-1-119-90, La Paz, pp. 60–91.

Serpenti, L.M. 1965. *Cultivators of the Swamps*. Van Gorcum, Assen.

Siemans, A. 1989. *Tierra Configurada*. Consejo para la Cultura y las Artes, Mexico City.

Smith, C.T., W.M. Denevan, and P. Hamilton. 1968. Ancient Ridged Fields in the Region of Lake Titicaca. *Geographical Journal* 134:353–367.

Steensberg, A. 1980. *New Guinea Gardens*. Academic Press, New York.

Stemper, D. 1987. Raised Fields and Agricultural Production, A.D. 1400–1600, Rio Daule, Guayas, Ecuador. In *Prehispanic Agricultural Fields in the Andean Region*, ed. W.M. Denevan, K. Mathewson, and G. Knapp, pp. 297–319. British Archaeological Reports, International Series 395. Oxford.

Turner, B.L. II and P. Harrison. 1983a. Pulltrouser Swamp and Maya Raised Fields: A Summation. In *Pulltrouser Swamp: Ancient Maya Habitat, Agriculture, and Settlement in Northern Belize*, ed. B.L. Turner II and P. Harrrison, pp. 246–270. University of Texas Press, Austin.

Turner, B.L. II and P. Harrison (editors). 1983b. *Pulltrouser Swamp: Ancient Maya Habitat, Agriculture, and Settlement in Northern Belize*. University of Texas Press, Austin.

Wiseman, F. 1984. *Pollen Analysis of Raised Fields and Canals, Northwest Margin of Lake Titicaca, Peru*. Unpublished manuscript on file at the Department of Anthropology, University of Pennsylvania.

Zucchi, A. and W.M. Denevan. 1979. *Campos elevados e historia cultural prehispánica en los llanos occidentales de Venezuela*. Universidad Católica Andres Bello, Caracas.

Chapter 7
The "Celtic" Field Systems on the Berkshire Downs, England

Stephen Ford, Mark Bowden, Vincent Gaffney, and Geoffrey C. Mees

Traces of former field systems are found over much of northwest Europe, where they are given names that reflect their supposed antiquity. In Britain some are commonly called Celtic fields to distinguish them from remains of Saxon or medieval date. Their very extent makes a study of these fields important for an understanding of landscape history and the economies of the societies that laid them out, provided, that is, we can say when they originated and for how long they remained in use. The imprecision of a term like "Celtic fields" is an acknowledgment of the difficulty of answering such questions.

This paper is concerned with the date of the extensive field systems that can still be seen on aerial photographs of the chalk downlands north of Lambourn in Berkshire, southern England and with the landscape in which they were laid out (Figures 7.1, 7.2). Fowler (1983) has reviewed the data on prehistoric field systems in Britain as a whole, and summaries for the Berkshire Downs have been provided by Bradley and Ellison (1975) and Richards (1978).

In the absence of documentary evidence, there are two commonly used ways to date archaeological features such as fields. One is by association with other features whose date is already known. Thus some fields can be assumed to belong to nearby settlements, or they may have a morphology reminiscent of securely dated fields elsewhere. Sometimes they are partially overlain by other features such as burial mounds which give at least a *terminus ante quem*. The second method of dating relies on finding artifacts to which field boundaries can be related. For example, if pottery of known date is located below a wall, the wall is probably younger than the pot.

Writing in 1978, Richards remarked that the chronology of the

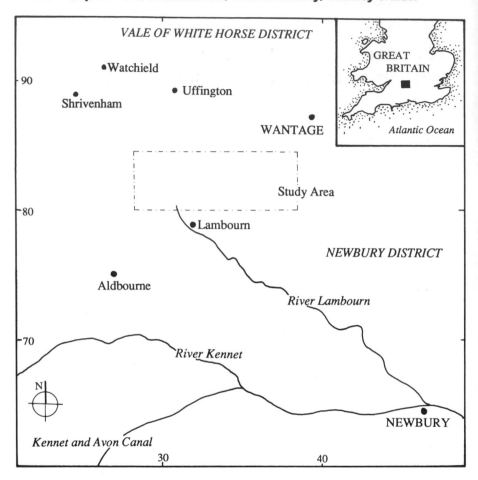

7.1. Southern England. (T. Hoffman)

field systems on the Berkshire Downs was for the most part vague and totally relative. At that time a few settlements in the area had been excavated and the nearby fields dated by association with them. The relationship of the fields to large earthworks, the linear ditches, that traverse the Downs had also been examined. About 48 km of these linear ditches were known, and although for the most part their dates were uncertain, some were assigned to the early first millennium B.C. Aerial photographs seemed to show that the ditches regularly cut elements of the field systems, which should therefore have been older (Bradley and Richards 1978). Furthermore, a general prehistoric date for the systems was not inconsistent with the results of a few isolated

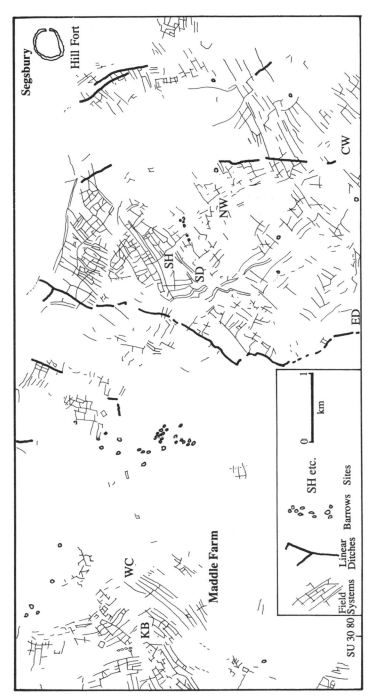

7.2. A composite plan prepared from aerial photographs of crop and soil marks. The location of trenches across lynchets are marked KB, WC, etc. Linear ditches are marked by heavy lines.

excavations of field boundaries (Atkinson 1965; Bradley and Ellison 1975; Mills 1948).

There were, however, indications contradicting a pre-Roman date. The long rectangular shape of some fields was like the classic Roman type described by Bowen (1961), and Roman settlements were known on the Downs. The largest was at Maddle Farm, where the extent of Roman agriculture has since been fully described by Gaffney and Tingle (1989). Nevertheless, Richards hesitated to say that the fields near these settlements had a Roman origin because, given prehistoric farming on the Downs, older fields may have been taken over after the conquest, perhaps with the removal of some boundaries to create the strip-like shapes suited to Roman ploughing. Thus Richards tended to favor the view that there had been continuity of land use in Britain from late prehistoric times through to the end of the Roman period. In support of this view he pointed out that the British evidence for centuriation—the allocation of blocks of land to army veterans—is doubtful.

A prehistoric date for the field systems on the Berkshire Downs has more recently been called into question by Ford (1982), who reexamined the relationship between the linear ditches and the field boundaries, both in photographs and on the ground. He concluded that the evidence for fields predating the ditches is very slight. It may indeed be confined to just one block of fields, and even there the aerial photographs are unclear. Furthermore, Ford found that small scale excavations on the linear ditches frequently recovered Roman pottery, indicating at least that Roman farming on the Downs was widespread.

Against this background of uncertainty we decided on an attempt to date the origin and period of use of the field systems north of Lambourn more precisely. Two blocks of these fields lie on high ground some 150 to 200 m above sea level, separated by a valley with modern villages and roads. The soils on which they are situated are rendzinas over chalk (i.e., highly calcareous soils with no marked zone of decalcification), or brown earths where the chalk is overlaid by silty drifts containing numerous flints. Up to the 1940s much of the high ground was under permanent grassland, and the physical remains of the ancient landscapes were extensively preserved in the form of lynchets (accumulations of soil on the downhill edges of fields laid out on a slope), banks, and hollow ways marking the position of tracks. Most have now been destroyed by modern cereal farming, but fragments can still be located in small woods and areas of grass that have escaped ploughing.

Our strategy was to excavate a sample of the surviving boundaries in both the western and eastern blocks of fields. Sampling such a large area adequately was an obvious problem, especially given the poor survival of excavatable structures. However, as Figure 7.2 shows, suitable sites were found in the center and along the southern edges of both blocks. Where the fields were laid out on a common alignment, near sites SH and WC, for example, the problem of where to locate the trenches was reduced. For, if the major axes of such alignments could be dated by digging at one position, the whole set of coaxial fields could reasonably be assumed to be of the same date.

Most of the surviving field boundaries near Lambourn are lynchets, formed when soil loosened by cultivation eroded downhill to accumulate at a permanent field edge. To the north edge of the study area, where few, if any, lynchets remained, we tried to locate and excavate ditches alongside tracks seen in the aerial photographs, unfortunately without success.

By excavating lynchets to date the fields, we assumed that once the bottommost layers of the soil accumulations had been covered, they would remain undisturbed except perhaps by burrowing animals. Artifacts finding their way from the ancient field surface into these basal layers should therefore give at least a coarse date for the origin of the fields, because the youngest artifact at the base of a lynchet will provide a *terminus post quem* for its formation.

The validity of this approach clearly depends on artifacts having been put on the fields in manure as soon as cultivation started. The very extensive spreads of potsherds and flint flakes that are found on the Downs are plausibly interpreted as material thrown onto household middens from which the manure derived (Fowler 1983). However, it would be rash to assume that household wastes were disposed of in this way at all times. Furthermore, if a field was cultivated for a time without manuring, the basal layers of the lynchets should contain no artifacts, making the field undatable. Worse still, the lynchets might contain artifacts present on the surface in a residual context—put there a long time before ploughing started. A Roman field created on the site of a Bronze Age settlement, and cultivated without manure for several years, could well accumulate Bronze Age potsherds at the bottom of the lynchet, clearly stratified below Roman material. Excavation would then suggest a Bronze Age origin for the field.

To minimize this problem, and to cope with the possibility of random mixing by burrowing animals, we intended to rely more on the totality of our results than on the findings from any one trench. We hoped to find a reasonably consistent pattern repeated across the whole area, and to the extent that we did so our confidence in dating the field systems would grow.

In all 21 trenches were dug across 13 individual lynchets. The trenches were 1.5 to 2 m wide and up to 7 m long, starting 2 to 3 m above the break of slope at the lynchet edge. All finds, except those in the modern topsoil, were located in three dimensions so that they could be plotted onto the section revealed at one side of the trench. In those cases where the ground sloped across as well as along a trench, an allowance for the lateral slope was made when the plots were prepared.

The stratigraphic sequence for most trenches was simple. Typically there was a stone line at the base of the modern topsoil, with a relatively loose layer below this representing the accumulation of eroded soil in the positive lynchet. The distribution of stones varied in this layer, but no horizons suggesting periods of stability without cultivation were to be seen within it. On the rendzina soils, calcium salts were redeposited toward its base. The lower limit of the soil accumulation was clear when the soils lay directly over chalk, but it was sometimes less obvious where the chalk was covered by a drift deposit. A buried soil was clearly visible in one trench only. It showed as a thin, dark, stone-free horizon between the lynchet accumulation and the chalk.

A few pieces of metal, 663 potsherds, and a large number of waste flakes were recovered from the 21 trenches. The flakes are likely to have been struck from the flint nodules that are abundant everywhere on the Downs, and indeed an area where flints had been knapped was discovered quite by chance below one of the lynchets. These flakes indicate prehistoric occupation of the area, but they cannot be used for more precise dating purposes. However, they helped locate the base of the eroded soil layer when it was not readily seen by inspection of a section.

Of the 663 potsherds recovered, 133 (20%) could not be dated because they were too fragmentary or too abraded. Of the remainder, 493 (74%) were identified as Roman (mid-first to late fourth centuries A.D.) and 37 (6%) as pre-Roman. Table 7.1 sets out the data by site. Though few sherds could confidently be assigned to the early and late Roman periods (roughly the first to the fourth centuries A.D.), those from the earlier period were usually better represented.

Roman pottery predominated at every site. Significant numbers of prehistoric sherds were found at only one (ED). Furthermore, no Saxon or medieval pottery was recovered. Such results strongly suggest that arable farming—or at least arable farming requiring the use of manure—was more intensive on the Lambourn Downs under the Roman occupation than before or since that time. They do not themselves demonstrate that the fields were first laid out after the Roman

TABLE 7.1. Potsherd Counts[a]

Site	Pre-historic	Early Roman	Late Roman	Undated Roman	Probable Roman	Undetermined	Total
KB1	2	3	.	59	.	1	65
KB2	.	2	.	9	.	.	11
KB3	.	1	.	2	2	1	6
KB4	.	.	1	9	.	.	10
KB5	.	1	2	7	1	.	11
KB6	.	1	1	22	.	.	24
KB7	.	.	.	3	.	.	3
KB8	.	1	.	3	1	2	7
KB9	.	3	.	11	2	5	21
WC1	.	4	2	48	4	1	59
WC2	.	8	1	53	1	6	69
AW1	.	.	2	3	3	4	12
AW2	1	3	.	20	2	9	35
CW	4	.	.	10	1	9	24
ED1	16	3	3	29	21	35	107
ED2	12	4	.	17	7	18	58
NW1	.	6	.	11	1	7	25
NW2	.	4	.	20	4	4	32
SH1	1	2	.	6	2	7	18
SH2	.	1	1	13	.	.	15
SD	1	3	.	16	7	24	51
Total	37	50	13	371	59	133	663

[a] Trenches 4–7 at Knighton Bushes (KB) were dug in close proximity across one lynchet to check a possible relocation of the field boundary.

conquest, but the stratigraphic placement of the finds was, for the most part, consistent with this view.

Nine of the 13 lynchets trenched had Roman pottery in their bottom-most layers. Figure 7.3 provides some examples, the first four of which (KB1, WC1, WC2, and NW2) illustrate this point, while the fifth (CW) does not. Relatively few sherds were found at CW, and ED is a better instance of a site that stood out from the majority. In one of the two trenches dug here (ED2) prehistoric finds lay fairly clearly in the lowest levels of the lynchet accumulation with Roman pottery of the first and second centuries A.D. above them (Figure 7.4). Flint flakes also lay below the pottery. A survey of the lynchets at ED revealed an alteration in the field pattern, and an analysis of mollusc shells from ED2 also supported the view that there were two phases of cultivation. Perhaps, therefore, this site provides evidence of prehistoric fields continuing in use after the Roman conquest. The majority of the data, however, support the conclusion that large parts of

POT FINDS IN POSITIVE LYNCHETS

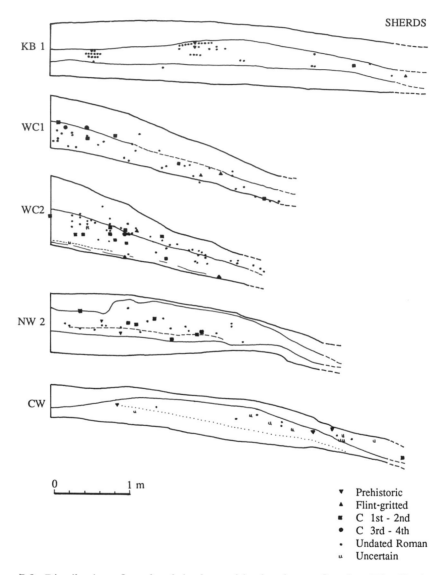

7.3. Distribution of potsherds in the positive lynchets at five sites. The distribution is discontinuous laterally in KB1 because the position of the sherds in the trench was recorded in meter squares.

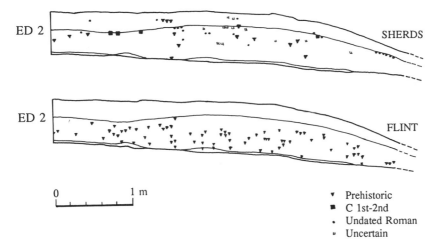

7.4. Distribution of sherds and flint in trench 2 at Eastbury Down.

the Lambourn Downs field systems were first laid out in the Roman period, perhaps (though the evidence is slight) in the first two centuries A.D.

The lack of any obvious stratification within the accumulations of eroded soil is evidence that, once established, the fields remained in continuous arable use. Had there been a reversion to grassland followed by a second arable phase, the remains of grassland soils should have shown up within the lynchet body, at least in some locations. Where the lynchets lay directly on chalk, snail shells were well preserved, and the species found could be analyzed to provide supporting evidence for such a view. Figure 7.5 shows the results of such an analysis at the site (WC) where a buried soil was seen. The diagram omits burrowing species and species with catholic ecological preferences that were present in small numbers throughout the profile. Three points can be made.

First, the total number of shells was high at the base of the modern topsoil and again in the buried soil; that is where stable conditions allowed them to accumulate. Throughout the horizon containing the eroded soil, snail numbers were smaller and roughly constant, indicating that the arable phase was not interrupted by long periods when the fields were uncultivated.

Second, the species composition remained much the same throughout the ploughsoil horizon, though it changed in the stony layer at the base of the modern topsoil where the proportion of *Pupilla muscorum*

SNAIL ANALYSIS   WC 2

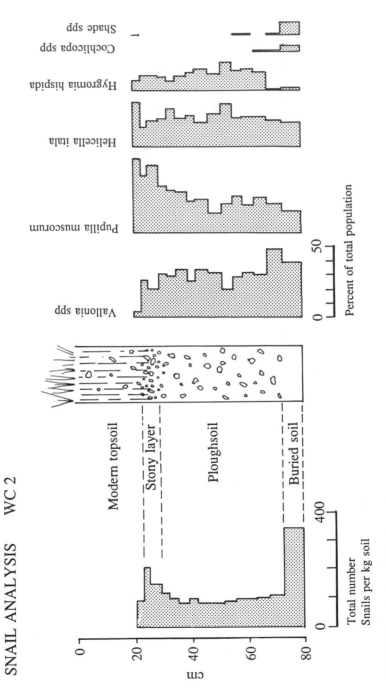

7.5. Snail analysis at Whit Coombe. The horizon labelled ploughsoil consists of the accumulation of eroded soil in the positive lynchet.

TABLE 7.2 Snail Taxa Mentioned in Text, with Authorities.

Snail	Full name
Cochlicopa spp. =	Cochlicopa lubrica (Müller 1774)
	and Cochlicopa lubricella (Porro 1838)
Carynchium tridentatum	Carynchium tridentatum (Risso 1826)
Clausilia spp. =	Clausilia bidentata (Ström 1765)
Discus rotundatus	Discus rotundatus (Müller 1774)
Helicella itala	Helicella itala (Linné 1758)
Hygromia hispida =	Trichia hispida (Linné 1758)
Hygromia striolata =	Trichia striolata (Pfeiffer 1828)
Pupilla muscorum	Pupilla muscorum (Linné 1758)
Retinella spp. =	Nesovitrea hammonis (Ström 1765)
	Aeginopinella pura (Alder 1830)
	Aeginopella nitidula (Dramarnaud 1805)
Oxychilus spp.	Oxychilus cf. cellarius (Müller 1774)
Punctum pygmaeum	Punctum pygmaeum (Draparnaud 1801)
Vallonia excentrica	Vallonia excentrica (Sterki 1892)
Vertigo pygmaea	Vertigo pygmaea (Draparnaud 1801)
Vitraea contracta	Vitraea contracta (Westerlund 1871)
Vitraea crystallina	Vitraea crystallina (Müller 1774)

increased substantially (see Figure 7.5). This result too is consistent with a single phase of arable (but see below).

Third, *Vallonia, Pupilla*, and *Helicella*, species characteristic of open habitats, dominated all the assemblages, even the one taken from the buried soil. This soil also contained species not found at higher levels in the profile, presumably because they were unable to tolerate the disturbance of cultivation.

Snail assemblages, of course, provide no direct information on the dates of the lynchets. They can, however, tell us something about land usage on the Downs before the fields in which we are interested were laid out. All the sites from which snail collections were made are considered together in Figure 7.6. This leaves out the burrowing species and those with catholic preferences (principally *Trichia hispida* and *Cochlicopa* spp.) that were present in small numbers throughout most profiles. The top row of histograms refers to snail populations found in the modern humic, relatively stone-free, topsoil. The second row (labelled ploughsoil) refers to the accumulations of eroded soil lying below the stony layer in the profiles. These accumulations were only moderately stony. Further down the profile the lowest horizons from which substantial numbers of snails could be collected were characterized (except at site WC) by a marked increase in stone content and the

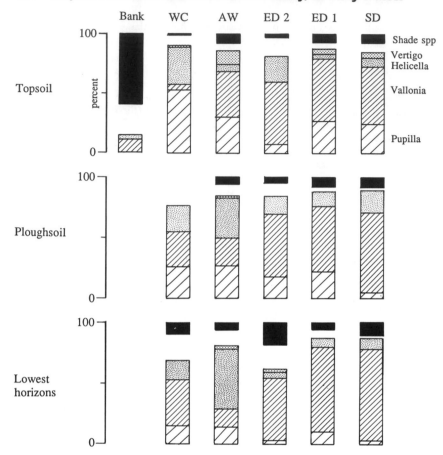

7.6. Histograms showing the proportion of the most important species in the snail assemblages from four sites. Species grouped as shade-loving include *Trichia striolata*, *Punctum pygmaeum*, *Vitraea* spp., *Nesovitrea* and *Aegopinella* spp., *Oxychilus* spp., *Carynchium tridentatum*, *Clausilia bidentata*, *Discus rotundatus*.

number of snails per kg of soil. These horizons are thought to represent the soils present before the lynchets formed.

It is immediately obvious that three open country species—*Pupilla muscorum*, *Vallonia excentrica*, and *Helicella itala*—dominated the assemblages at all sites and all levels. The representation of species characteristic of damp, sheltered environments (shade species) was not substantially greater in the lowest horizons, though it did increase somewhat at this level at WC and ED2. We may therefore conclude that the field systems were imposed on a landscape long since cleared of the natural climax vegetation, deciduous woodland.

Furthermore the area studied had probably been cultivated at least intermittently, although, as we have shown, such cultivation did not usually lead to the formation of lynchets. (Perhaps the form of cultivation caused little soil erosion, or the field boundaries were not in fixed positions.) The evidence is found in the contrast between the assemblages in the lowest horizons and the modern assemblage from the topsoil of a bank alongside a farm track, included in Figure 7.6 for comparison. The bank was covered in long grass and hawthorn (*Crataegus monogyna*) scrub, and is thought not to have been cultivated for a very long time. The snail fauna taken from it was dominated by shade species (*Vitraea* spp. and *Carynchium tridentatum*), open country types constituting only 14% of the total.

Additional evidence for cultivation before the Roman fields were laid out resides in the small numbers of *Pupilla muscorum* and *Vertigo pygmaea* in the lowest horizons. These taxa are characteristic of stable grassland (Drewett 1982; Evans 1972). Indeed, both species were better represented in the modern topsoils, which do lie below permanent grassland.

The interpretation of fine differences in these assemblages is not easy. The contrast between the two trenches at site ED makes this clear. The topsoil from ED1 contained slightly more *Pupilla* than the levels below, and *Vertigo pygmaea* was present. By contrast, in the topsoil of ED2 the proportion of *Pupilla* declined and *V. pygmaea* was absent. The numbers of snails were also very different: 166 snails per kg of soil in ED1, but only 15 per kg in ED2, yet the lynchets trenched were only 40 m apart, in the same field and subject to the same macroenvironment. Thus it seems that microenvironmental factors can have at least as big an influence on the snail populations as a major change in land use from intensive cultivation to grassland.

In any case, the differences between the assemblages in the lynchet soils and the modern topsoils were rather small. The steepness of the sites makes it likely that AW has not been cultivated since the early first millennium A.D., and the other sites cannot have been frequently cultivated or the lynchets would have been destroyed. If such small changes as those that are seen take such a long time to become established, it is perhaps unlikely that a relatively short sequence of cultivation-grass-cultivation within the lynchet body would show up as a change in species composition, though an increase in the total number of shells might be detected.

In summary, then, our work has shown that the majority of the ancient field systems on the Lambourn Downs are likely to have been laid out in the Roman period, perhaps early on. They were imposed on a landscape already cleared and probably already cultivated to some extent. (In addition to the evidence from the snail analyses, the widespread flint scatters on the Downs are also reasonably accounted for as the result of prehistoric manuring [Fowler 1983].) However, arable farming during the Roman occupation was more intensive, and the Roman fields appear to have remained predominantly in arable for a long time, perhaps 200 years, after which they reverted to grassland until very recently. Our success in dating them probably owes much to this uncomplicated history, as well as to the need to manure the shallow downland soils heavily if they are to remain productive. Excavations are clearly not likely to be helpful for dating fields unless datable artifacts were scattered over them while they were in cultivation. Even then, for the reasons set out earlier, isolated excavations may give seriously misleading results, making the accumulation of evidence from as large an area as possible very desirable.

Our findings are of interest in the wider context of Roman studies because the intensification of agriculture, with the heavy use of fairly marginal land on the Downs, has to be fitted into a general picture of economic expansion after the Roman conquest. It would seem that the transition from the later prehistoric to an early Roman organization of the rural landscape was not so smooth as has sometimes been suggested.

And finally, our conclusions reopen the question of the economies of downland communities in the last two millennia B.C. If we cannot continue to associate these communities with the ancient fields that we now see, we need to look for fresh evidence of their means of subsistence, the way they organized the landscape, and their farming practices.

References

Atkinson, R.J.C. 1965. Waylands Smithy. *Antiquity* 39:126–133.

Bowen, H.C. 1961. *Ancient Fields: A Tentative Analysis of Vanishing Earthworks and Landscapes*. British Association for the Advancement of Science, London.

Bradley, R. and A. Ellison. 1975. *Rams Hill, A Bronze Age Defended Enclosure and Its Landscape*. British Archaeological Reports 19. Oxford.

Bradley, R. and J.C. Richards. 1978. Prehistoric Fields and Land Boundaries on the Berkshire Downs. In *Early Land Allotment in the British Isles: A Survey of Recent Work*, ed. H.C. Bowen and P.J. Fowler, pp. 53–60. British Archaeological Reports 48. Oxford.

Drewett, P. 1982. *The Archaeology of Bullock Down, Eastbourne, East Sussex: The*

Development of a Landscape. Lewes Monograph 1. Sussex Archaeological Society, Lewes.

Evans, J.G. 1972. *Land Snails in Archaeology*. Seminar Press, London.

Ford, S. 1982. Linear Earthworks on the Berkshire Downs. *Berkshire Archaeological Journal* 71:1–20.

Fowler, P.J. 1983. *The Farming of Prehistoric Britain*. Cambridge University Press, Cambridge.

Gaffney, V. and M. Tingle. 1989. *The Maddle Farm Project. An Integrated Survey of Prehistoric and Roman Landscapes on the Berkshire Downs*. British Archaeological Reports 200. Oxford.

Mills, A. 1948. A Section of Celtic Field Terraces at Streatley Warren, Berks. *Berkshire Archaeological Journal* 50:51–53. Berkshire Archaeological Society, Reading.

Richards, J.C. 1978. *The Archaeology of the Berkshire Downs: An Introductory Survey*. Berkshire Archaeological Committee Publication 3. Reading.

Chapter 8
Techniques for Excavating and Analyzing Buried Eighteenth-Century Garden Landscapes

Anne E. Yentsch and Judson M. Kratzer

In this essay we draw on experience with a half dozen eighteenth-century garden sites in the mid-Atlantic region of the United States to discuss the ways historical archaeologists read the land to find barnyards, social forecourts, pathways, vegetable gardens, and, especially, pleasure gardens with all their frills (Figure 8.1).[1] In many ways landscape archaeology is unlike the archaeology done on domestic units from the historic period, which are frequently characterized by artifact-rich deposits. In fact, many historical archaeologists routinely search for such deposits because their contents are time capsules that enable reconstruction of daily life in a great house, a boarding house, a family home. Reading the landscape presents, instead, an exterior view that is only intermittently pierced with richly filled privies or wells. Pleasure gardens, in particular, leave an artifact-poor imprint created by features whose dimensions vary from a few inches in diameter (individual plantings such as those in the Victorian garden at Grumblethorpe shown in Figure 8.2) or a hundred feet or more in length or width (a garden walk, a terrace as shown in Figures 8.6 and 8.7). Since narrow windows (i.e., small test pits) do not reveal the big picture, landscape archaeologists need to draw upon analytical techniques with a broader reach.

In some regions, old gardens have been abandoned or become ploughed farm fields (e.g., Carter's Grove [Kelso 1984a], Kingsmill [Kelso 1984a, 19984b], Bacon's Castle [Luccketti 1990]). Thus in the

1. A list of elements often found in eighteenth-century ornamental gardens would include statues, urns, water elements (canals, fish ponds, fountains), summerhouses, grottos, arbors, privies, functional outbuildings (dairies, wash houses), walks, groves, planting beds, specimen trees and plants, decorative animals and birds, gates, fences, garden steps, and tree-lined avenues.

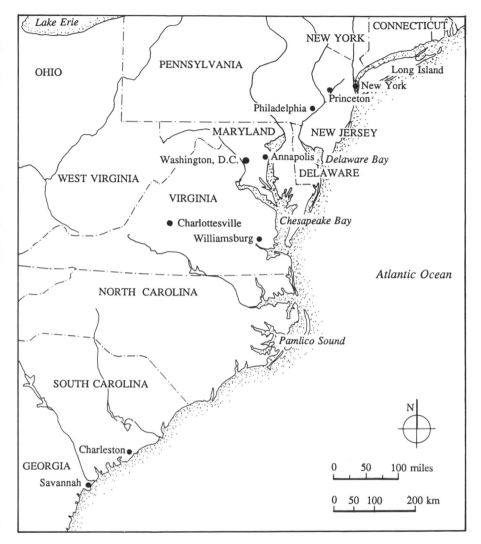

8.1. Location of garden sites discussed in text. (E. Brescia)

Chesapeake archaeologists often apply heavy machinery to remove plough zones, stripping large expanses of soil. The stripping opens to view the pattern created by fence posts, walks, and planting beds within a garden and its peripheral space. The technique is not as useful in the mid-Atlantic, where country estates have gradually been swallowed by towns and cities (cf. McLean 1984 on Philadelphia gar-

dens and Yentsch 1992a on the Cliveden estate). As cities and towns
grew outward, many country estates were divided again and again,
then cut by streets, power line trenches, and deep building foundations. Since ornamental gardens usually lay adjacent to a great
house, they were afforded some protection as country estates con-
tracted. At the same time, if protected, they were continuously
planted and, depending on the wealth of their owners, adapted and
recreated to follow the latest garden styles (e.g., Grumblethorpe,
Morven, Cliveden). Complicating already complex stratigraphic sequences, the explosion of garden activity in the late nineteenth century produced glorious Colonial Revival gardens like the one Helen
Hamilton Shields planted at Morven.

To take a continuously planted garden down to its earlier levels,
recording all later reincarnations, is laborious, hence expensive. Restoration schedules do not allot sufficient time; funding is rarely adequate. The preservation community normally grants more importance
to a house and its furnishings than to the exterior surrounding.
Houses set in their gardens in the eighteenth century, however, were
meant to be seen by neighbors, and families "tried to outdo each other
in the creation of their architecture and garden schemes" (Racine et
al. 1987:48). The importance of gardens in eighteenth-century society made them dynamic arenas for symbolic manipulation; pastiches
created from a test unit here and another unit there do not do justice
to the dense symbolic meaning pleasure gardens carried within the
culture. A variety of archaeological techniques allows one to balance
the need for more extensive exposure with the economic realities of
preservation-based archaeology.

Strategies for recovering old landscapes have been developed by a
generation of landscape archaeologists working on sites along the
Eastern seaboard of the United States, beginning with William Kelso
at Carter's Grove (Kelso 1971, 1984a; see also Kelso and Most 1990)
and Noël Hume at Williamsburg and Carter's Grove (Noël Hume
1974). For the most part, the field techniques can be applied cross-
culturally. The one exception is the set of expectations that derive
from knowledge of the eighteenth-century planters' own ideas (i.e.,
world view), how they viewed nature and its constituents, and how
they transformed these into garden designs by combining land, water,
plants, trees, birds, and vistas. Their world view also ordered how
planters viewed what needed to be done to keep their pleasure gardens, which were always a family's pride and joy, on a par with their
neighbors' or, perchance, to outdistance their neighbors' garden realm.

Archaeological manifestations of these basic ideas have been studied since 1982 by Barbara Paca (then of Historic Annapolis, Inc.;

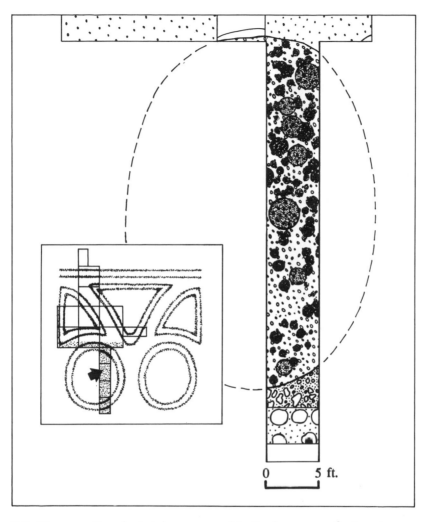

8.2. Many smaller plant stains appeared in the large goosefoot parterre—a decorative planting bed installed at the Grumblethorpe garden in the Victorian era. (J. Hunter-Abbazia, based on Bescherer et al. [1990a])

Paca-Steele and Wright 1987) and were a major focus in our landscape study of Morven in Princeton, New Jersey (Miller et al. 1990; Yentsch 1990a; Yentsch et al. 1987, 1990). Paca drew on St. Clair Wright's knowledge of the principles of dynamic symmetry. Working with Paca, Leone (1984) integrated these same principles into his concept of the William Paca Garden while Paul Shackel expanded them in a discussion of the Charles Carroll Garden (Leone and Shackel 1990). We also drew on these constructs to orient the excavation program at Belmont, an eighteenth-century mansion now incorporated into Fairmount Park in Philadelphia (Yentsch 1990b) while applying more technical models for garden study to our work at three country estates in northwest Philadephia: Grumblethorpe (in Germantown [Bescherer et al. 1990a]), Cliveden (the Chew mansion also in Germantown [Yentsch 1992a]), and the more rural Highlands (Bescherer et al. 1990b). The ideas governing planting activity and garden design constituted a set of informal rules, a social logic for space (Yentsch et al. 1987). Familiarity with them is of great utility in deciding where to dig, how deep to go, and what to expect. It is part and parcel of a landscape archaeologist's skill in the field. It is an explicit element in field strategies for recovering earlier landscapes.

Mental models for eighteenth-century gardens in the mid-Atlantic cannot be transferred to non-western cultures, but they are applicable wherever garden design drew on the well-spring of Renaissance garden tradition, settings as diverse as colonial South and West Africa, France, Italy, England, Spain, and the Caribbean. In fact, it would not surprise us to see their expression in the tea islands of the Indian Ocean or in colonial South America. Obtaining ethnographic knowledge of past cultures involves reading old texts, studying old paintings, and analyzing present-day gardens whose eighteenth-century boundaries remain intact.[2] One looks for the elements people used to build their gardens, considers their range of variability, and adds time-depth whenever possible. More broadly, a methodology that identifies mental models based on knowledge of the culture the archaeologist studies can apply to many archaeological situations where ethnographic information about past cultures is available in documents. The strategy would work with Chinese gardens dating to the Ming dynasty, Persian gardens of Anatolia or Iran, or the coral gardens Bronislaw Malinowski wrote about on the Trobriand Islands (see also Erickson, this volume). Because it enables a field crew to take ordinary procedures and produce extraordinary results, it is part of the toolkit that skilled landscape archaeologists use in their excavations.

Field Methods and Techniques

Hole et al. (1969:24) observed that "digging down into the unknown" may be a romantic and exciting idea, but it constitutes clumsy and

2. There are a number of gardens where the old landscape is just below the present day garden; change has been in plantings and, to varying degrees, in interior design, but the overall boundaries have remained constant.

poorly-planned archaeology. Until archaeologists learn the cultural grammar that organized the original garden, modern previewing techniques are indispensable. These include remote sensing, mechanical stripping, trenching, the excavation of intermittent units along east-west or north-south lines, topographic analysis, a checkerboard sampling plan, and various types of probes into the soil.

The first step is remote sensing (see Bevan, this volume). Nondestructive techniques of geophysical exploration were tried with disappointing results at Morven (Bevan 1987), where large areas of fieldstone paving did not show up on the recorder. The results at Long Hill in Wicomico County, Maryland on the eastern shore (Bevan 1991) also failed to reveal a sterile, packed clay layer that formed a garden surface off the kitchen wing (Betweiler 1991). The reason these buried surfaces did not appear is not clear, but may be related to differences between built garden strata and those formed naturally. Nothing dramatic appeared at the Frederick Law Olmsted garden site in Brookline, Massachusetts, either.

At the Olmsted garden, the radar successfully located several drainpipes (previously known from an early twentieth-century map) and what may be some areas of intensive landscape alteration (filling; filling and regrading). In addition, several unidentified anomalies were detected by radar, but no ground verification was conducted. The proton magnetometer proved virtually useless; it detected largely modern features: powerline, street, metal objects. The electromagnetic survey identified several anomalies. Certainly a number of landscape features can be detected in some conditions through the use of remote sensing. But ground verification is imperative (R. Elia, pers. comm. 7 February 1992).

Even if remote sensing studies have uninformative results, some type of preview is essential; we have had more luck with topographic surveys that pinpoint subtle changes in ground contours, locating tree lines, planting beds, and access areas. In this area, work at Boston University has led the way with a sophisticated survey system using an electronic theodolite and EDM (electronic distance measuring device). This type of mapping saves time, is accurate, and overlays by stratum or feature type can be produced easily. Individual numbers can also be assigned to trees, shrubs, and planting areas. It is a flexible, elegant method that has a reasonable cost. The results let an archaeologist look at the landscape from a bird's eye view and begin reading the underlying garden plan. Since many new gardens at historic houses play on elements present in earlier ones, there are many advantages to planning a testing program with such a map in hand.

Still, exploring a large area expeditiously requires a system whereby one segment of the excavation moves downward prior to the rest. At Morven, for example, we tried several previewing techniques to get an overall impression of a garden or yard area while work was in progress. Augering to obtain soil cores (small and large), probing, a checkerboard excavation strategy, and trenching allowed us to place test units that would maximize information about the garden plan. The least destructive technique was sampling the lower layers with a split spoon auger. Although it does not produce results adequate to construct stratigraphic sections with known elevations, the geologist's split spoon gives an archaeologist a qualitative feel for what lies below, and disturbs a site no more than a good-sized locust larva's burrow.

A steel T-probe is effective in locating buried brick paths and tracing building walls. It works better in towns like Annapolis and Williamsburg, where rubble is concentrated and stone is culturally deposited (very little natural stone occurs on the Chesapeake flood plain), than at mid-Atlantic sites, like Morven, Belmont, Grumble-thorpe, and the Highlands, where brick rubble and fieldstone is abundant across the entire site. At Morven, the probe enabled archaeologists to locate large sections of a brick-paved mid-nineteenth century walkway/work area leading to an ice-house, and to trace a fieldstone forecourt (Figure 8.3). At Belmont, it was useful in tracing a north garden wall built from fieldstone (Yentsch and Kratzer 1991). In all cases, however, it has to be accompanied by additional below-ground testing.

Occasionally a post-hole digger can test the depth of deep fill layers; used judiciously the stratigraphic evidence it produces is informative and time-saving. For example, to create a level garden terrace land-owners brought in additional soil, sometimes from distant sources, but often from nearby areas on site. Deep fill sequences give an archaeologist the impression he or she is digging through subsoil—an impression further intensified if soil from preparing a new cellar or cellar extension (which comes from subsoil layers) was used. Yet the technique does not have overall usefulness and as a sampling strategy is less informative than when it is used in a single unit to answer a particular question.

In 1982 at Reynolds Tavern (Annapolis, Maryland), we used large cores placed 10 to 15 ft apart, a spacing too great to pick up lateral boundaries or transition zones between strata; artifact recovery was also inadequate for close dating. Although this technique has been used successfully at St. Augustine (Deagan 1981) and at Providence (Rubertone and Gallagher 1981), the research at Reynolds Tavern and the difficulties noted by McManamon (1981, 1984) and Elia (1987) dissuaded us from using large-diameter cores to locate or de-

8.3. Fieldstone courtyard at Morven. The distinct line between paved area and yard was discerned by use of the T-probe. (courtesy of the New Jersey State Museum)

fine features and levels at the mid-Atlantic sites. They were, however, occasionally taken to evaluate fill deposits. Small split spoon cores were routinely used in a variety of ways to preview and assess work in progress. Note that we used both these techniques to work outward from a known point, not as part of a general sampling strategy (cf. Elia 1987).

A variant of a sampling strategy based on large-diameter cores uses quick STPs (shovel-test pits) to subsoil. At Cliveden, for example, this strategy was used to identify artifact concentrations across a four acre yard (Lewis 1991). However, the problems of linking soil layers that represent garden parterres, of distinguishing deliberate variations in garden elevations (i.e., the creation of slopes, sunken gardens, or raised beds), or tying artifacts to eighteenth- and nineteenth-century occupations makes this technique inappropriate for refined landscape analysis. Its benefit remains its ability to identify the presence of broad areas that require further work (Yentsch and Kratzer 1993) and, in the case of Cliveden, of suggesting the richness of the artifact deposition in particular areas—a critical factor in financial and logistic planning.

There is no gainsaying that the Virginia approach, in which archaeologists mechanically remove large areas of ploughed fields and take a garden down to earlier levels across wide areas a level at a time, gives the best information if the original garden surface was deep enough to escape destruction by the farmer's plough. When this is impossible, a checkerboard plan (especially in a small area or on a town lot) can be highly advantageous. The technique has not been as productive in the preparation of long profiles. Braidwood and Howe (1960) noted that underlying strata at sites can pitch and toss in unanticipated ways; it often seemed at Morven that they did so precisely in those units which, in terms of the checkerboard, fell within the not-to-be excavated sequence of units.

Trenching is another technique whose popularity has waxed and waned (see Erickson, this volume). It was useful at the Calvert site in Annapolis for understanding grading and filling across the site, and hence was incorporated into the excavation strategy at Morven. The initial trench plans were designed to obtain a long north-south profile across the entire yard by means of a five-foot wide gradall trench (Figure 8.4). Because critical, sensitive features are often located close to buildings, the excavation of the mechanically dug trenches arbitrarily stopped 75 ft from the house, and hand excavation took its place. Clues concerning the ca. 1760 garden immediately appeared in the first north trench, whose profile revealed the existence of an early terraced garden. Trench No. 3 also uncovered the edge of a wide set

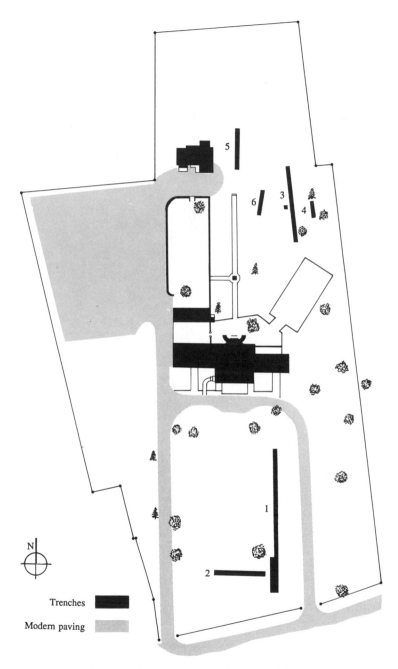

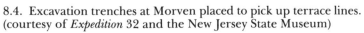

8.4. Excavation trenches at Morven placed to pick up terrace lines.
(courtesy of *Expedition* 32 and the New Jersey State Museum)

8.5. Terrace steps cut by trench at Morven in 1987. (A. Yentsch)

of fieldstone steps that provided passage from the main terrace to a lower garden (Figures 8.4, 8.5). Continuation of the terrace fall line to the west was found in Trench 6; to the east, Trench 4 uncovered a profile containing no evidence of terracing. Thus the 1987 trenching located one corner of the garden, but without further information on other boundaries the garden's formal design could not be delineated. Trenching is a technique we have since used successfully in other gardens in the Philadelphia region (Bescherer et al. 1990a, 1990b; Yentsch and Kratzer 1991), and it is a particularly effective means to establish variations in earlier surface grades or the existence of terracing. We pay careful attention to the elevation of different soil strata within the trenches because even when we have to use segmented trenching (skipping portions one would normally like to open up), variations in elevation will often reveal whether or not a site was terraced.

Garden Terraces

Terraces were the basis of many eighteenth-century gardens. Essentially they were artificial slopes, usually carved from a hillside, consisting of falls and level parterres that Italians, drawing on planting techniques developed in the ancient Near East, made popular in the fifteenth century. Terraces and their staircases visually elevated a mansion. A sign of refined taste, terracing allowed an owner to look out over the countryside and view pleasing focal points in the garden itself—a temple, a mound, a pond, a summerhouse, a statue. Variations in terrace boundaries altered visual perspectives that further manipulated a view by making it seem further away or close and large (see Weber et al. 1990: figs. 9.6, 9.7). Ornamental garden terraces were brought to North America by ca. 1720–1730, constructed in Governor Calvert's garden in Annapolis (Yentsch 1994, Yentsch et al. 1987) and in Governor Spotswood's gardens at Williamsburg and Germanna (Martin 1991; Noël Hume 1974; Sanford 1990).

The benefits of terracing extended beyond the symbolic ascendancy they expressed. Terraces unified the appearance of the disparate vegetation and planting beds that formed the garden. In garden historian Peter Martin's words, terraces "created that blessed quality of variety as well as a theatrically conceived and shaped space" (Martin 1991:50). Furthermore, European horticulturalists found terraces to be an excellent way to prevent soil erosion, control rain water runoff, and provide level garden beds. Plants grew better on a terrace because they received more uniform sunlight. Landscape archaeologists are discovering that terracing was a technique used in many pe-

8.6. Water features from the eighteenth-century garden at Middleton Place have remained a dominant element in the Middleton landscape. (courtesy of Middleton Place, Charleston, South Carolina)

riods and regions (see Treacy and Denevan, this volume; Pulsipher, this volume).

We study terracing (and other forms of planting beds) by visualizing a garden as a series of flat horizontal planes, relatively shallow, that are tied together. In a terraced garden these horizontal planes contain the parterres and are linked by the terrace falls, by garden walks that follow major axes, and by exterior boundaries—fences, hedge-rows, or lines of trees—that encompass the garden as a single unit, all of which bind together the different levels and provide verticality. The horizontal planes and their walkways provide passage through the garden, create different social spaces within it, and provide varying access to these social spaces and their related vistas (Figures 8.6, 8.7).

Key steps towards understanding the spatial relationships utilized within a garden's design are (1) establishing its boundaries, (2) finding its major axis, and (3) locating other passageways through it. Boundaries, major axis, and passages vary in terms of their above-ground or archaeological visibility. At the William Paca Garden in Annapolis, the eighteenth-century boundaries were established by thick brick walls (Little 1967/68). Once located archaeologically, variations in the depths of their baselines delineated the terrace fall lines (see Yentsch et al. 1987: fig. 11). At the later Paca Garden on Wye Island, the boundaries were provided by more naturalistic elements, by land contours, and by the meeting of sky and land (Bescherer and Yentsch 1989). Because the site underwent no major alteration in the nineteenth century, its naturalistic boundaries are still seen today. At Morven, Grumblethorpe, and Belmont, the garden boundaries were also provided by walkways and terraces, but major episodes of subsequent landscape change effectively covered and hid them, while their construction material (local field and limestone, or, in later gardens, gravel, ash, and charcoal) and microstratigraphy (created because the construction materials required periodic replenishment) gave them less archaeological visibility than the sturdy brick features or water-based elements in the southern gardens of rich planters (cf. Middleton Place in South Carolina, Figure 8.6).

If eighteenth-century gardeners had a passion for vertical space, then their nineteenth-century counterparts had an equally strong attraction to level ground. The recovery of older landscapes is complicated by later efforts to flatten earlier gardens. In addition, the Victorian predilection for adding fill was the means normally chosen to enrich garden soils and hide unsightly or out-of-fashion activity areas, a practice that has been observed in many New England yards

(Beaudry 1988; Beaudry and Blosser 1982; Deetz 1977; Moran et al. 1982; Reinke and Paynter 1984) and created immensely deep stratigraphic sequences at East and West coast cities (Yentsch 1992b). We have also seen it in Philadelphia gardens. At Belmont, for example, more than 4 ft of fill, created in large part from 2 to 3 ft deep boulder/ rubble, hides the ca. 1740–1760 front yard (Yentsch and Kratzer 1991: fig. 9). Equivalent or deeper layers have been found at the Bordley-Randall site in Annapolis (Yentsch 1988), at the Calvert site (Yentsch 1994) while at the retaining wall on the old Carroll property near the Annapolis harbor, fill is more than 8 ft deep (Sanchez 1982). Men usually went to rural locations to obtain garden soil and fill, so it often contains subsoil that introduces an artificial sterility into profiles.

Considering the Victorians' passion for raising yard surfaces from the perspective of the Grumblethorpe garden, Bescherer et al. (1990a) suggest such earth-moving may have been prompted by the ungainly encroachment of urban/suburban construction onto an aesthetically beautiful "prospect." In some cases, nineteenth-century lot division actually cut and divided the eighteenth-century terraces themselves; in other cases, it simply inserted visual distractions into the rural vista. Raising the land helped hide the view, especially when paired with judicious tree plantings. Nowadays it is difficult to find an in situ terrace except on isolated, rural estates or on steep hillsides. Old terraces are still visible at Tulip Hill in Anne Arundel County, Maryland, on the Eastern Shore, and along the James River in Virginia. Yet even where old terraces survive, the division between house and land is not what it was when an early eighteenth-century garden was first born, for by the late eighteenth century gardeners were planting groves of trees near their homes to create park-like settings and impose visual distance from farm work buildings (cf. George Washington's revamping of Mt. Vernon [de Forest 1982; Martin 1991] and trees planted after the Revolution at Cliveden [Yentsch 1992a]). John Dixon Hunt (1992:285) writes of this era as a "watershed in landscape architecture." It is one that left a deep archaeological imprint on the land, one we must dig through to uncover older forms and styles in gardens.

Garden Grids

The new aesthetic tore apart the earlier spatial unity conferred on a garden through its terracing and fencing. It privatized the home by visually separating a house from working buildings. On country estates, families obtained a heightened sense of living in a natural park by erecting artificial mounds and groves of trees to shield their homes from casual view. Garden walls hid behind ivy; statues were sequestered in secluded spaces. There was a deliberate unshaping of space; boundaries were blurred to suggest a merging of social landscape with nature. As the formal symmetry of the earlier landscape was displaced and its social divisions rewritten, so too was the dynamic symmetry implicit in the older use of garden space.

Dynamic symmetry is a term adopted in the 1920s by artist and designer Jay Hambidge (1920) to describe a way of analyzing a work of art (and he included gardens) that highlights the design and proportions used to bind it together as a composition (Fisher 1985:40). The proportions Hambidge was particularly interested in were ones that used the Euclidean geometric principles that first saw expression in ancient Egyptian and Greek architecture. It is not surprising that these principles would structure many gardens in the eighteenth century, for it was a time when Western cultures drew on classical antecedents in many domains of life. What planters sought to do with their gardens was shape space in a particular way working within a *predetermined* area.

We do not yet understand the spatial decisions behind the predetermined areas they chose as garden space. In some cases it is easy to see how city boundaries affected these. Thus William Paca bought land in Annapolis, consolidating two square lots into one rectangular parcel that ran between Prince George's and King George's Streets, with a length of 24 perches and a width of 12 perches[3] (South 1967:31). In the countryside, landowners had more options. Yet it is our impression, as we study more gardens, that there was an "ideal" size for an ornamental garden, derived in part by size similarities in Georgian house plans, but also influenced by the available labor base for garden construction and maintenance. Having first decided what width his garden was to be (normally three times the length of the house in the mid-Atlantic) and what length (by taking into consideration topographic attributes of a site, especially elevation), a gentleman then designed elements to fit within its confines.

Fisher (1985:52–53) points out that this use of space, in which the articulating principles shift and change, is quite different from that based on a Cartesian grid, which displays a static, repetitive manipulation of space built from uniform "blocks." Archaeologists are familiar with the Cartesian grid. It is the basis of the grid laid down over a site to plot locations of features and track sub-surface findings. Based on the multiple repetition of a given unit (whether measured in me-

---

3. A perch (also called a rod or a pole) is 16.5 ft long. It is derived from the Gunter Chain (66 ft), the basic unit of measurement in the eighteenth-century surveying system.

ters or feet), it is essentially infinite, a character that enables us to extend it here, not use it there. This "static treatment of space," Fisher points out, "tends to emphasize *measured, counted* space over *shaped* space" (ibid:52, original emphasis). And that, of course, is precisely its value to archaeologists.

Eighteenth-century horticulturalists *shaped* space using non-uniform building blocks that included rectangles formed from the dimensions of the houses that sat within their gardens. Thus at Tulip Hill the height of the building is also the width of the first terrace or mansion platform (Figure 8.7). At times garden designers emphasized the right triangle from which the rectangles were formed, while maintaining the pairing of elements that reflects the Georgian preference for static space. Gardens where triangular shapes underlay the design include Charles Carroll's ca. 1720 Annapolis garden, which abutted his private chapel and framed the area of his yard devoted to religious space. At Middleton Place, too, the triangle controlled the garden layout. Within the context of Georgian design, the triangle inspired more complex gardens, because it is more difficult to create bilateral symmetry with a design based on a right triangle. More often, gardens and house space were designed by emphasizing rectangular or square units.

There is an inherent contradiction created by the use of static archaeological space to measure and identify dynamic garden space. How to transcend it? One strategy is to begin by searching for a garden's boundaries so that its elements can be visualized within the preconceived whole, framed and contained. Another is to set aside temporarily our own measuring tools (i.e., the grid built in meters or feet) and conceive of the site's space using the eighteenth-century unit of measurement (i.e, the 16.5 ft rod or perch). A third is to begin within the garden and trace portions of it outward until original spatial divisions become apparent. In some ways the latter strategy is the easiest because all it involves is taking very precise measurements of different soil strata and mapping their occurrence. Finding a garden's boundaries, on the other hand, involves having good control over the original dimensions of an extant home and its related outbuildings, structures which rarely survive in precisely the same form or pattern they originally exhibited, and sometimes houses have simply vanished. Viewing a site using an alien system of measurement is sufficiently difficult for those of us who are not visually oriented that as a strategy it is much easier to bring it into play after one has archaeological facts to join with it. With this is mind, let us begin using variations in depth to identify horizontal planes, and conjoining the planes to pinpoint terrace locations by drawing on a Morven example.

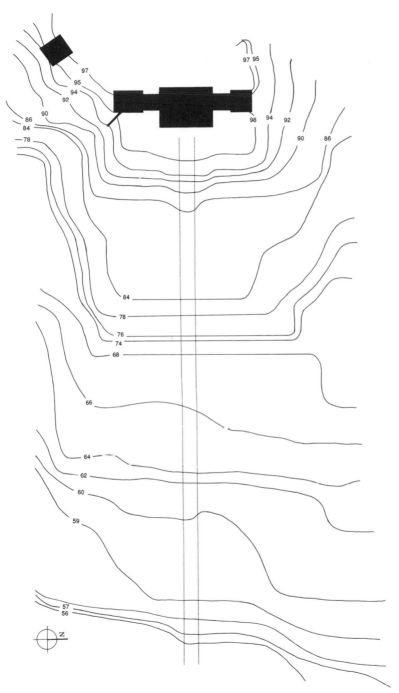

8.7. Plan view of surviving eighteenth-century garden at Tulip Hill in Anne Arundel County, Maryland. (J. Hunter-Abbazia, after original by J. Kratzer)

This reveals how verticality was used to distinguish one area from another in eighteenth-century social space.

A Garden's Horizontal Planes

First, we note elevations in feet-above-sea-level (ASL) rather than as feet-below-datum, and determine the ASL readings, preferably day by day. An advantage of daily readings, particularly on a large site where several datum points may be in use, is that the field crew know, as they excavate a feature or level, precisely what its depth is relative to similar features or levels elsewhere. The elevations often suggest spatial relationships not apparent to the naked eye. The use of ASL measurements expedites timely testing and tracing of linkages between garden features over a broad area.

At Morven it was difficult to compare strata and depths between two sets of excavation units because they were located 130 ft apart, separated by a brick wall. In one area archaeologists found a pair of stone slabs, a narrow stone pathway, and a three-foot layer of fill over an oval fieldstone floor. In the other they found a set of stone steps. While no one was sure of the relationship between the two gardens within the original garden, the absolute elevations of the features was quite close: the top of the eastern steps (F12) at 213.48 ASL was at virtually the same level as the top of the stone slabs (F225) at 213.46 ASL; the elevation of the bottom of the steps at 211.78 ASL closely matched that of the surface of the fieldstone floor (F231) at 211.67 ASL. Midway between the features was either a fieldstone ramp or another set of steps (F303) whose top elevation was 213.8 ASL. While this area was not fully excavated, the elevations indicate two planes each extending in a band 10 ft wide on a east-west line across the site 160–165 ft or 10 perches distant from the house. They were connected by an east-west fieldstone walk (F283), also at the slightly higher elevation of 213.8 ASL. That is, the variation in depth at which these features were placed marked the terrace fall and the northern edge of the second, or major terrace (Figure 8.8).

Excavation units nearer the house revealed a third plane that extends no more than 30 ft from the original building at a depth of about 215.5 ASL. There is a fourth level, on the west side of the site whose precise depth remains undetermined, although it is probably at 211 ASL if not lower (ca. 209 ASL); it represents the working gardens and also held outbuildings associated with the family farm. Additional terraces extended northward from the terrace represented by the 211 ASL horizontal plane and dropped lower. Remnants of these exist on old topographic maps. Finally, immediately in front of

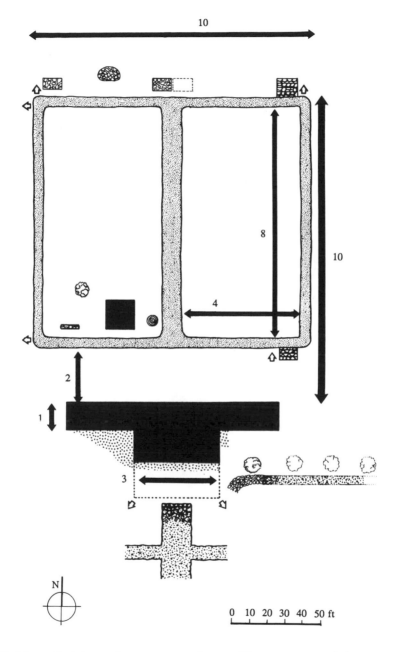

8.8. Map of eighteenth-century garden at Morven as revealed through archaeology. Note that arrows show linear measurement in perches. (J. Hunter-Abbazia, after original by J. Kratzer)

TABLE 8.1 Morven Above-Sea-Level Elevation Analysis of Eighteenth-Century Landscape Elements

Feature no.	Descriptions	Elevation (ft ASL)	Designated perch
North Yard			
Garden features close to house by east wing			
329	Limestone walk (abuts east wing)	215.5	N1
298	Limestone scatter (continuation of walk?)	215.3	N2
Garden features close to center block of house			
263	Set of N–S and E–W fieldstone walks	215.5	N1
264	Planting bed associated with F263	215.4	N1
278	Tree-hole off center block	214.6	N2
134(L)	Original topsoil on north side of house (center block)	214.8	N1
Garden features between west wing and outbuildings			
009	Well (stone lining)	215.6	N2
035	Ice-house doorstoop (fieldstone)	215.5	N2
025	Ice-house fieldstone foundation (first build)	215.2	N2
334	Fieldstone foundation or east walk (east of ice-house)	215.3	N3
038	Fieldstone-flagstone walk or wall	215.5	N2
342	Red shale (disintegrated paving stone?)	215.3	N1–2
134(L)	Original topsoil in courtyard area	215.0	N2
Garden features in the center section of the first major terrace			
327	Western N–S walk across terrace (by parking lot)	213.4	N6
170(L)	Eighteenth-century garden topsoil—west sector	214.1	N6
286A	Center N–S walkway across terrace in perch 3	214.8	N3
328	Narrow garden bed abutting center N–S walkway	214.8	N3
338	Eastern N–S walkway across terrace	214.9	N4
335	Tree-hole or garden outbuilding(?)	214.8	N5
024	Flat stones—Unit 34	215.1	N3
	Garden bed east of east N–S walkway—Unit 34	215.0	N3
Garden features found in association with the fall line of the first major terrace			
012	Stone steps (east) at top	213.5	N10
012	Stone steps (east) at base	211.8	N11
303	Stone steps (center) at top	213.8	N10
303	Stone steps (center) at base	211.7	N11

TABLE 8.1 (*continued*)

Feature no.	Descriptions	Elevation (ft ASL	Designated perch
North Yard (continued)			
Garden features found in association with the fall line of the first major terrace			
283	Northern E–W walkway (mid-level) across terrace	214.3	N10
002	Northern E–W walkway across terrace (by F12)	214.8	N10
338	Eastern N–S walkway across terrace (near F12)	214.8	N10
286C	Center N–S walkway across terrace (near F303)	214.5	N10
225	Stone slabs on upper terrace (in west)	213.5	N10
231	Possible fieldstone walk on lower terrace	211.7	N11
South Yard (facing Stockton Street)			
Garden features close to center block of house or aligned with it			
059	2nd fieldstone doorstoop (front door)	217.7	S1
070	Refuse deposit by front door	217.1	S1
078	Fieldstone forecourt on lower terrace	216.6	S4–6
Garden features close to house by east wing			
195	E–W fieldstone walk by east wing	215.5	S0
214	Limestone walk to east wing (north)	215.8	S0
194	Brick rubble off east wing	215.8	S1
218	Shale parallel to house (center block east wall) (walk?)	215.1	S0
Garden features by west wing			
341	Red shale apron (disintegrated paving stone?)	216.5	S0
	Planting bed in red shale	216.4	S0
141	Cobble apron abutting brick paving	216.3	S0

the house there was a fifth and higher level (217 ASL) which formed a small terrace, 32 ft x 48 ft (2 x 3 perches), leading out and gently dropping off to the fieldstone forecourt at 216 ASL. Thus the house was set on a slightly raised platform above a terraced garden (and adjacent to it) while the working area beyond the dependencies was conceptually demoted by its slightly lower working plane (Table 8.1).

Whereas Morven sat on a small rise on the plateau the town of Princeton occupied, Belmont was set in the side of a hill overlooking a river; a similar variation in yard levels was seen there, although the testing was insufficient to tie the horizontal planes together. These eighteenth-century horizontal planes are the remains of level yard surfaces created through landscaping. They are occupation layers qualitatively different from those formed when people serendipitously scatter household refuse which eventually forms a midden. They represent a deliberate manipulation of vertical space for symbolic and aesthetic ends.

Normally these different garden surfaces are formed in a series of short term, intensive land manipulations. Because of the rapid deposition of soil, artifact densities are unusually low for a historic site. The layers result, in some cases, from carving away the hillside (Morven, Belmont, Middleton Place) or from building it up (William Paca Garden on Wye Island). Terraced gardens can be found up and down the Eastern seaboard from the Carolinas to Maine. Their creation is why one writer observed: "Every Man Now be his fortune what it will, is to be [found] doing something at his place, as the fashionable Phrase is; and you hardly meet with any Body, who, after the first Compliments, does not inform you that he is in Mortar and moving of Earth; the modest terms for Building and Gardening" (1739 article in "Common Sense" quoted in Hunt and Willis 1988:25). And, when styles changed, "Every man's" sons and grandsons altered the effects of these different vertical planes surrounding the houses they inherited by filling the land to make their homes fashionably sited on the land once again.

Knowledge of relationships among and between the various sets of horizontal planes tell of the way in which the garden evolved over time and how its present day contour lines gradually developed. Yet the vertical relationships provide only a fragmentary view of the garden. The features must also be perceived within a horizontal framework—the garden's boundaries—before its design can be seen.

Using the House to Find Garden Boundaries and Date Garden Layers

William Kelso uses the house to find the garden, observing that the garden fence line normally articulates with one or another corner of the house. He conceives of the house as consisting of a main block and its attached or adjacent dependencies. And he works in the Chesapeake where plough zone stripping can be done (see above). The way that fence lines often align with a house and its dependencies shows clearly in the posthole pattern and field plans of Kingsmill (Figures 8.9, 8.10; see also Kelso [1984b]) and in photographs of

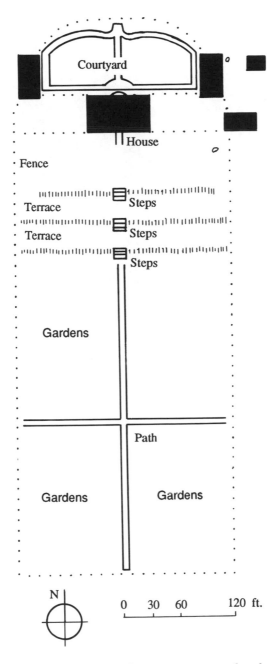

Courtyard

House

Fence

Terrace   Steps

Terrace   Steps

Steps

Gardens

Path

Gardens   Gardens

N

0   30   60   120 ft.

8.9. Arrangement of entrance courtyard and
fences at Kingsmill Plantation. (courtesy of
the Virginia Department of Historic
Resources)

8.10. Postholes at Kingsmill show the outline of garden fences. (courtesy of the Virginia Department of Historic Resources)

Kingsmill excavation units. We have not observed such a tight alignment in the mid-Atlantic, although we too have found that a house is one of the best places to begin to date different occupation layers across a yard.

Because doorways provided access to different sectors of the pleasure garden or working yards, they are logical starting points for reading the stratigraphic sequence before one moves outward into the garden itself. Doors are also areas of a site that normally have extremely complex stratigraphy; many features representing sequences of paths and walkways converge upon them. Doorstoops or stairs must be rebuilt or repaired with each change in yard level. Yet doorways have also enabled us to locate eighteenth-century yard surfaces with sufficient certainty that, using ASL measurements for similar strata in other sectors of the garden, we could begin to trace the contours of the earliest surfaces.

The eighteenth-century yard surface outside the front door of Belmont, for example, not only indicated that a stairway to the original door was essential, but also located the original ground surface at a depth four feet below present grade—a depth consistent across the entire front facade of house and dependencies. A line of three 5 ft by 5 ft excavation units were sufficient to tell us this (Basalik 1990, 1991; Yentsch and Kratzer 1991).

Morven is perhaps the best example of using entryway changes to begin reading a site. At its main doorway facing Stockton street, archaeologists inferred five periods of change (Goodwin et al. in press; Yentsch et al. 1990). Initially there was a small fieldstone doorstoop opening onto a level terrace that led, in turn, to a fieldstone forecourt. After the occupying British Army left, the Stocktons renewed their terrace and installed a larger fieldstone doorstoop. The new terrace surface covered the older red shale 'apron' abutting the house. A front porch was the third change. It was probably in place before the family "dismantled" their home in the 1790s, for there is no accumulation from ca. 1795–1820 of household or architectural debris beneath the porch floor and over the terrace. The new house, built on the foundations of the old, was different; its first front porch was renovated ca. 1820 (Albee 1990).

The next era of doorway change was ca. 1850 when Commodore Robert Field Stockton "built upon Morven." He enlarged and raised the roof lines in both wings, renovated the main block, and attached a small, exterior bathroom with a tub and running water, thereby creating new activity areas for house and yard. These, in turn, necessitated new and/or differently marked access routes. Those in the north yard and off the kitchen wing were converted to wide brick-paved areas that clearly demarcated the servants' passageways to and from the domestic workspace.

The profile drawing in Figure 8.11 clearly depicts the build-up of the landscape off the East Wing and shows the sequence from the original occupation to the present-day brick walk and boxwood hedge (seen in the upper right corner). At its base is a 2 to 3 inch stratum (215.5 ASL) that was the original ground surface prior to construction of the ca. 1760 house. Within 6 to 8 inches of the modern surface (at 216.3 ASL), is the surface of the Commodore's nineteenth-century Horse Chestnut Walk. A trench through the walk exposed its sub-base of recycled cut stone, and the adjacent decorative border (indicated by the presence of two linear features containing crushed red shale) cutting the brown loam of his father's lawn. Apparent below the sub-base are several occupational levels and a critical architecturally-related layer—the sandy sterile yellow clay (or cellar excavate) spread out when the cellar foundation was dug ca. 1760. The lowest section of fieldstone is a ca. 1760 walkway.

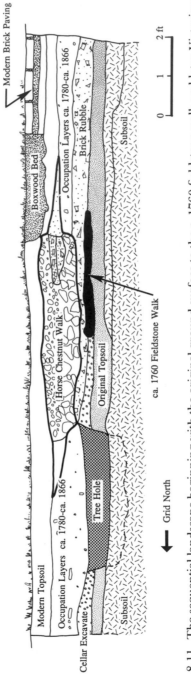

8.11. The sequential landscape beginning with the original ground surface to the c. 1760 fieldstone walk and later Victorian gravel path as well as tree locations, lawns, and modern paving appear in this stratigraphic profile off the east wing at Morven. (courtesy of *Expedition* 32 and the New Jersey State Museum)

The convergence of paths on the Stockton Street side of the house and their articulation with one another, particularly off the East wing, is a dramatic illustration of stratigraphic complexity. The layering enabled us to grasp the relationships between the different architectural phases of the house and the sequences of levels (read as horizontal planes) in the ornamental garden. It also enabled us to establish that the original foundation (ca. 1760) was re-utilized in the rebuilding. Eighteenth-century gardens served as ornaments to the main dwelling and as components of a broader landscape design. One way designers subsumed them within the whole was by drawing upon the dimensions of a mansion's front and side walls for the core shape. They then cast this unit outwards as part of a network of rectangles in the garden design (Paca-Steele and Wright 1987). Thus house and lot dimensions are critical data for discovering the basic outline of the ca. 1760 gardens.

Rediscovering the Substructure of Gardens

Archaeologically, the use of proportions drawn from a main house is well defined in the William Paca Garden (Paca-Steele and Wright 1987). Yet Paca's original research left unanswered the question whether an archaeologist can understand how the garden was built and predict where its significant features lie using geometric analysis as a planning tool. That is, can an archaeologist use his or her knowledge of fashionable garden designs and the designs' articulation with a house and lot on an individual basis, and then use to advantage knowledge of the spatial constraints the dimensions of the house and lot put on the garden plan? At the outset, all any archaeologist has to work with is some abstract sense of the rectangles from which gardens were made and the knowledge that these were created from measurements made in perches.

The modern application of perch measurements and their aesthetic analysis began when Barbara Paca (Paca 1982; Paca-Steele and Wright 1987; Yentsch et al. 1987) noted that eighteenth-century garden design often used a proportional grid based on a simple geometric form, the 3:4:5 rectangle, ideal proportions in Renaissance design, advocated by Italian architects such as Serlio and Palladio. In the eighteenth century, the basic unit of measurement was the perch. Because the measuring rule was a chain created of lengths of metal, it could be stretched tighter or looser, thus introducing a deviation into the absolute measurements. This resulted in an approximation rather than an exact replication each time it was used. In other words, the proportional units do not always appear precisely as they would if modern instruments were used and house and garden walls were uniform. Instead, there is often an approximation of measurement masked by the overall visual appearance of a building or garden.

The importance of the proportional units lies in the way they were used to situate key elements in the garden to (1) punctuate the space in terms of garden height and (2) to define areas where building foundations would lie, thus defining space on a flat plane as well. They ordered height, depth, and width, thereby giving an ornamental garden form that introduced visual movement inside its bounds and ordered the garden's spatial relationships within the larger cultural landscape of house, yard, and human-shaped surroundings.

In sum, Paca and Wright (drawing on Hambidge) rediscovered a provocative idea about the manipulation of spatial relationships by classical artists and were able to establish that its expression could be seen in the articulation of design elements within Chesapeake gardens. With our work on the Stockton family garden at Morven (Yentsch 1990a; Yentsch et al. 1990), we extended the use of this idea and integrated it into an approach for testing the presence of these principles within other gardens. Assuming that the Morven garden was symmetrical and that the eastern eighteenth-century north-south fieldstone walk was a major boundary provided us with a square garden measuring about 165 ft (10 perches) on a side. Using garden symmetry as a predictive model, an east-west trench was placed where it would intersect the walkway on the western side of the site that would be parallel to the eastern eighteenth-century north-south walk, were the model accurate. Here we found Feature 327, a fieldstone walk exhibiting lesser workmanship and cruder stone than its eastern counterpart. However, since the western side of the garden lay toward the working gardens and working buildings, the variation in the composition and quality of the walks was not significant in terms of defining the garden's original dimensions. Bilateral Georgian symmetry in eighteenth-century Princeton only approximated Palladian dicta; the variation in building material showed how different elements fit within the dynamic symmetry denoting hierarchical division of social space even as they bound together the garden as a single unit. Knowing the garden's bounds opened other aspects of it to view (see Yentsch et al. 1990 for a detailed summary).

We learned that ca. 1760, Richard and Annis Stockton designed a garden that integrated the axes provided by the original main block of the house and its wings in its interior design. Once the original dimensions of the Stockton home were defined and recognized, the archaeological team was able to pinpoint specific areas in the garden where major features might be located. Knowledge of the below-surface depths of the different horizontal planes told how deep we would have to dig before finding the features. Contextual knowledge of the way public space and private space, work areas and pleasure gardens intermingled also served as a guide to the site.

Since 1989 we have used this strategy in looking at other old garden landscapes. As one example, at Belmont, the main house is 2 + perches in length (c. 36 ft) and 1.5 perches in width (c. 24 ft), which forms a rectangle whose quarter divisions become 9 ft (or 1/2 perch) in length and 12 ft in depth. This subdivision, in fact, "predicts" the width of the stairway (or south) division of the house and the location of the two smaller rooms on the north whereas the larger rectangle predicted the location of the original dependencies (demolished ca. 1785). Their distance from the main house was equivalent to the length of the house—something that could only happen if the proportions of the house were projected onto the landscape. The same principles have been observed at Tulip Hill (Figure 8.7).

Conclusion

Jay Hambidge saw root-rectangles as integral to the creation of a work of art exhibiting dynamic symmetry. Fisher (1985:47–51) summarizes the criticism of the Hambidge theory, but for the archaeologist what is important is how these select proportions make possible different, rich spatial relationships with "subtle potentials for transformation which afford the designer immense scope of variation while yet preserving the mathematical grounds of unity of theme." In other words, select proportions of root-rectangles could be used wisely to create a work of art—as in a pleasure garden—fluid, sophisticated, beautiful. The genius of eighteenth-century landscaping is encapsulated in the descending terraces and butterfly ponds at Middleton Place, in a magnificent sense of scale that created monumental platforms for public display and for slave labor. Genius too can be seen in William Peters's siting of his house and garden at Belmont in such a way that it opened upon (and appropriated) the panorama of the Philadelphia skyline, a majestic view that survives today, qualitatively different yet unreduced in grandeur. More modest applications are seen elsewhere, and there are undoubtedly gardens poorly designed from the perspective of a model based on dynamic symmetry. In fact, we suspect that one could even apply the geometric principles of the root-rectangle in rote fashion to create new gardens sharing an eighteenth-century sensibility, though they would never equal the brilliance of the best originals.

When the idealized proportions of a house are projected onto a garden landscape, they can create an illusion of magnificent scale (as they did at the William Paca Garden in Annapolis, at Middleton Place, and at Belmont). They thus become one means to separate small houses from great houses, ordinary folk from extraordinary families—ones with wealth, power, prestige, *and* knowledge. They help a garden attain the numinous quality all great gardens possess (Cabot 1992). When archaeologists learn how to read their use and to see how the principles of dynamic symmetry bind together old cultural space, applying these principles as a way of finding what time has masked, they literally bring the past present and make its ideas live again.

The research on which this paper is based was funded in part by a grant from the James Marston Fitch Charitable Trust in 1990–91. The excavation at Morven was sponsored by the New Jersey State Museum; the study of Belmont was done for Martin Rosenblum, R.A. and Associates in conjunction with a Historic Structures Report (Rosenblum 1992) and draws on archaeological findings by Cultural Heritage Research Services, Inc. As always, the support and encouragement of St. Clair Wright helped us find a way to give attention to the aesthetic as well as the practicalities of garden archaeology.

References

Albee, P.A. 1990. Historic Structures Report for Morven. Report on file, Historic Morven, Princeton, NJ.

Basalik, K.J. 1990. Field Report [A] of the Archaeological Investigations at Belmont Mansion, Fairmount Park, Philadelphia County, Pennsylvania. Cultural Heritage Research Services, Inc. Report prepared for Martin Rosenblum and Associates, Philadelphia.

——. 1991. Field Report [B] of the Archaeological Investigations at Belmont Mansion, Fairmount Park, Philadelphia County, Pennsylvania. Cultural Heritage Research Services, Inc. Report prepared for Martin Rosenblum and Associates, Philadelphia.

Beaudry, M.C. 1988. Comments on the Historical Archaeology of North American Households. Paper presented at the 21st Annual Meeting of the Society for Historical Archaeology, Reno, NV.

Beaudry, M.C. and T. Blosser. 1982. Filling in Round Pound: Refuse Disposal in Post-Revolutionary Boston. Paper presented at the Council for Northeast Historical Archaeology, Windsor, CT.

Bescherer, K., C.M. Goodwin, and J.M. Kratzer. 1990b. Report on the 1989 Garden Archaeology at the Highlands. Morven Landscape Archaeology Report 3. Report on file, New Jersey State Museum, Trenton.

Bescherer, K., C.M. Goodwin, J.M. Kratzer, and A.E. Yentsch. 1990a. Report on the 1989 Garden Archaeology at Grumblethorpe Garden, Germantown, Pennsylvania. Morven Landscape Archaeology Report 2. Report on file, New Jersey State Museum, Trenton.

Bescherer, K. and A.E. Yentsch. 1989. Initial Archaeological Testing at Wye House, Wye Island, Maryland. Report on file, Historic Annapolis Foundation, Annapolis, MD.

Betweiler, H. 1991. Testing the Kitchen Wing at Long Hill, Maryland. Report on file, Maryland Historic Trust.

Bevan, B. 1987. Remote Sensing Survey of Morven Gardens. Report on file, New Jersey State Museum, Trenton.

————. 1991. Remote Sensing Survey of Long Hill, Maryland. Report on file, Maryland Historic Trust.

Braidwood, R.J. and B. Howe. 1960. *Prehistoric Investigations in Iraqi Kurdistan.* Studies in Oriental Civilization 31. Oriental Institute, Chicago.

Cabot, F. 1992. Interview with Mac Griswold. *House and Garden,* January, p. 116.

Deagan, K. 1981. Downtown Survey: The Discovery of 16th Century St. Augustine in an Urban Area. *American Antiquity* 46 : 626–634.

Deetz, J. 1977. *In Small Things Forgotten: The Archaeology of Early American Life.* Anchor Books, Doubleday, New York.

deForest, E.K. 1982. *The Gardens and Grounds at Mount Vernon: How George Washington Planned and Planted Them.* University Press of Virginia, Charlottesville.

Elia, R. 1987. Needle-in-a-Haystack Archaeology: The Use of Soil Cores to Discover Archaeological Sites. Paper presented at the 27th Annual Meeting, Northeast Anthropological Association, Amherst, MA.

Fisher, H.J. 1985. Dynamic Symmetry, a Theory of Art and Nature. *St. John's Review* (Winter):40–55.

Goodwin, C.M., K. Bescherer, J. Kratzer, and A.E. Yentsch. In press. Techniques Used in Excavating the Stockton Gardens at Morven in Princeton, New Jersey. *Historical Archaeology.*

Hambidge, J. 1920. *Dynamic Symmetry: The Greek Vase.* Yale University Press, New Haven, CT.

Hole, F., K.V. Flannery, and J.A. Neely. 1969. *Prehistory and Human Ecology on the Deh Luran Plain.* University of Michigan Museum of Anthropology Memoir 1, Ann Arbor.

Hunt, J.D. 1992. *Gardens and the Picturesque: Studies in Landscape Architecture.* MIT Press, Cambridge, MA.

Hunt, J.D. and P. Willis. 1988. *The Genius of the Place: The English Landscape Garden 1620–1820.* MIT Press, Cambridge, MA.

Kelso, W.M. 1971. A Report on Exploratory Excavations at Carter's Grove, James City County, Virginia (June 1970–September 1971). Report on file, Colonial Williamsburg Foundation, Williamsburg, VA.

————. 1984a. Landscape Archaeology: A Key to Virginia's Cultivated Past. In *British and American Gardens in the Eighteenth Century,* ed. R.P. Maccubbin and P.M. Martin, pp. 159–169. Colonial Williamsburg Foundation, Williamsburg, VA.

————. 1984b. *Kingsmill Plantation, 1620–1790.* Academic Press, New York.

Kelso, W.M. and R. Most (editors). 1990. *Earth Patterns: Essays in Landscape Archaeology.* University Press of Virginia, Charlottesville.

Leone, M. 1984. Interpreting Ideology in Historical Archaeology: Using the Rules of Perspective in the William Paca Garden, Annapolis, Maryland. In

Ideology, Power, and Prehistory, ed. D. Miller and C. Tilley, pp. 25–35. Cambridge University Press, Cambridge.

Leone, M. and P.A. Shackel. 1990. Plane and Solid Geometry in Colonial Gardens in Annapolis. In *Earth Patterns: Essays in Landscape Archaeology*, ed. W.M. Kelso and R. Most, pp. 153–168. University Press of Virginia, Charlottesville.

Lewis, L. 1991. The Cliveden Survey Project Report. Report on file, Cliveden, Germantown, Philadelphia.

Little, J.G. II. 1967/68. Archaeological research on Paca Garden, correspondence 8 November 1967–24 May 1968. On file at the William Paca Garden Visitors' Center, Historic Annapolis Foundation, Annapolis, MD.

Luccketti, N. 1990. Archaeological Excavations at Bacon's Castle, Surry County, Virginia. In *Earth Patterns: Essays in Landscape Archaeology*, ed. W.M. Kelso and R. Most, pp. 23–42. University Press of Virginia, Charlottesville.

Martin, P. 1991. *The Pleasure Gardens of Virginia*. Princeton University Press, Princeton, NJ.

McLean, E. 1984. Town and Country Gardens in Eighteenth-Century Philadelphia. In *British and American Gardens in the Eighteenth Century*, ed. R.P. Maccubbin and P.M. Martin, pp. 136–147. Colonial Williamsburg Foundation, Williamsburg, VA.

McManamon, F.P. 1981. Probability Sampling and Archaeological Survey in the Northeast: An Estimation Approach. In *Foundations of Northeast Archaeology*, ed. D.R. Snow, pp. 195–227. Academic Press, New York.

———. 1984. Discovering Sites Unseen. *Advances in Archaeological Method and Theory* 7:223–292.

Miller, N.F., A.E. Yentsch, D. Piperno, and B. Paca. 1990. Two Centuries of Landscape Change at Morven, Princeton, New Jersey. In *Earth Patterns: Essays in Landscape Archaeology*, ed. W.M. Kelso and R. Most, pp. 257–275. University Press of Virginia, Charlottesville.

Moran, G.P., E. Zimmer, and A.E. Yentsch. 1982. *Archaeological Investigations at the Narbonne House, Salem Maritime National Historic Site, Salem, Massachusetts*. U.S. National Park Service, Washington, DC.

Noël Hume, A. 1974. *Archaeology and the Colonial Gardener*. Colonial Williamsburg Archaeology Series 7. Colonial Williamsburg Foundation, Williamsburg, VA.

Paca, B. 1982. Maps of the William Paca Garden. On file at the William Paca Garden Visitors' Center, Historic Annapolis Foundation, Annapolis, MD.

Paca-Steele, B. and St. C. Wright. 1987. The Mathematics of an Eighteenth Century Wilderness Garden. *Journal of Garden History* 6:299–320.

Racine, M., E.J.-P. Boursier-Mougenot, and F. Binet. 1987. *The Gardens of Provence and the French Riviera*. MIT Press, Cambridge, MA.

Rosenblum, Martin Jay and Associates. 1992. Final Historic Structures Report for Belmont Mansion.

Reinke, M. and R. Paynter. 1984. *Archaeological Excavation of the Surroundings of the E. H. Williams House, Deerfield, Massachusetts*. University of Massachusetts Archaeological Series, Amherst.

Rubertone, P.E. and J. Gallagher. 1981. *Archaeological Site Examination: A Case Study in Urban Archaeology*. Cultural Resource Management Study 4. Roger Williams National Memorial. U.S. Department of Interior, National Park Service, North Atlantic Regional Office, Boston.

Sanchez, F. 1982. Report on Archaeological Testing for Stabilization of the

Retaining Wall, Victualling Warehouse, Annapolis, Maryland. Unpublished report on file at Historic Annapolis, Inc., Annapolis, MD.

Sanford, D. 1990. The Gardens at Germanna. In *Earth Patterns: Essays in Landscape Archaeology*, ed. W.M. Kelso and R. Most, pp. 43–57. University Press of Virginia, Charlottesville.

South, S. 1967. The Paca House, Annapolis, Maryland: A Historical Archaeology Study. Report on file at Historic Annapolis, Inc., Annapolis, MD.

Weber, C.A., E.A. Comer, L.E. Akerson, and G. Norman. 1990. Mount Clare: An Interdiscipinary Approach to the Restoration of a Georgian Landscape. In *Earth Patterns: Essays in Landscape Archaeology*, ed. W.M. Kelso and R. Most, pp. 135–152. University Press of Virginia, Charlottesville.

Yentsch, A.E. 1988. Report on the Preliminary Testing of the Bordley-Randall Site in Annapolis, Maryland. Report on file, Historic Annapolis, Inc., Annapolis, MD.

——. 1990a. The Archaeological Reappearance of an 18th Century Princeton Garden. *Expedition* 32(2):14–23.

——. 1990b. A Plan for Excavation at Belmont Mansion, Fairmount Park, Philadelphia. Report submitted to Martin Rosenblum and Associates, Philadelphia.

——. 1992a. Cliveden's Landscape, 1763–1920, with Emphasis on the Earlier Gardens. Report prepared for Martin Rosenblum and Associates, Philadelphia. On file at Cliveden, Philadelphia.

——. 1992b. Working with Fill in San Francisco. In *Tar Flat, Rincon Hill, and the Shore of Mission Bay: Archaeological Research Design and Treatment for SF-480 Terminal Separation Rebuild*, vol. 2, ed. M. Praetzellis and A. Praetzellis, pp. 4.103–4.120. Anthropological Studies Center, Sonoma State University, Academic Foundation Inc., Rohnert Park, CA.

——. 1994. *A Chesapeake Family and Their Slaves: A Study in Historical Archaeology*. Cambridge University Press, Cambridge.

Yentsch, A.E. and J.M. Kratzer. 1991. An Archaeological Strategy for the Recovery of the 18th-Century Gardens at Belmont in Fairmount Park, Philadelphia. Prepared for Martin Rosenblum Associates, Philadelphia. Report on file, Fairmount Park Commission, Philadelphia.

——. 1993. Landscape Archaeology at Cliveden: A Review of Prior Work and Strategies for Future Study. Report prepared for Cliveden, National Trust, Philadelphia.

Yentsch, A.E., K. Bescherer, and J.M. Kratzer. 1990. Management Summary of the 1989 Field Season at a National Historic Landmark: Morven in Princeton, New Jersey. Report on file, New Jersey State Museum, Trenton, NJ.

Yentsch, A.E., N.F. Miller, B. Paca, and D. Piperno. 1987. Archaeologically Defining the Earlier Garden Landscapes at Morven: Preliminary Results. *Northeast Historical Archaeology* 16:1–29.

Chapter 9
The Landscapes and Ideational Roles of Caribbean Slave Gardens

Lydia Mihelic Pulsipher

To a geographer interested in the complex interactions between the Old World and the Americas that began with the voyages of exploration, the Eastern Caribbean is a particularly attractive study area. On these tiny volcanic and sedimentary islands, Northern Europeans with little or no experience in tropical environments and enslaved Africans with a long tradition of tropical resource management encountered Native American tropical cultivators. The Europeans, for the most part, rejected anything they might have learned from either the Africans or the indigenous people about how best to use the resources of the tropics, and set up a mercantilist cash-crop economy. The island Native Americans were annihilated by disease and warfare with the Europeans, and Africans were brought in, first by the hundreds and then by the thousands, to work on the European-owned plantations.

Up to the time of European contact the landscapes of the Eastern Caribbean, while bearing the marks of hunting, gathering, fishing, cultivation, and domestic activities, probably were not severely modified by human agency (Harris 1965; Sauer 1969; Watt 1966, 1986). By comparison, the changes wrought by Europeans and the slaves who worked for them during the first fifty years of colonial settlement, 1632–1680, were quite drastic and had a distinctly European flavor (Merrill 1958; Pulsipher 1985a; Watt 1966, 1986). Complex tropical forests were cleared and the open land marked off into geometric landholdings bordered with hedgerows and fences. The colonists introduced commercial monocropping of exotic plants such as sugar and cotton, or of newly commercialized New World plants such as cocoa, tobacco, and indigo (Table 9.1). They brought large draft animals and the plough, and they built roads, grid-pattern towns, fortifications and harbors. During this era African slaves had little direct influence on the landscape, principally because they were very few in number, being outnumbered by Europeans three or four to one, and their effect on land use policy was limited. By the late seventeenth century and during the eighteenth, however, when slaves outnumbered Europeans by nine or ten to one, their impact on Caribbean landscapes increased.

Throughout the eighteenth and nineteenth centuries, though the dominant land use continued to be European-managed plantations, slaves and their descendants increasingly had an impact on plantation landscapes, particularly in marginal zones such as low-elevation steep slopes, upland ravines, and mountainous interiors. It was in these zones, difficult to reach and unsuited to plantation cultivation, that the slaves first seized the right to grow their own food crops and then expanded production in order to sell surplus crops at market.

In this paper I combine historical sources from the British Caribbean with ethnographic and geographical field research on the island of Montserrat to produce a profile of the physical features of slave gardens and of the perceptions of the environment and organization of time, space, and resources they embody. This research was conducted as part of a continuing interdisciplinary study of Galways, an eighteenth-century sugar plantation on Montserrat, which I co-direct with archaeologist Conrad M. Goodwin. My study of slave gardens was designed to enhance our understanding of the human landscape surrounding Galways, and to help us interpret the archaeological evidence from the plantation core, especially the slave village. It also was intended to elicit the ideational role that gardens and gardening may have played in the lives of slaves and to help us see what, if any, connections there might be between past and present uses and perceptions of the land by slaves and their descendants (Figure 9.1).

There were, in fact, three contexts for slave gardening: (1) common grounds, (2) ravine and mountain grounds and (3) houseyard gardens. The impact of this threefold system of slave cultivation on Caribbean landscapes was significant and remarked upon at the time (Barclay 1826; Beckford 1790; Edwards 1793; Leslie 1739; Long 1774; Sloane 1707; Stewart 1823; Wentworth 1834); and the patterns of crops and techniques survive into the present in houseyards and subsistence gardens. The first type was plantation-managed; the second and third were established and managed by the slaves, sometimes surreptitiously, but eventually with at least the tacit consent of the plantation management.

Evidence for this study of the location, scope and character of the slave gardens comes from three main sources: (1) historical documents such as travelers' accounts, plantation maps, laws, colonial reports, and

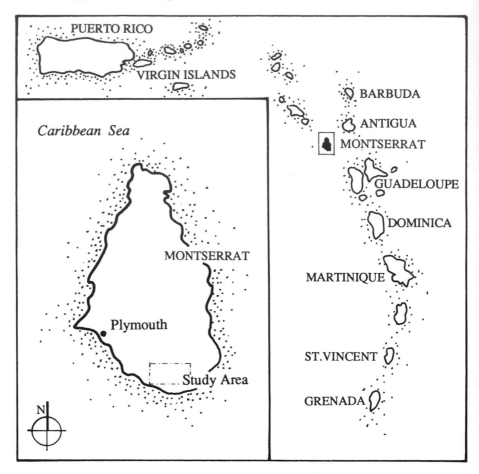

9.1. The site of the field research for this study, Galways Mountain, lies in the southwest of Montserrat, an Eastern Caribbean volcanic island of 39 square miles. Montserrat was settled by the British in 1632 and eventually contained more than 50 sugar plantations. It remains, by choice, one of the very last British colonies. (T. Hoffman, after original by Will Fontanez)

artists' impressions; (2) oral tradition and folk geographies from Galways Mountain on the island of Montserrat; and (3) geographical field analysis of past and present human uses of the landscape, including:

(a) the definition of environmental zones,
(b) the assessment of plant and microenvironmental management in present-day gardens, and
(c) the analysis of relict landforms and vegetative complexes.

A fourth source of evidence, actual archaeological excavation of slave gardens on Galways mountain, has not been completed and remains problematic, not only because of the high rates of decay in hot, moist tropical environments, but also because commercial and subsistence cultivation of these sites has continued to the present, churning the evidence and making it difficult to locate sealed deposits or those with good stratigraphic context. Nonetheless, some proposals for the use of excavation, and pollen and phytolith evidence in analyzing slave gardens will be made, such proposals being tuned to the specific qualities of the island's tropical environments and the particular characteristics of slave and more recent cultivation practices.

Types of Slave Gardens

Common Grounds

Plantation-supervised "common grounds" were actually required by law in the mid-seventeenth century. To ensure that slaves were adequately fed and not forced to steal provisions, owners or managers of plantations were to see that so many acres of roots and tubers were grown by and for specific numbers of servants and slaves. A typical example is a 1669 law in Montserrat.

. . . all Masters of Families . . . residing on this Island, shall plant or cause to be planted One acre of Provision for every two working persons, Whites or Black, in their or any of their Families (that is to say) Potatoes or Cassad' [cassava], or both. . . . (Laws of Montserrat, #15 1669; see also #36 1693)

Maps of plantations throughout the British Caribbean confirm that such fields, given names like "potato piece" or "plantain walk," were consistently a part of plantation layout (Higman 1988; Porter 1710) (Figure 9.2).

At least during the seventeenth century these plantation managed plots were European in conception, location, shape, size, and methods used. First, they were located on plantations proper. Although the location of plantations varied greatly from island to island, level lowland or upland valleys were favored overall; hence common grounds tended to be on relatively flat land. According to European custom, they were clear-cut rectangular plots, each planted with a single, or at most two crops. They were cultivated by a gang of laborers who moved rapidly through the plot, giving little attention to variation in microenvironments within a field or to the needs of individual plants. Therefore, even though the laborers in common grounds were African, the agricultural practices used were those derived from the Eu-

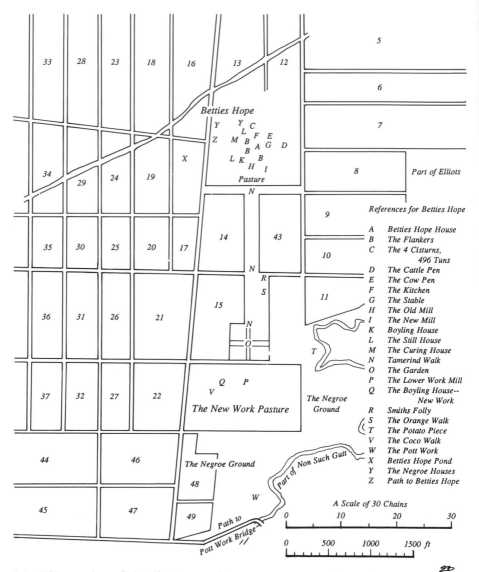

9.2. This portion of the 1710 map of Bettys Hope estate in Antigua and the cartouche, shows that some fringe plantation land was given over to the systematic production of food, both tree crops and ground provisions. (Drawn originally by James Porter and redrawn by C.M. Goodwin and E. Brescia)

ropean mid-latitudes. While the crops chosen for common grounds were not European, they tended to be those that did well in open sunny fields, that were drought resistant, that needed little special attention, and that produced large quantities of hunger-relieving carbohydrates. Typical crops were cassava, sweet potatoes, and plantain. These garden crops lacked essential nutrients, which, depending on the island and the situation of the planter, may or may not have been provided by imported items such as salt fish and dried beans.

Slave-grown common grounds persisted into the nineteenth century because planters remained ultimately responsible for feeding their slaves a minimum diet, especially during hard times caused by droughts or hurricanes. Such grounds appeared to planters to be an efficient way to ensure basic food needs for slaves. At Galways, though no maps survive, oral tradition indicates at least one such plantation provision field, "Common Ground," lying well down slope of the plantation yard in a zone that, due to moisture deficit, is just marginally cultivable during much of the year.

Ravine and Mountain Grounds

Early evidence for ravine and mountain grounds planned and managed by the slaves themselves is partially circumstantial and rests on later, better documented descriptions. Indications are that in Montserrat the early slave-managed plots were grown surreptitiously, perhaps as early as the 1650s, when laws seeking to control the rambunctious behavior of slaves on Sundays were passed.

> Whereas . . . our Slaves have ranged to and fro at their own Pleasure, without Controlment, to our great Damage . . . we do again order . . . That if any Negro . . . go out of his Master's Plantation upon the Lord's Day, or any other day of Liberty, . . . [he] shall be either bound and sent securely to the Marshal's or . . . to the Master of the Family where he shall be taken, whipt, and sent home again. (Laws of Montserrat, #10, 1668, orginally passed in 1659)

Later laws of the same type make it clear that the real point was to keep slaves from marketing surplus produce on Sundays, partly because it was hard to tell whether slave-sold produce was self-grown or stolen.

> . . . the Labour and Industry of many of the poorer Sort of People of this Island is defeated by the Thefts of Slaves, who, under Colour of planting Indigo, Cotton, Ginger, Coffee, and Cocoa, for their own Use, do often steal the said Commodities, to the great Loss and Detriment of the Planters thereof . . . the said Commodities . . . [being] easily disposed of . . . at the public Market, which Slaves have been suffered to keep on the Lord's Day. (Laws of Montserrat, #112, 1736)

But more important, the general tone of these laws indicates a hidden agenda, namely, that the entrepreneurial success of slave craftspersons and cultivators alarmed those who were trying to preserve the economic niche of small plot cash producer and skilled craftsperson for the freed Irish indentured servants who, it was hoped, would bolster the numbers of white settlers by staying on Montserrat. Despite the fact that by law slaves were forbidden to offer their produce for sale in the Sunday markets or in any other context, we know that the custom persisted, because laws forbidding slaves to cultivate cash crops and to sell in Sunday markets were passed repeatedly well into the later eighteenth century, the text often alluding to the impossibility of stamping out the custom (Laws of Montserrat #37, 1693; #112, 1736; #209, 1779).

Just where such slave-managed plots would have been grown during the early years of colonization is not clear. Modern cultivators, who are free to choose place and time for their work, usually have several plots, some on the sunny drier lower slopes at about 1000 feet above the sea and some in the cooler, shaded, moist upland zones above 2000 feet. In the case of slaves, however, given the restrictions on their time and movement and the need to work covertly, their plots were probably in nooks and crannies around plantation fringes where the choice of ecological niches was restricted. On mountainous islands such as Montserrat, these plots were almost inevitably on steep slopes, either on the banks of ravines or on high volcanic fingers too narrow or precipitous for sugar cultivation and well out of sight of plantation managers, yet not too distant from slave villages.

In 1986 at Galways I learned of such a covert garden from several descendants of the people who once cultivated there. In Germans Ghaut, a dramatically deep ravine bordering Galways on the north, is a raised "island" of six to ten acres of gently sloping land surrounded by deep, heavily forested ravines (Figure 9.3). This formation was created when the mountain stream running in German's Ghaut divided, forming two ravines that then rejoined further down slope. Although the area, known as Little Island, is now covered with a thick secondary forest of medium height, the garden is still clearly identifiable by the contour cultivation banks that underlie this forest and by the relict food-crop trees (breadfruit, breadnut, mango, sour-sop, and sugar apple), that surround the area. While completely hidden from view, Little Island is no more than a brisk ten-minute hike from the Galways slave village.

In the eighteenth century, even while laws were still being passed against slave cultivation, planters, recognizing the advantage to themselves, allowed slaves Saturday afternoons and Sundays to cultivate.

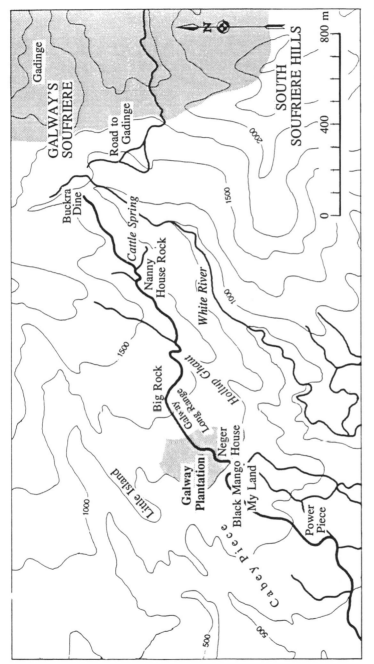

9.3. These folk place names of the environs of Galways Mountain do not appear on official charts; but they mark well known landmarks and convey the intimacy with which the people regard their landscapes. The shading marks Galways Plantation and Gadinge, a high mountain region with many gardens. (W. Fontanez, after original by L. Pulsipher)

This extra time made it possible for slaves to cultivate in more remote upland zones. William Beckford, writing about Jamaica, observed:

> They generally make choice of such sorts of land for their ground as are encompassed by lofty mountains; and I think that they commonly prefer the sides of hills, which are covered with loose stones, to the bottoms upon which they are not so abundant. Some will have a mixture of both, and will cultivate the plantain-tree upon the flat and their provisions [root crops] upon the rising ground. . . . (Beckford 1790)

All available sources of evidence indicate that the tools and techniques used and plants grown in these ravine and mountain grounds were very similar to those that survive today in the mountain grounds of traditional cultivators descended from slaves. The garden plant complex represented an amalgamation of tropical plants brought from Africa (yams, okra, dasheen, and guinea corn), including several originally from Asia (pigeon peas, banana, oranges, ginger); plants borrowed in the early years from surviving Native Americans (cassava, maize, peppers, pineapples, christophines, sweet potato, beans, arrowroot, edible canna lily); other native American plants diffused from the mainland like peanuts and cocoa; and some European plants that adapted to tropical conditions (cabbage, carrots, onions, thyme, rosemary, shallots). At the end of the eighteenth century, when plants were introduced from the Pacific, the New World complex of tree crops was enhanced with the addition of mangoes, breadfruit, and breadnut.

The tools were surely very simple, including at best a cutlass and a hoe (both probably of European origin but used by subsistence cultivators in Africa by the seventeenth century); the cultivation techniques were those of the African and American wet tropics, including forest fallowing, complex intercropping, and the banking of soil to inhibit erosion (Sauer 1969:51). Contemporary descriptions of slave-managed gardens (Sloane 1707; Leslie 1739; Beckford 1790) and lists of the produce they yielded (Long 1774), coupled with modern cultural ecology studies (Berleant-Schiller and Pulsipher 1986; Brierley 1974; Handler 1971; Hills 1988; Wilken 1972), indicate that these gardens represented a completely different concept of agriculture from the common grounds described above. They were complex systems of environmental management that took into consideration angle of slope (note the quote from Beckford above), moisture availability, cycles of soil fertility, wind patterns, propitious lunar phases for planting, tending and harvesting, and the specific ecological requirements of the dozens of species grown. Plants were treated as individuals with their microenvironments carefully managed for sustained or prolific

TABLE 9.1 Economic plants mentioned and their Latin names[a]

Common English name	Latin name
Almond	*Terminalia catappa*
Aloe vera	*Aloe vera*
Arrowroot	*Maranta arundinacea*
Avocado	*Persea americana*
Banana	*Musa sapientum, M. paradisiaca*
Beans	*Phaseolus vulgaris* (varieties)
Breadfruit	*Artocarpus altilis*
Breadnut	*Brosimum alicastrum*
Cabbage	*Brassica oleracea*
Canna	*Canna edulis*
Carrot	*Daucus carota* var. *sativa*
Cassava	*Manihot esculenta*
Chaney bush	*Philodendron sagittifolium*
Christophine	*Sechium edule*
Cocoa	*Theobroma cacao*
Coconut	*Cocos nucifera*
Coffee	*Coffea arabica*
Colita	*Sansevieria liberica*
Corn	*Zea mays*
Cotton	*Gossypium barbadense*
Dasheen	*Colocasia esculenta*
Eggplant	*Solanum melongena*
Genip	*Melicocca bijuga*
Ginger	*Zingiber officinale*
Guinea corn	*Sorghum vulgare*
Indigo	*Indigofera tinctoria*
Lemon grass	*Cymbopogon citratus*
Maize	*Zea mays*
Mango	*Mangifera indica*
Okra	*Hibiscus esculentus*
Onion	*Allium cepa*
Orange	*Citrus sinensis, C. aurantium* (varieties)
Papaya	*Carica papaya*
Peanut	*Arachis hypogaea*
Pepper	*Capsicum annuum* (varieties)
Pigeon pea	*Cajanus cajan*
Pineapple	*Ananas comosus*
Plantain	*Musa paradisiaca*
Pot-scrubber bush	*Helianthus hirsutus*
Prickly pear	*Opuntia monacantha*
Rosemary	*Rosmarinus officinalis*
Shallot	*Allium ascalonicum*
Sweet potato	*Ipomoea batatas*
Tamarind	*Tamarindus indica*
Tannia	*Xanthosoma sagittifolium*
Thyme	*Thymus vulgaris*
Tobacco	*Nicotiana tabacum*
Yam	*Dioscorea* (varieties)

[a] *Source*: Kermath and Pulsipher (Forthcoming)

production, and like traditional cultivators world-wide, Caribbean slaves continuously selected the most desirable genetic characteristics in plants, thereby fostering improvement of the system over time.

The fact that these slave-managed plots were frequently on steep slopes, as they still are by choice today, necessitated erosion control strategies, the most important being the contour banking of soil. The geographer Carl Sauer (1969:51–58) suggests this technique was first learned from the indigenous people in the early contact period, though African and European customs are similar. The banks are constructed of soil hoed into a series of ridges running across the slope at intervals of three feet. My observations of cultivation practices today indicate that, as Sauer suggested, the soil banks present certain advantages beyond interrupting the flow of runoff. First, on very steep slopes they act as a sort of staircase from which workers can more easily reach to work on rows upslope. Second, tuber production is fostered by the loose soil and moisture availability is controlled. Third, the banks provide protection from excess sun and wind for seedlings planted in the furrows between banks. As they mature, soil is pulled down around the seedlings from the ridge above, hence the entire ridge system actually moves half a ridge or so down slope over the course of a growing season as the plants move to the top of a bank where they can receive more intense sun. Over time a large bank of soil develops at the bottom of a field serving to inhibit erosion into lower fields (Pulsipher 1978; see also Treacy and Denevan, this volume) (Figure 9.4).

Abandoned ridged fields are to be found in many places at Galways, especially on the steep mountain slopes above the plantation. Like those described at Little Island, the age of these ridged fields is indicated by the fact that they now are often covered with a tall stand of secondary tropical rainforest and by the fact that European and Asian ceramics found in the soil banks indicate that these ridges may have been used as early as the mid-eighteenth century.

A landmark study done by Sidney Mintz and Douglas Hall in 1960 established conclusively that by the beginning of the eighteenth century planters recognized the advantage of allowing slaves to cultivate their own food and to sell their surpluses, not only because this relieved the planter from supplying sufficient food, but also because the slaves were more attached to a particular place as a result of their ability to tend gardens, keep animals, and enjoy the little luxuries these entrepreneurial activities allowed. The authors document that the practice grew steadily, especially on hilly islands like Jamaica, where plantations contained land unusable for cane cultivation. Custom allotted Saturday afternoons and Sundays for slaves to attend to

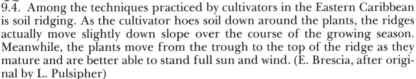

9.4. Among the techniques practiced by cultivators in the Eastern Caribbean is soil ridging. As the cultivator hoes soil down around the plants, the ridges actually move slightly down slope over the course of the growing season. Meanwhile, the plants move from the trough to the top of the ridge as they mature and are better able to stand full sun and wind. (E. Brescia, after original by L. Pulsipher)

their plots, especially remote mountain grounds and eventually entire islands became dependent on slave-cultivated produce, which was sold in regular weekly markets (Mintz and Hall 1960). By the nineteenth century, when attention was turning to the need to maintain slave populations through natural reproduction, on Montserrat women slaves who had borne five or more live children were relieved from most field work in order that they could tend their garden plots (British Sessional Papers, 1789; Acts Respecting the Treatment of Slaves, Montserrat, 1824).

Slave Houseyard Gardens

The gardens that slaves planted around their houses are referred to in numerous descriptions, for example:

> Adjoining to the house is usually a small spot of ground, laid out into a sort of garden and shaded by various fruit-trees . . . . (Stewart 1823)

The cottages of the Negroes usually compose a small village . . . . They are seldom placed with much regard to order, but being always intermingled with fruit-trees, particularly the banana, the avocado pear and the orange (the Negroe's own planting and property) they sometimes exhibit a pleasing and picturesque appearance . . . (Edwards 1793)

These gardens are also portrayed in a number of contemporary sketches and paintings (Craton 1978:144, 240, 252; Wentworth 1834). They differed from the ravine and mountain grounds in that they tended to be in somewhat drier zones and were smaller and stationary, as opposed to shifting. They contained a less extensive and somewhat different complex of plants that could be tended and harvested on a daily basis.

Slave villages were nearly always located near the central works of plantations; therefore the ecological zones common for slave villages were coastal regions or relatively level upland flanks of mountains or interior valleys (Edwards 1793; Higman 1987). Because there were at least minimum moisture requirements for cane cultivation, houseyard gardens probably were rarely in truly dry zones, but certainly on low dry islands such as Antigua and Barbados slave cultivators would have had to cope with drought. Furthermore, on such islands cultivable land was at a premium, hence all structures, including slave villages, usually occupied land not well suited for cultivation. On mountainous Montserrat slave villages also were not placed on the best land, although it was probably better than on neighboring Antigua.

The reduced complex of plants was due partly to drier conditions and partly to the small spaces in slave villages. According to plantation maps and archaeological evidence, slave houses were normally only a few yards apart (Clapham 1755; Porter 1710; Goodwin 1987). Illustrations and descriptions indicate that in all zones trees were an important component of houseyard gardens just as they are today (Kimber 1966), in part because tree crops were especially susceptible to thievery and needed constant surveillance. Coconuts were especially popular, probably because of their many uses as food, fiber, and containers; in dry sunny coastal zones coconuts tended to be the dominant tree species. Bananas and plantains were also popular, in part for the cooling ambience their large swaying leaves created. Other houseyard trees are less consistently prominent in surviving records, perhaps because seedlings were hard to obtain, but possibilities include tamarind, almond, papaya, breadfruit (where rainfall was sufficient), and perhaps mango. Ethnographic evidence from the early twentieth century on Montserrat indicates that ownership of valuable trees like mango and breadfruit was the purview of the planter class and laborers were punished even for picking fruit up off the ground under roadside trees. Nelly Dyer, who has lived her entire life on Galways Mountain, recounted such an experience in the 1920s:

When me 14, me ride me donkey through Black Mango and swat three mango with me cutlass 'cause they bump me head. Fat Boy [an assistant to the plantation manager] see me pick them up and haul me in to Mr. French. He take me to court and me have to pay 14 shilling, which was seven days pay. (Pulsipher, taped interview, summer, 1989)

On the other hand, descriptions of gardens and of the slave-supplied market in Jamaica indicate that all types of fruit were grown by slaves (Long 1774, 2:105). Very likely freedom of access to land for gardens and to valuable plants varied over time and space, being related perhaps most of all to the plantation manager's personality.

Depending on the amount of shade and moisture availability, other plants in houseyard gardens would have included herbs, plants often used in cooking, medicinals, cosmetics, ornamentals, and plants used in performing household chores or in making household items. Examples would be pigeon peas and beans, eggplant, tannia, "pot-scrubber bush" (a rough-leaved member of the Compositae family used to clean dirty dishes), colita (*Sansevieria*, whose fibrous leaves were used to make ropes, collars and lashes for small animals and pads for carrying heavy loads on the head), aloe vera (used for burns and as an emetic), prickly pear cactus (used for hair conditioner and as "slime" to thicken certain dishes), tobacco, "chaney bush" (a large-leaved philodendron used as packaging and the tendrils used as fiber), and lemon grass for a medicinal tea. Contemporary illustrations indicate that the plants in houseyards were often arranged in an ornamental fashion, but historic accounts and modern research indicate that nearly all plants had a useful as well as a decorative function (Pulsipher 1985b).

The tools and techniques used in houseyard gardens were the same as those in mountain grounds, except that in houseyard gardens special care was given to maintaining fertility since only crop-rotation (not plot-rotation) and short term fallowing were possible. Slope management was less needed, but the moving contour ridging system described above was still used because of its other advantages for soil and microclimate management.

Slave houseyard gardens appear to have been very similar in most respects to modern houseyard gardens such as that of Miss Jane Ryan and her eighteen-member extended family in Kinsale, Montserrat (Pulsipher 1985b) (Figure 9.5).

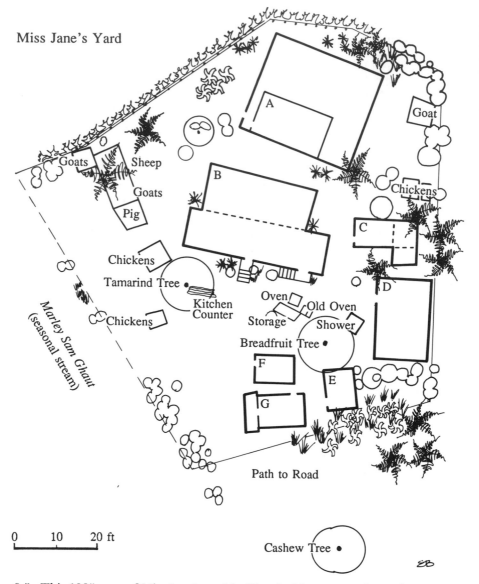

Miss Jane's Yard

Goats
Sheep
Goats
Pig

A

Goat

B

Chickens

C

D

Chickens

Tamarind Tree •

Kitchen Counter

Chickens

Oven
Storage
Old Oven
Shower

Breadfruit Tree •

F

E

G

Marley Sam Ghaut (seasonal stream)

Path to Road

0   10   20 ft

Cashew Tree •

9.5. This 1985 map of Miss Jane's yard in Kinsale, Montserrat, shows the arrangement of houses, plants and animal pens that is still common in the West Indies. (E. Brescia, after original by L. Pulsipher)

The Ideational Role of Slave Gardens

Slave gardens originated in early colonial days, and mountain ground and houseyard gardens were important strategies employed by slaves to construct a decent life for themselves within a hostile system. These gardens remained important long after emancipation and, indeed, are still central in the subsistence economy of traditional West Indian people (Hills 1989). My field work over the past seventeen years with present-day gardeners indicates that they were early taught by their elders that along with the economic function of the gardens is a corresponding ideational role.

Cultivating on high remote slopes early in the morning calls up feelings of freedom and independence, of affinity with nature, of the solidarity of black people in landscapes where whites rarely tread. The cultivators feel close to ancestors who worked the same spots and and their labors give them the sense of prosperity that abundant food symbolizes. The folk names attached to particular plots and to places along the paths to the high fields convey these ideas as well. "My Land" (a perversion of the original name, Milaun) carries obvious meaning. "Cabey Piece" recalls Jim Cabey who long ago worked that parcel. "Neger House" marks the remains of the Galways slave village and calls up distant childhood memories of grandparents who cultivated there. "Buckra Dine" humorously identifies the place near the sulfur-smelling Soufrière (volcanic fumerole) where white folks inexplicably choose to picnic. "Little Island" names a secret cultivation plot near Galways nearly impossible to reach because it is surrounded by dramatically deep, thickly forested ravines. "Galway Long Range" designates a long straight section in the climb to 2000 feet. "Nanny House Rock" was a natural shelter from the rain where friends and lovers agreed to rendezvous during trips up and down the mountain. "Power Piece," named for a seventeenth-century Irish Catholic cultivator, Andrew Power, identifies a spot where in the nineteenth century missionaries established a school for the children of ex-slaves (Pulsipher 1987) (Figure 9.3).

Houseyard gardens also symbolized independence, security, and pride of ownership, in the past just as they do in the present. In slavery times many writers observed the charming ambience of slave houses surrounded by gardens and noted the sense of pride with which the slave proprietors took care of their plants and domestic animals:

Behind the house is the garden filled with plantains, ochras, and other vegetables, which are produced at all seasons . . . . Every family has a hogsty:

poultry houses are not wanted [as] the chickens are carefully gathered at night, and hung in baskets, to preserve them from the rats. (Barclay 1826)

Today the obvious pride of ownership taken in a small house surrounded by flowers and garden plants is celebrated in the countless paintings and picture postcards traded to tourists. And for West Indian sojourners in the labor markets of northern European and American cities, images of these small "estates" in the tropics have sustained many a homesick migrant through long years of toil while she saved to support her mother and children back home and planned for her own eventual retirement to her native island.

Implications for Archaeology

This paper has used many of the methods common to archaeology, except that of excavation. While this most notable archaeological technique is not ruled out for the future, the study has demonstrated that in most cases the use of excavation in assessing slave cultivation practices in the Galways landscape would be futile. Beyond the problem of rapid decay of plant remains in the wet tropics is the fact that shifting cultivation has continued in most known slave garden zones right up to the present. Furthermore, the custom of forming contour banks of soil and then moving these banks down slope over the course of a season churns up the soil in such a way that stratigraphy is lost. Although datable artifacts are often found even in mountain grounds, their context has been disturbed uncounted times. Even when occasionally relict soil banks are found under mature forest, dating the last use of such a bank is made problematic due to the inability to correlate tree rings with annual cycles because of the lack of regular cycles of temperature or moisture seasonality in mountain rainforests. The site of the Galways slave village also has been cleared and cultivated repeatedly since its abandonment in the nineteenth century. Nonetheless, it is hoped that an apparent sealed context in the Galways Village discovered in the summer of 1987 will prove to contain some phytolith evidence (Howson 1987). Irene Good established in her study of pollen samples taken from acid-rich microenvironments around the Galways sugar works that pollen grains can survive in special cases (though only very sparsely) and are occasionally identifiable to the species level (Good 1985). She found evidence of genip (*Meliocca bijuga*), a popular fruit tree native to the West Indies, corn (*Zea mays*), and unspecified citrus, native to Southeast Asia. If sealed and datable contexts can be isolated in slave houseyards, Good's preliminary study indicates that further pollen analysis might make it possible to reconstruct actual gardens, especially when used in connection with studies of opal phytoliths, which she found in abundance but did not analyze. A study in Hawaii demonstrated the usefulness of phytolith analysis in reconstructing field patterns and plant complexes in tropical zones (Pearsall and Trimble 1984), and one in Israel suggests that it is possible to distinguish irrigated farming, which leaves multiple-celled phytoliths, from dry farming, which leaves single-cell phytoliths (Rosen 1987).

The reconstruction of past landscapes has been a favorite endeavor for geographers for centuries; in fact, some of the first warnings about human-induced environmental deterioration came out of this tradition (Marsh 1864). Such work always requires the integration of many types of information. In this reconstruction of the landscapes wrought by slaves I have used historical documents and illustrations from the wider Caribbean to help me interpret the Montserrat historical, ethnographic, and field evidence. It must be emphasized that this methodology is dependent on an intimate familiarity with the landscape being studied and with the physical processes and human impacts it has undergone; whereas the methodology is applicable in nearly any environmental and cultural context, it requires background knowledge, several types of research skills, time, reflection, and continuous re-evaluation.

The information for this paper was gathered under grants funded by the Center for Field Research/Earthwatch, the Association of American Geographers, the Wenner-Gren Foundation for Anthropological Research, the Skaggs Foundation, and the University of Tennessee. The contributions of my colleague Jean Howson and especially those of my husband, C.M. (Mac) Goodwin, are gratefully appreciated.

References

Barclay, A. 1826. *A Practical View of the Present State of Slavery in the West Indies*. London.

Beckford, W. 1790. *A Descriptive Account of the Island of Jamaica*. 2 vols. Printed for T. and J. Egerton, London.

Berleant-Schiller, R. and L.M. Pulsipher. 1986. Subsistence Cultivation in the Caribbean. *Nieuwe West-Indische Gids* 60:1–40.

Brierley, J.S. 1974. *Small Farming in Grenada, West Indies*. Manitoba Geographical Studies 4. Winnipeg, University of Manitoba, Department of Geography.

Clapham, S. 1755. Map of Bettys Hope Estate, Antigua. Copy housed in the Museum of Antigua and Barbuda, original in the Codrington Papers.

Craton, M. 1978. *Searching for the Invisible Man: Slaves and Plantation Life in Jamaica*. Harvard University Press, Cambridge, MA and London.

Edwards, B. 1793. *The History, Civil and Commercial of the British West Indies.* 2 vols. John Stockdale, London.

Good, I. 1985. Plants and Humans at Galways: A Preliminary Floral Analysis. Galways Symposium, Annual Meeting of the Society of Historical Archaeology. January 10, Boston.

Goodwin, C.M. 1987. Sugar, Time and Englishmen: A Study of Management Strategies on Caribbean Plantations. Ph.D. dissertation. Boston University.

Great Britain. 1789. British Sessional Papers, 1731–1800. Accounts and Papers, Vol. XXVI, No. 646A, pp. 110–209.

―――. 1824. Acts respecting the treatment of slaves in Montserrat. Accounts and Papers, 1801–1852, Vol. XXII, manuscript p. 605.

Handler, J. 1971. The History of Arrowroot and the Origin of Peasantries in the British West Indies. *Journal of Caribbean History* 2:46–93.

Harris, D. 1965. *Plants, Animals and Man in the Outer Leeward Islands, West Indies.* University of California Press, Berkeley.

Higman, B. 1987. The Spatial Economy of Jamaican Sugar Plantations: Cartographic Evidence from the Eighteenth and Nineteenth Centuries. *Journal of Historical Geography* 13:17–39.

―――. 1988. *Jamaica Surveyed.* Institute of Jamaica Publications Limited, Kingston.

Hills, T. 1988. The Caribbean Peasant Food Forest, Ecological Artistry or Random Chaos? In *Small Farming and Peasant Resources in the Caribbean,* ed. J.S. Brierly and L. Rubenstein, pp. 1–28. Manitoba Geographical Studies, Manitoba.

―――. 1989. Tropical Intensive, Mixed Garden Cultivation: Lessons for the Designing of Agricultural Ecosystems. Paper presented at the annual meeting of the Association of American Geographers, March, 1989, Baltimore.

Howson, J. 1987. Report of 1987 Fieldwork at Galways Village, Montserrat, West Indies. Galways Project unpublished report on file at Department of Geography, University of Tennessee, Knoxville.

Kermath, B. and L. Pulsipher. Forthcoming. *Native and Introduced Food Plants of the Americas.* Smithsonian Institution Press, Washington, DC.

Kimber, C. 1966. Dooryard Gardens of Martinique. *Yearbook of the Association of Pacific Coast Geographers* 28:97–118.

Laws of Montserrat 1668–1740. 1740. John Baskett, London.

Laws of Montserrat 1741–1788, Index. 1790. Robert Hindmarsh, Printer to His Royal Highness, the Prince of Wales, for J. Anderson, No. 62, Holborn Hill.

Leslie, C. 1739. *A New and Exact Account of Jamaica.* Printed by R. Fleming for A. Kincaid, Edinburgh.

Long, E. 1774. *The History of Jamaica.* 3 vols. London.

Marsh, G.P. 1864. *Man and Nature.* Charles Scribner, New York.

Merrill, G. 1958. *The Historical Geography of St. Kitts and Nevis.* Instituto Panamericano de Geografía y Historia, Mexico.

Mintz S. and D. Hall. 1960. *The Origins of the Jamaican Internal Marketing System.* Yale University Publications in Anthropology 57. New Haven, CT.

Pearsall, D.M. and M.K. Trimble. 1984. Identifying Past Agricultural Activity Through Soil Phytolith Analysis: A Case Study from the Hawaiian Islands. *Journal of Archaeological Science* 11:199–233.

Porter, J. 1710. The Plan of Bettie's Hope & Cotton, Plantations Belonging to the Honorable William Codrington, Esquire. Copy housed in the Museum of Antigua and Barbuda, original in the Codrington Papers.

Pulsipher, L.M. 1978. Ridged Fields of Montserrat, West Indies. Proceedings of the Middle States Division of the Association of American Geographers.

———. 1985a. *Seventeenth Century Montserrat*. Historical Geography Research Series 17. Geo Books, Norwich, England.

———. 1985b. The Ethnoarchaeological Study of West Indian Houseyards. Presented at the Johns Hopkins University symposium on plantation archaeology. February, Baltimore.

———. 1987. Folk Placename Study. The Geography of Galways Mountain. Galways Project unpublished manuscript on file, Department of Geography, University of Tennessee, Knoxville.

———. 1989. Taped interviews with the residents of Galways Mountain, Summer, 1989.

Rosen, A. 1987. Phytolith Studies at Shiqmim. In *Shiqmim I*, ed. T.E. Levy, pp. 243–249. British Archaeological Reports, International Series 356(i). Oxford.

Sauer, C.O. 1969. *The Early Spanish Main*. University of California Press, Berkeley.

Sloane, H. 1707. A Description of a Voyage to the Islands of Madera, Barbados, Etc. Vol. I. In *After Africa*, ed. R. Abrahams and J. Szwed, p. 281. Yale University Press, New Haven, CT. 1983.

Stewart, J. 1823. *A View of the Past and Present State of the Island of Jamaica*. Oliver and Boyd, Edinburgh.

Watt, D. 1966. *Man's Influence on the Vegetation of Barbados 1627–1800*. Occasional Papers in Geography 4. University of Hull Publications, Hull, Yorkshire.

———. 1986. *The West Indies: Patterns of Development, Culture and Environmental Change Since 1492*. Cambridge University Press, Cambridge.

Wentworth, T. 1834. *A West India Sketch Book*. Vol. II, London.

Wilken, G. 1972. Microclimate Management by Traditional Farmers. *Geographic Review* 62:544–560.

Contributors

Bruce Bevan is a geophysicist and owner of the firm, Geosight. He specializes in the geophysical exploration of archaeological sites.

Mark Bowden is a Field Officer with the Royal Commission on the Historical Monuments of England. He undertakes topographical surveys of archaeological landscapes throughout northern England and his research interests include the history of archaeological survey techniques.

William M. Denevan is Carl O. Sauer Professor of Geography and Environmental Studies at the University of Wisconsin-Madison. His research has been on the historical geography and cultural ecology of Indian agriculture, settlement, and demography in the Amazon and the Andes.

Clark L. Erickson is an Assistant Professor in the Department of Anthropology and an Assistant Curator in the University Museum of Archaeology and Anthropology at the University of Pennsylvania. His research focuses on prehispanic land use and indigenous agricultural technology in the Andean region and Amazonia.

Suzanne K. Fish is a research archaeologist at the Arizona State Museum. Her primary research interests are the archaeology and traditional agriculture of the southwestern United States and archaeological palynology.

Stephen Ford, a graduate of Reading University, is Director of Thames Valley Archaeological Services, a small independent archaeological unit, and a Member of the Institute of Field Archaeologists. His research interests include British Prehistoric settlement and land use.

Vincent Gaffney is computer officer and Research Fellow at the Birmingham University Field Archaeology Unit in Great Britain. He has worked extensively in Britain and mainland Europe, but has a specialist interest in the later Prehistory of Croatia. His other specialist fields include the analysis of landscape archaeological data through the use of Geographic Information Systems.

Kathryn L. Gleason is Assistant Professor of Landscape Architecture at the University of Pennsylvania. Project Director of the Penn Excavations at Caesarea Maritima, her research focuses on the design and archaeology of ancient Roman gardens and landscapes.

Judson M. Kratzer is currently a graduate student at the History Department, Armstrong State College, Savannah, Georgia. His research interests are focused toward the archaeological investigation of formal American gardens of historic age with a particular emphasis on the relationship between viticulture and greenhouses.

Geoffrey C. Mees was a biologist working in the chemical industry. Since retiring he has taken an interest in archaeology and the evolution of the British landscape.

Naomi F. Miller is a Research Specialist in archaeobotany at the Museum Applied Science Center for Archaeology (MASCA), The University Museum, The University of Pennsylvania. Her research focuses on environment, agriculture, and plant use in the ancient Near East.

Lydia Mihelic Pulsipher is Professor in the Department of Geography at the University of Tennessee. She is a cultural/historical geographer interested in human adaptation to the New World tropics in the post-Columbian era. Her research focuses on the Eastern Caribbean.

John M. Treacy was Visiting Assistant Professor of Geography and Regional Science at George Washington University at the time of his death in 1989. Earlier that year he completed his Ph.D. dissertation at the University of Wisconsin-Madison on the terraces of the Colca Valley of Peru. He had also undertaken field research on indigenous agriculture in the Guayas Basin of Ecuador and the northeast Amazon of Peru.

Anne E. Yentsch is Associate Professor of Historical Archaeology in the Public History Program, History Department, Armstrong State College, Savannah, Georgia. She has published widely on anthropological history and historical archaeology; her research focuses on the contextual use of varied data sources to reconstruct eighteenth-century Anglo-American and African-American cultures.

Index

This book was set in Baskerville and Eras typefaces. Baskerville was designed by John Baskerville at his private press in Birmingham, England, in the eighteenth century. The first typeface to depart from oldstyle typeface design, Baskerville has more variation between thick and thin strokes. In an effort to insure that the thick and thin strokes of his typeface reproduced well on paper, John Baskerville developed the first wove paper, the surface of which was much smoother than the laid paper of the time. The development of wove paper was partly responsible for the introduction of typefaces classified as modern, which have even more contrast between thick and thin strokes.

Eras was designed in 1969 by Studio Hellenstein in Paris for the Wagner Typefoundry. A contemporary script-like version of a sans-serif typeface, the letters of Eras have a monotone stroke and are slightly inclined.

Printed on acid-free paper.